ıich
the
ınce
ents

ə in
our
ing.
ıilt
and
reen
vely
n of
: are
ent,
pics
lity,

Built
ıese
: the

PROFESSIONAL ETHICS
General Editor: Ruth Chadwick
Centre for Professional Ethics, University of Central Lancashire

Professionalism is a subject of interest to academics, the general public and would-be professional groups. Traditional ideas of professions and professional conduct have been challenged by recent social, political and technological changes. One result has been the development for almost every profession of an ethical code of conduct which attempts to formalise its values and standards. These codes of conduct raise a number of questions about the status of a 'profession' and the consequent moral implications for behaviour.

This series seeks to examine those questions both critically and constructively. Individual volumes will consider issues relevant to particular professions, including nursing, genetic counselling, journalism, business, the food industry and law. Other volumes will address issues relevant to all professional groups such as the function and value of a code of ethics and the demand of confidentiality.

Also available in this series:

ETHICS AND THE BUILT ENVIRONMENT

Edited by Warwick Fox

London and New York

First published 2000
by Routledge
2 Park Square, Milton Park, Abingdon, Oxon, OX14 4RN

Simultaneously published in the USA and Canada
by Routledge
270 Madison Ave, New York NY 10016

Routledge is an imprint of the Taylor & Francis Group

Transferred to Digital Printing 2006

Typeset in Times by
Prepress Projects Ltd, Perth, Scotland

British Library Cataloguing in Publication Data
A catalogue record for this book is available
from the British Library

Library of Congress Cataloging in Publication Data
Ethics and the built environment/edited by Warwick Fox
p. cm. – (Professional ethics)
Includes bibliographical references.
1. Architecture – Environmental aspects. 2. Environmental ethics.
3. Architecture and society. I. Fox, Warwick. II. Series.
NA2542.35. E88 2000
720′.47–dc21   00-042487

ISBN 0-415-23877-3 (hbk)
ISBN 0-415-23878-1 (pbk)

Publisher's Note
The publisher has gone to great lengths to ensure
the quality of this reprint but points out
that some imperfections in the original may be apparent.

Printed and bound by CPI Antony Rowe, Eastbourne

CONTENTS

CONTENTS

CONTENTS

CONTENTS

ILLUSTRATIONS

Figures

Tables

CONTRIBUTORS

Isis Brook is Director of the Distance Learning Programme in the Institute of Environment, Philosophy and Public Policy at Lancaster University. She teaches philosophy there and for the Open University. Her research focus is on the philosophical issues that bear on our knowledge of places and whether our relationship to place needs to be enhanced before we make aesthetic judgements or planning decisions.

Christopher Day is an architect, former Visiting Professor at Queens University, Belfast, and author of *Building with Heart* (Green Books 1990), *A Haven for Childhood* (Starborn Books 1998) and *Places of the Soul* (Thorsons 1990; HarperCollins 1999).

Graham Farmer is a practising architect, a studio design tutor and Lecturer in environmental design at the Department of Architecture, University of Newcastle. His research interests include sustainable buildings and technologies, environmental assessment methods and the impact of environmen'   ᵔ architectural pr ᵔᵔ

Saul Fisher is a philosopher an
 Andrew W. Mellon Foundati
 philosophy of architecture, i
 recent articles include: 'Archi
 Design' (*Journal of Aesthe*
 'Architectural Aesthetics in the
 (*Journal of Architectural Ec*

Bob Fowles is Senior Lecturer
 Cardiff University. His work
 approach to achieving increase
 To that end, his work focuses
 and practice in the areas
 architecture and ecological

Warwick Fox is Senior Lecturer in Philosophy at the Centre for Professional Ethics, University of Central Lancashire. He is the author of many papers on environmental philosophy and serves on a number of editorial advisory boards, including that of the US-based journal *Environmental Ethics* (the oldest academic journal devoted to that subject). He is the author of *Toward a Transpersonal Ecology: Developing New Foundations for Environmentalism* (State University of New York Press 1995 and Green Books, UK, 1995) and *The New Ethics* (forthcoming).

Herbert Girardet is a cultural ecologist, writer, film maker, Visiting Professor for environmental planning at Middlesex University and Chairman of the Schumacher Society (UK). He is the author of, *inter alia, The Gaia Atlas of Cities* (Gaia Books 1996) and *Creating Sustainable Cities* (Green Books 1999). His documentary on London's metabolism, *Metropolis*, was shown on Channel 4 in 1994, and he has also produced many short films for that channel on the human impact on the planet. In 1992 he received a UN Global 500 Award for Outstanding Environmental Achievement.

Simon Guy is a sociologist and Lecturer in the Department of Architecture, University of Newcastle, UK. His research interests revolve around the social production of the material environment. He has undertaken research into environmental innovation, the role of architecture in urban regeneration and the links between environmental building design and infrastructure provision.

Keekok Lee was Reader in Philosophy and Programme Director of the MA in Philosophy and Environment, University of Manchester, until late 1999 and is now based at the Department of Philosophy, University of Lancaster. She has published widely on environmental philosophy, her most recent book being *The Natural and the Artefactual: The Implications of Deep Science and Deep Technology for Environmental Philosophy* (Lexington Books 1999).

Gian Carlo Magnoli is a private architect and Lecturer in the Faculty of Architecture at the Polytechnic of Milan. He is currently undertaking postgraduate research in the field of social sustainability in the Department of Architecture at the University of Edinburgh.

Oliver is Director of the Centre for Vernacular Architecture ies at the School of Architecture, Oxford Brookes University. he editor of *The Encyclopedia of Vernacular Architecture rld* (Cambridge University Press 1997, three volumes) and the author of, *inter alia, Dwellings: The House Across the World* (Phaidon Press 1987).

Mustafa Pultar is Professor of Building Science in the Faculty of Art, Design and Architecture, Bilkent University, Ankara, Turkey. He has also taught at both Princeton University and the Middle East Technical University, and has researched at MIT and Strathclyde University. His research focuses on building culture and building theory.

Antony Radford is Professor at the School of Architecture, Landscape Architecture and Urban Design, The University of Adelaide, Australia. His current research interests are in computer-aided design and environmentally responsible contemporary Australian houses.

Roger Talbot is a Senior Lecturer in the Department of Architecture at the University of Edinburgh, Director of the Edinburgh Sustainable Architecture Unit, and Managing Director of the private consultancy 'thirdwave'. He served as a member of the Lord Provost's Commission on Sustainable Development for the City of Edinburgh and is currently involved, in both Scotland and the USA, in developing and operationalising a Community Learning Toolkit as a practical demonstration of the ideas discussed in his contribution to this book.

Nigel Taylor is Principal Lecturer in the School of Planning and Architecture at the University of the West of England, Bristol. He holds both a PhD in philosophy and an MPhil in town planning and teaches courses in the philosophy and theory of town planning, the aesthetics of urban design, and architectural theory. He has published papers in all the major planning journals on planning theory and philosophy, as well as papers on aesthetics, and is the author of *Urban Planning Theory Since 1945* (Sage 1998).

John Whitelegg is Professor of Environmental Studies at Liverpool John Moores University. He is the Managing Director of the environmental consultancy 'Eco-Logica Ltd', the editor of the journal *World Transport Policy and Practice* and the author or co-author of some eight books including, most recently, *Greening the Built Environment* (with Maf Smith and Nick Williams) (Earthscan Publications 1998).

Terry Williamson is Associate Professor at the School of Architecture, Landscape Architecture and Urban Design, The University of Adelaide, Australia. He has dual architecture and engineering qualifications and, in a series of papers, has examined both the technical and the philosophical dimensions of theory and practice underpinning the thermal performance design of buildings.

Tom Woolley is Professor of Architecture at Queens University, Belfast, and a practising architect with Rachel Bevan Architects in County Down. He is editor of the journal *Green Building Digest* and the author/editor of both the *Green Building Handbook* and *Rehumanising Housing*. He is a founder member of both the Ecological Design Association and the Ecological Building Foundation, a member of the Association of Environment Conscious Builders, chairman of the Northern Ireland Building Regulations Advisory Committee and was chairman of ACTAC, the Technical Aid Network.

ACKNOWLEDGEMENTS

The editing of this book is one of several projects largely completed during a period of research leave funded jointly by the Arts and Humanities Research Board and the University of Central Lancashire. I am grateful to both organisations for their support. I am also grateful to Professor Ruth Chadwick, Head of the Centre for Professional Ethics, University of Central Lancashire, for her support for this project from its inception. Finally, I would like to extend my sincere thanks to all the contributors for their thoroughly enthusiastic support for this project.

Warwick Fox
September 2000

1

INTRODUCTION

Ethics and the built environment

Warwick Fox

Major theoretical and practical developments dating back variously over the last century, and in some cases longer, have contributed to a revolution in ethics in the last two to three decades. On the theoretical side, I have in mind developments as significant as those of post-Big Bang physics, post-Darwinian evolutionary biology and ecology, the emerging cognitive sciences and the emerging study of complex adaptive systems – in short, the sciences of matter, life, mind and complexity-in-general. These sciences have collectively fuelled the development of a naturalistic, evolutionary understanding of the universe and all that it contains, which, in turn, has stimulated (at least for many) a fundamental rethinking of humanity's place in the larger scheme of things. On the practical side, the emerging anthropogenic (i.e. humanly caused) ecological crisis has been leading us to question the ways in which we dwell upon the Earth. Taken together, these major theoretical and practical challenges to our previous self-understandings and ways of living have led, just since the 1970s, to the development of an emerging field of philosophy known as 'environmental philosophy' or, more particularly, 'environmental ethics'.

As its name suggests, environmental ethics is, or at least ought to be, concerned with examining any and all ethical questions that arise with respect to a moral agent's interactions with any and all aspects of the world around her or him. This *includes* other humans, since environmental ethics typically *begins* with an analysis of the reasons why we believe humans to be deserving of moral consideration and why we have, until quite recently, denied such consideration to the non-human world. Thus, if its full implications are grasped, environmental ethics represents the most general form of ethics we have. Far from being a minor, 'applied ethics' offshoot of the field of enquiry hitherto known simply as *ethics*, environmental ethics actually represents a vast enlargement of that field

1

of enquiry. This is because, as just implied, the field of ethics to date has been profoundly human-centred in its range of concerns and therefore effectively constitutes a *subset* – albeit an astonishingly elaborated subset – of the range of concerns addressed by environmental ethics (see, for example, Fox 1995 and 1996; Zimmerman 1998). There is therefore a strong case for referring to environmental ethics as 'general ethics' and referring to traditional human-centred ethics as 'anthropocentric ethics', that is, as that subset of general ethics that deals with human-centred ethical concerns.

However, just as traditional, anthropocentrically focused forms of ethics have exhibited a major blind spot in their theorising with respect to the non-human world, so the development of environmental ethics has thus far exhibited a major blind spot of its own – and, to that extent, not fully realised its own implications. This 'blind spot' flows from the following basic fact: the world around us – what we call 'the environment' – consists of both spontaneously occurring and humanly constructed environments. For convenience, we label these the 'natural environment' and the 'built environment', and this natural/built environment distinction is perhaps the most obvious division that we can make in the day-to-day world in which we live. When you look out of your window, you may see, on the one hand, trees, the sky and, perhaps, some birds; on the other hand, houses, roads and cars. These things are all mixed together in your field of view, but some of them belong to the spontaneously self-organising natural world and some of them belong to the intentionally organised built environment (including cars and other artefacts on the broad understanding we are employing here, since cars are part of the intentionally organised, built – or constructed – environment even though they are not 'buildings'). In addition there are many, many examples of what we might call 'mixed' environments all around us. These are becoming increasingly common as humans intentionally engineer and put to use the spontaneous self-organising processes of the natural world – from the back garden to the brave new world of genetic modification.

Yet, despite the fact that the world around us – 'the environment' – consists of both natural and built environments (and their various admixtures), environmental ethics, as a formal field of enquiry, has been overwhelmingly focused upon the spontaneously self-organising, 'natural' environment, as opposed to the humanly created, or intentionally organised, *built* environment. It seems, then, that *environmental* ethics has not yet truly earned the name that it presently goes under, let alone the name *general ethics*, which would be an even better way of describing the field if its full implications were realised.

On the one hand, this bias towards concerns with the natural environment is completely understandable: environmental ethicists have wanted to escape the almost exclusively anthropocentric focus that has pervaded traditional ethical approaches and so have deliberately directed their attentions to the non-human world in order to redress this imbalance. On the other hand, however, this bias is decidedly odd for at least two reasons. First, the development of any truly comprehensive environmental ethics (which would then amount to a general ethics) obviously demands the development of an ethic which is broad enough to address ethical questions that arise in all manner of environments – natural, built and mixed. Second, whereas humans evolved in natural, or spontaneously self-organising environments, we now increasingly live in built, or intentionally organised environments, and these built environments draw mightily upon the free 'goods and services' provided by the spontaneously self-organising realm of Nature (see Chapter 2, by Girardet, 'Greening Urban Society'). In consequence, it should be obvious that how we build these environments and how we live in them is a question of prime importance, not only for the preservation and flourishing of humans themselves, but also for the preservation and flourishing of the whole non-human realm of Nature. The fate of the 'green bits' of the planet is now inextricably bound up with – indeed, effectively at the mercy of – the future of the 'brown bits'.

However, as significant as these theoretical and practical issues are, no field of enquiry presently exists that is clearly and explicitly devoted to the subject of what we would call *the ethics of the built environment* or (perhaps more simply, and with more of an emphasis on process rather than outcome) *the ethics of building*. That said, it is true that some philosophers have occasionally attempted explicitly to address ethical issues associated with the *built* environment, and it is also true that some commentators coming more from a design and architecture background have also occasionally attempted explicitly to address *ethical* issues in this area. We can point to various contributions that might come to be viewed as 'early developments' in the field of the ethics of the built environment, once this field gets going as a formally recognised field of enquiry. For example, the art historian David Watkin's *Morality and Architecture* (1977) (critically discussed by Nigel Taylor in this volume); the philosopher Dale Jamieson's paper on 'The City Around Us' (1984) (thanks to Andrew Light for drawing this paper to my attention); the philosopher Avner De-Shalit's paper 'Urban Preservation and the Judgement of Solomon' (1994) (thanks to Doris Schroeder for drawing this paper to my attention); the designer Victor Papanek's *The Green Imperative: Ecology and Ethics in Design and Architecture* (1995); the Heideggerean-influenced philosopher Karsten Harries' *The Ethical*

Function of Architecture (1997) (critically discussed by Saul Fisher in this volume); the philosopher Alastair Gunn's paper 'Rethinking Communities: Environmental Ethics in an Urbanized World' (1998); and, as this book is going to press, the philosopher Roger King's paper 'Environmental Ethics and the Built Environment' (2000). On the whole, however, contributions that attempt explicitly to address ethical issues associated with the built environment have thus far been few and far between, whether they have come at this topic from the philosophical side or the design and architecture side. This point is reinforced by most, if not all of the philosophical contributions in the preceding list (as it is by a number of the contributors to this volume). For example, Jamieson began his 1984 paper by saying:

> It may seem *odd* to many people that a book devoted to environmental ethics includes an essay on the city. We often speak of the environment as if it is everywhere except where we live (italics added).
>
> (Jamieson 1984: 38)

Fourteen years later, Gunn began his paper along similar lines:

> Unfortunately, the central concerns of environmental ethics have been and largely continue to be heavily slanted towards animals, plants, endangered species, wilderness, and traditional cultures and not toward the problems of life in industrialized, urbanized society where most people now live.
>
> (Gunn 1998: 34)

In short, the discussion of the built environment was unusual in environmental ethics then (Jamieson 1984) and still remains unusual (Gunn 1998). King (2000: 115) rightly sees this 'lack of attention' (to the built environment) as 'a lost opportunity for environmental ethics.'

The aim of this volume, then, is to contribute towards the accumulation of a critical mass of ideas and questions that will enable the discussion of *the ethics of the built environment* (or *the ethics of building*) to take off as a field of enquiry in its own right. This volume therefore brings together, on the one hand, philosophers (especially ethicists) with an interest in architecture, planning and building and, on the other hand, philosophically oriented architects, planners and other analysts of the built environment. The aim is to create an informed interdisciplinary forum in which to:

4

1 widen and deepen the debate on the ethical dimensions of building in all its forms from a variety of disciplinary perspectives and approaches;
2 contribute significantly towards establishing an agenda for the future development of these issues; and
3 propose some tentative solutions to the kinds of questions that arise when we contemplate the ethics of building.

To this end, excluding the introduction and the conclusion, the chapters that constitute this volume have been divided into three parts of five chapters, grouped under the headings: The Green Imperative – and its Vicissitudes; Building with Greater Sensitivity to People(s) and Places; and Steps Towards a Theory of the Ethics of the Built Environment. As a generalisation, the book moves from contributions that are more empirically, practically or policy oriented to those that are more theoretically oriented.

The volume opens by examining 'The Green Imperative – and its Vicissitudes' (the first part of the title being borrowed from Papanek's 1995 book of the same name). Any book on the ethics of the built environment produced at this point in global history simply has to begin with the 'green' imperative of sustainability, which links directly to issues of human intra-generational justice, human intergenerational justice, the ethics of the human–non-human relationship (including the preservation of global biodiversity) and, ultimately, questions concerning the richness, beauty and even survival of life on Earth. Although the objective of sustainability carries a 'green' tag, it is now endorsed (in theory at least) by governments internationally. As Roger Talbot and Gian Carlo Magnoli point out in their contribution to this volume, before the 1987 report of the Brundtland Commission (the World Commission for Environment and Development) 'it was difficult to identify any official social, economic or indeed environmental policies that recognised sustainable development as a significant policy objective' (see p. 91), whereas since the publication of Agenda 21, following the Earth Summit in Rio de Janeiro in 1992 (the United Nations Conference on Environment and Development), 'it is difficult to identify government policy statements that do not'(see p. 91).

The principle of sustainability is now also endorsed by internationally recognised architectural leaders (see, for example, Richard Rogers, *Cities for a Small Planet*, based on his Reith Lectures of 1995) as well as by the profession of architecture as a whole. At the level of the profession of architecture itself, for example, The Union of International Architects declared at their World Congress in 1993 that they would commit themselves, individually and professionally, to 'place environmental and social sustainability at the core of our practices and professional responsibilities.' Their 'Declaration of Interdependence for a Sustainable Future' goes on to commit the profession, *inter alia*, to educate all their professional contacts, including others in the building industry, clients and students, about the 'critical importance and substantial opportunities of sustainable design', and to 'establish policies, regulations and practices in government and business that ensure *sustainable design becomes normal practice'* (my italics). Thus, as Simon Guy and Graham Farmer note (this volume, p. 73, quoting Sudjic), it is now the case that 'for any architect not to profess passionate [ethical] commitment to "green" buildings is professional suicide'.

Why has this transformation come about? The basic reasons are now well known. First, an increasing proportion of the planet's still wildly increasing numbers of people are choosing or being forced to live in densely built urban developments. These developments constitute such massive resource sinks and waste generators on a global scale that, as Talbot and Magnoli put it (this volume, p. 92), '...present forms of urban development are clearly and unequivocally unsustainable'. Yet, second, and realistically, 'it is simply not possible to envisage a future that is not rooted in urban living' (ibid.). Crunch! These facts of the matter explain, in essence, why the green imperative of sustainability must now lie at the heart of considerations regarding the built environment in general. Indeed, it is becoming increasingly clear that few matters are of more importance to the future of both humanity *and* the non-human world than the ways in which humans construct their built environments and live their day-to-day lives in those environments. This applies particularly in the case of our most densely built, most densely populated and fastest growing built environments – cities. Thus, as Maf Smith, John Whitelegg (one of the contributors to this volume) and Nick Williams argue in their important recent book *Greening the Built Environment* (1998: 214): 'The built environment must be seen not only as the major source of environmental problems, but also as the locus of the solution to these problems.'

But why should a book concerning the *ethics* of building begin with the issue of sustainability? Why not leave that issue to the technical skills of architects, builders, planners, and so on, and just let them 'get on with it'? Again, the reason should be obvious – *achieving a sustainable way of living is not just a technical issue (although it is often discussed as if it were), but also (and fundamentally) an ethical one.* As Terry Williamson and Antony Radford put it (this volume, pp. 57–58): 'If ethics deals with the standards by which human actions can be judged right or wrong, appropriate or inappropriate, then the notion of a 'sustainable' architecture expressed in these statements [i.e. by national and international organisations of architects] is fundamentally an ethical issue.'

Notwithstanding the many fine words endorsing the principle of sustainability in government policy statements and from the architecture profession in general, those architects who are most genuinely and deeply committed to this principle typically see a massive gap between 'the talk' and 'the walk' – an observation that goes to basic moral questions concerning governmental honesty and professional integrity. But, as ever in the real world, the issues here are rarely so clear-cut. Even with the best will in the world, there are tremendously difficult questions involved in surmounting the gap between support in principle for the objective of sustainability ('the green imperative') and translating that support into practice – or even into a shared understanding at a more detailed level. Thus, the chapters in Part I of this volume go beyond simply extolling the cause of sustainability and explore the technical and especially the ethical complexities of the issues involved.

Herbert Girardet ('Greening Urban Society') sets the stage with a detailed overview of the present urban situation worldwide, drawing particular attention to the 'ecological footprint' and 'metabolism' of cities. He points out, for example, that the ecological footprint of London, 'the city that started it all', 'the mother of megacities', now extends to around 125 times its surface area – the equivalent of Britain's entire productive land! In the face of this sort of unsustainable situation, and drawing upon a worldwide perspective, Girardet outlines the directions in which urban society now needs to move and the resources that can be drawn upon to effect this change. John Whitelegg ('Building Ethics into the Built Environment') then proceeds with a case study approach in which he examines a range of ethical issues raised by some major recent projects – Heathrow Terminal 5, the Lancaster Local Plan and Calcutta's flyover project. Reflection upon these leads him to focus, in particular, on the ethically saturated issues of place identity, empowering local residents and communities, the ethics/economics tension and the role of professional ethics. He finds, among other things, that the transformation of the built environment along 'industrial and consumerist lines is creating future inequalities, inequities, social injustice, loss of community, loss of place identity and loss of a spiritual dimension to life.' Of particular relevance to the overall theme of this book is his follow-up observation to this point: 'All of these issues are ethical issues, *as is the absence of an ethical perspective from the built environment agenda itself*' (my italics), which speaks precisely to the rationale for this volume.

The next three chapters in Part I speak in various ways to the complex questions of translating the principle of sustainability into practice – and even of understanding exactly what is meant by the green imperative of sustainability. Tom Woolley ('Green Building: Establishing Principles') addresses the ubiquity of 'greenwash' and 'enviro-speak' with respect to sustainable building practices and calls for the establishment of rigorously thought through principles in order to sort the genuinely sustainable (or at least more-sustainable-than-the-alternatives) from the greenwash. *En route*, Woolley observes that, despite the fact that we spend most of our lives in buildings, 'the issues of green building have failed to make much of an impact on public consciousness when compared with public concerns over food, medical and pollution issues'. Indeed, as Woolley notes, these issues have even failed to make much of an impact upon environmental organisations: 'Few [environmental organisations] take more than a passing interest in the subject of building. Most environmental organisations emphasise protecting the natural environment, and a recent study showed that many did little to change the environment in their own offices.' This constitutes an interesting parallel to my previous remarks regarding the overwhelming focus of environmental ethicists upon the natural environment and, hence, the built environment blind spot in environmental ethics. Terry Williamson and Antony Radford ('Building, Global Warming and Ethics') then focus on the single, but hugely significant, environmental issue of global warming and greenhouse gas emissions in order to explore in some detail the complexities of the link between sustainable building as an ethical issue and building design as a pragmatic activity. Finally in this section, Simon Guy and Graham Farmer ('Contested Constructions: The Competing Logics of Green Buildings and Ethics') provide a detailed analysis of six competing sets of interlocking ideas ('competing logics') that vie with and/or jostle each other in the literature on green building, and that we need to be aware of in order to make sense of the full range of debate in this area.

Part II of the volume is devoted to 'Building with Greater Sensitivity to People(s) and Places.' Roger Talbot and Gian Carlo Magnoli ('Social Inclusion and the Sustainable City') discuss the importance of social inclusion to the goal of ecological sustainability, with reference to urban developments/cities in general and the example of Edinburgh in particular. They devote particular attention to community learning as the primary means by which social inclusion can be facilitated. Bob Fowles ('Transformative Architecture: A Synthesis of Ecological and Participatory Design'), like Talbot and Magnoli, adopts systems ideas and a holistic perspective in discussing the importance of architects involving the people for whom they are designing in the design process itself. Based on practical experience, he observes that when people do this 'they begin to critically examine broader ecological aspects of building design' and that 'the experience of many participants indicates that the synthesis of participation with an ecological agenda results in a significant personal level of change within themselves.' Fowles sees this personal transformation as an 'important ingredient in contributing to sustainable communities...and just as important as the creation of a socially responsible and ecologically sound architecture.' Paul Oliver ('Ethics and Vernacular Architecture') likewise emphasises the ethical lesson that 'Housing that involves the active participation of the community...is the most likely to succeed'. He graphically illustrates the importance of respect for 'the values, mores, building skills, experience and wisdom of the cultures whose housing needs are to be met' with a variety of examples drawn from his long-standing study of vernacular architecture around the world and argues that 'If the housing of the billions in the twenty-first century is not to result in design debacles of unprecedented scale, these are lessons in the ethics of building that must be learned.'

Following on the vernacular theme of building in the 'everyday environment', the architect Christopher Day ('Ethical Building in the Everyday Environment: A Multilayer Approach to Building and Place Design') seeks to overcome the false oppositions with which we often seem to be confronted (humanity *or* Nature, utility *or* beauty, society *or* ecology) by offering a thoroughly 'process-oriented' approach to building that takes into account the different 'levels of being' of a building and its place. These levels of being include its physical substance, its flow through time (its biography if you will), our own emotional responses to what we openly refer to as its moods, and, finally, what the place itself would say if it could speak (as distinct from us merely projecting a voice upon it), that is, if its essence, *genius loci* or spirit of place could speak. This is truly a 'multilayer approach' to building – one that might go further than some people would want to go, but then you should see the results! Finally in this section, Isis Brook ('Can "Spirit of Place" Be a Guide to Ethical Building?') follows on from Christopher Day's paper by focusing specifically on sensitivity towards 'place' as a guide to ethical building. She offers a critical but sympathetic analysis of the conceptually slippery, yet ancient and apparently indispensable notion of 'sense of place', '*genius loci*' or 'spirit of place'. Considering a phenomenon that seems to many to be both as real, yet as difficult to pin down as consciousness itself, Brook distinguishes and examines some ten or more 'shades of meaning' of this notion and points the way to its future development as a guide to ethical building.

Part III of the volume is overtly philosophical (a movement begun with Brook's paper) and explores various 'Steps Towards a Theory of the Ethics of the Built Environment.' Mustafa Pultar begins this section ('The Conceptual Basis of Building Ethics') by reinforcing the point made in the opening section of this introduction when he says that 'there appears to be no well-established, coherent and systematic framework for a discussion of value-related issues in the analysis of building(s)'. He then provides a detailed overview of the range of values that need to be considered if we are to develop a firm and comprehensive 'basis for discussing building ethics.' Saul Fisher ('How to Think about the Ethics of Architecture') also reinforces the point made in the opening section of this introduction when he says that 'Philosophical ethicists have not yet fully explored, or even mapped out, the problems posed by architectural practice'. Advancing a number of reasons for 'why architecture merits its own branch of applied ethics', he then critically examines three current models of addressing ethical problems in architecture and finds each of them flawed in different ways. In contrast, he argues for the advantages of pressing the tried-and-tested analytical philosophical approach to ethics into the realm of the built environment and draws our attention to the guidance that can be offered in this task by drawing upon the already existing wealth of argument in the realm of architectural law.

As a generalisation, the chapters by Pultar and Fisher are formal in their approach, in the sense that they offer valuable general frameworks within which progress can be made in developing the ethics of the built environment: a range of values that pay close attention to the actual practices of building, in the case of Pultar's paper, and the analytical philosophical approach to ethics, amplified by the body of architectural law, in the case of Fisher's paper. In contrast, the remaining three chapters in this section are concerned more with arguing for substantive philosophical positions.

Keekok Lee ('The Taj Mahal and the Spider's Web') considers the ontological differences (i.e. the differences in fundamental modes of being or existence) between the purposively built, artefactual environment and its obvious contrast – the natural environment. She argues that these realms are 'two different types of being – they belong to two different and distinct ontological categories' and that our moral obligations towards these two realms differ in some rather fundamental ways. For example, while we might feel we have a moral obligation to preserve or repair great works of art (including buildings) with as little alteration as possible, it would be a serious mistake to adopt this approach towards the natural realm (effectively 'deep freezing' the natural world) because this would rob the natural realm of an essential ontological feature, namely, its dynamic and, by the same token, transient nature.

10

Where Lee considers the ontology/ethics nexus, Nigel Taylor ('Ethical Arguments About the Aesthetics of Architecture') turns his attention to the equally deep and tangled question of the ethics/aesthetics nexus and asks 'Are there any *ethical* grounds for praising, or criticising, the *aesthetic* content of buildings?' (my italics). This is a very important question to address in a volume of this kind precisely because many people have had the experience of wishing to register what they feel is an essentially moral objection against the form of a building (even that 'There ought to be a law against it!') only to have their objection interpreted as (and often, in their own eyes, *reduced* to) an *aesthetic* objection that carries no *moral* weight. Taylor carefully considers (and rejects) three likely candidate answers to the question of whether there are ethical grounds for praising or criticising the aesthetic content of buildings before then advancing a positive answer to this question, based on the degree of *care* or aesthetic *attentiveness* that has gone into a building.

I begin the concluding contribution ('Towards an Ethics (or at Least a Value Theory) of the Built Environment') to Part III by asking whether questions concerning the ethics of building are in fact reducible to other, more familiar, kinds of ethical concern. If this were the case then, at a fundamental level, the very idea of an ethics of the built environment *per se* would be unnecessary – 'surplus to moral requirements'. I argue against this that there is a foundational principle at work in value theory in general and ethics (as a subset of value theory) in particular, and that the recognition of this foundational principle provides a basis for both (1) recognising the ethics of the built environment as a legitimate (non-theoretically reducible) area of enquiry in its own right and (2) judging some forms of the built environment as better or worse than others *in principle* (i.e. irrespective of the preferences, interests or desires of observers).

The book concludes on an agenda-setting note ('Conclusion: Towards an Agenda for the Ethics of the Built Environment'). This conclusion briefly sets out, in an ethically systematic way, the kinds of questions that have been discussed herein and that will set the agenda for the future development of enquiry into the ethics of the built environment.

It remains to say two things. First, that it is the collective hope of the authors who have contributed to this volume that it will contribute both fruitful ideas and inspirational energy to the, by now, well overdue development of a vigorous and full-blown area of enquiry into the ethics of the built environment. Second, that it is likewise the collective hope of these authors that the most critically robust ideas in this area of enquiry will inspire, guide and increasingly come to be reflected in the real-world practices of creating, preserving and, where appropriate, destroying the built environment.

References

De-Shalit, A. (1994) 'Urban Preservation and the Judgement of Solomon', *Journal of Applied Philosophy* 11: 3–13.

Fox, W. (1995) *Toward a Transpersonal Ecology: Developing New Foundations for Environmentalism*, New York: State University of New York Press, and Dartington, Devon: Green Books.

Fox, W. (1996) 'A Critical Overview of Environmental Ethics', *World Futures* 46: 1–21.

Gunn, A. (1998) 'Rethinking Communities: Environmental Ethics in an Urbanized World', *Environmental Ethics* 20: 341–60.

Harries, K. (1997) *The Ethical Function of Architecture*, Cambridge, MA: MIT Press.

Jamieson, D. (1984) 'The City Around Us', in T. Regan (ed.) *Earthbound: New Introductory Essays in Environmental Ethics*, Philadelphia: Temple University Press.

King, R. (2000) 'Environmental Ethics and the Built Environment', *Environmental Ethics* 22: 115–31.

Papanek, V. (1995) *The Green Imperative: Ecology and Ethics in Design and Architecture*, London: Thames and Hudson.

Rogers, R. (1997) *Cities for a Small Planet*, London: Faber and Faber.

Smith, M., Whitelegg, J. and Williams, N. (1998) *Greening the Built Environment*, London: Earthscan.

Watkin, D. (1977) *Morality and Architecture: The Development of a Theme in Architectural History*, Oxford: Clarendon Press.

Zimmerman, M.E. (ed.) (1998) *Environmental Philosophy: From Animal Rights to Radical Ecology*, 2nd edn, Englewood Cliffs, NJ: Prentice Hall.

Part I

THE GREEN IMPERATIVE –
AND ITS VICISSITUDES

2

GREENING URBAN SOCIETY

Herbert Girardet

The urban age

City growth is changing the condition of humanity and the face of the Earth. In one century, global urban populations will have expanded from 15 to 50 per cent, and this figure will increase further in the coming decades. At present, half of humanity live and work in cities, while the other half depend increasingly on cities and towns for their economic survival. In most developed countries over 70 per cent now live in cities.

The size of modern cities, too, in terms of numbers as well as physical scale, is unprecedented: *in 1800*, London was the only city with one million inhabitants. At that time the largest 100 cities in the world had twenty million inhabitants, with each city usually extending to just a few thousand hectares. *In 1990*, the world's 100 largest cities accommodated 540 million people and 220 million people lived in the twenty largest cities, mega-cities of over ten million people, some extending to hundreds of thousands of hectares. In addition, there were thirty-five cities of over five million and hundreds of over one million people.[1]

In the nineteenth and early twentieth centuries, urban growth was occurring mainly in the North, as a result of the spread of industrialisation and the associated rapid increase in the use of fossil fuels. Today, the world's largest and fastest growing cities are emerging in the South, because of population growth, migration from rural areas and unprecedented industrial development.

In discussing urban issues, the urban *social* agenda has had much attention. We are used to thinking about cities as places where great wealth is generated, and also where social disparities and tensions have to be addressed.

The urban *health* agenda has also been widely discussed – under headings such as inadequate sanitation and poor working and housing conditions. Diseases such as cholera, typhoid and TB, well known in northern cities such as London 150 years ago, are now occurring in many developing cities, with epidemics threatening particularly the poorest districts.

However, an issue that has had much less exposure is the huge *resource consumption* of modern cities – and the potential to reduce impacts on both local and global environments.

Worldwide, urban development is closely associated with increased resource consumption. Compared with rural dwellers, city people in developing countries have much higher levels of consumption, with massively increased throughput of fossil fuels, metals, timber, meat and manufactured products.

Much of Asia, in particular, is currently undergoing the most astonishing urban-industrial development. China alone, with some 10 per cent economic growth per year, is increasing the number of its cities, from just over 600 to over 1,200 by 2010. Some 300 million people are expected to be moving to cities, converting from peasant farming to urban-industrial lifestyles. The increased purchasing power is already leading to increased demand for consumer goods and a more meat-based diet.[2]

The unprecedented impacts of cities require a wide range of responses – technological, organisational and legislative. Evidence from all over the world proves that the challenge of making cities more resource efficient is being taken seriously in a growing number of places.

Cities as superorganisms

Urban systems with millions of inhabitants are unique to the current age and they are the most complex products of collective human creativity. They are both *organisms* and *mechanisms* in that they utilise biological *re*-production as well as mechanical production processes.

Large cities have unique characteristics, developing extraordinary degrees of specialisation. The vast array of productive enterprises, capital and labour markets, service industries and artistic endeavour could be described as a *symbiotic cultural system*. However, unlike *natural systems*, they are highly dependent on external supplies: for their sustenance large modern cities have become dependent on global transport and communication systems. This is not *civilisation* in the old-fashioned sense, but *mobilisation,* dependent on long-distance transport routes.

Demand for energy defines modern cities more than any other single factor. Most rail, road and aeroplane traffic occurs between cities. All their internal activities – local transport, electricity supply, domestic living, services and manufacturing – currently depend on fossil fuels. To my knowledge there has never been a city of more than one million people that was not running on fossil fuels. Without their routine use, the growth of mega-cities of ten million people and more would not have occurred. But there is an environmental price to pay. Waste gases, such as nitrogen dioxide and sulphur dioxide, discharged by chimneys and exhaust pipes, affect the health of city people themselves and, beyond urban boundaries, forests and farmland downwind. A large proportion of the global increase in carbon dioxide is attributable to combustion in the world's cities. Climate change from fossil fuel burning is becoming a worldwide concern.

Concentration of intense economic processes and high levels of personal consumption increase the resource demands of an urbanising humanity. Apart from a monopoly on the use of fossil fuels and metals, humans now consume nearly *half* of the world's total photosynthetic capacity. Cities are the home of the 'amplified man', an unprecedented amalgam of biology and technology, transcending his biological ancestors. Beyond their limits, cities profoundly affect distant ecosystems as a result of their demand for exotic timber, rare plants for domestic display, cage birds and unusual pets. The annual turnover of illegal wildlife trade, emanating from cities, is second only to the drugs trade.[3]

Cities also affect traditional rural economies and their cultural adaptation to biological diversity. With better roads and rail links, and ever improving telecommunications, rural people tend to abandon their own indigenous cultures, often defined by sustainable adaptation to their local environment, adopting urban culture and products into their daily lives. Over time, they tend to acquire urban standards of living and the mind set to go with these.

Cities also have vast impacts on the world's oceans, consuming the bulk of the world's fish catch. Half of the world's population lives close to the sea and much of its sewage is flushed into coastal waters. Urban expansion itself has often been to the detriment of mangrove forests and coral reefs.

Thus, urbanisation has profoundly changed humanity's relationship to its host planet, with unprecedented impacts on forests, farmland and aquatic ecosystems. The human species is changing the way in which the 'the web of life'[4] on Earth itself functions, from a *geographically distributed* interaction of a myriad of species, into a highly *centralised system* dominated by the resource use patterns of just the one species. Cities take up only 2 per cent of the world's land surface, yet they use over 75 per cent of the world's resources.

With Asia, Latin America and parts of Africa now joining Europe, North America and Australia in the urban experiment, it is crucial to assess whether large-scale urbanisation and sustainable development can be reconciled. Whilst urbanisation is turning the living Earth from a self-regulating interactive system into one dominated by humanity, we have yet to develop and deploy the skills to create a new, sustainable equilibrium.

Urban sprawl

Mega-cities of ten million people or more are the largest artificial structures ever to appear on the face of the Earth, extending to hundreds of thousands of hectares. Urban sprawl is typical of cities of increasing affluence in which people often prefer the spaciousness of suburbs to denser city centres. Metropolitan New York's population, for instance, has grown only 5 per cent in the last twenty-five years, yet its surface area has grown by 61 per cent, consuming much forest and farmland in the process.

Sprawl is above all else the result of the routine use of the motor car. Los Angeles is the epitome of a sprawling city. Some 90 per cent of its population drive to work by car and most people live in detached houses surrounded by their own gardens, often more than an acre in size.

Phoenix, Arizona, is the ultimate sprawling city, extending to three times the surface area of Los Angeles. LA is famous for the way it sprawls along its vastly complex freeway system. A city of eleven million people, it covers an area three times larger than London, which has a population of seven million. London itself, where semi-detached houses are the norm in the suburbs, is several times larger than Hong Kong, which has six million inhabitants and where most people live in high-rise blocks. Not surprisingly, Hong Kong makes far more efficient use of available road space than London. High urban density made it possible for Hong Kong to develop an efficient public transport system.

Sprawl can be contained by the enforcement of planning policies. London's outward growth, for instance, was curtailed by policies that were drawn up after 1945. A clearly defined green belt, which cannot be built upon, stopped the expansion of the city and preserved the rural hinterland. Similar policies now in place in Portland, Oregon, have dramatically curtailed the outward growth of that city. Promoting housing development that is dense enough to reduce the need for car use is vital for curtailing urban sprawl. In the USA, researchers found that seventeen dwellings per hectare support a fairly frequent bus service; twenty-two dwellings support a light railway network and thirty-seven people support an express bus service that people can reach on foot, from their homes.

Increasing urban density by deliberate land use policies is a key for reducing urban sprawl. However, to persuade people to give up suburbs and their quasi-rural qualities, they have to be offered the special urban qualities that are absent in sprawling cities: vitality, diversity, mixed activities, social amenities and cultural facilities. We have much to learn from historical cities and their lively pedestrian culture of markets, public squares and convivial meeting places. Some of the most fashionable and popular urban areas, such as Chelsea, Montmartre or Manhattan, are, all in their own different ways, places of high density and mixed activities. We have to relearn the art of building of cities with lively and safe centres that are easily accessible on foot.

The ecological footprint of cities

A few years ago I produced a TV documentary on deforestation in the Amazon basin and the resulting loss of biodiversity. Filming at the port of Belem, I saw a huge stack of mahogany timber with 'London' stamped on it being loaded into a freighter. I started to take an interest in the connection between urban consumption patterns and human impact on the biosphere. It occurred to me that logging of virgin forests, or their conversion into cattle ranches and into fields of soya beans for cattle fodder (in Brazil's Mato Grosso region) or of manioc for pig feed (in the former rainforest regions of Thailand), was perhaps not the most rational way of assuring resource supply to urban 'agglomeration economies'.[3]

Recently, the Canadian economist William Rees[5] started a debate about the *ecological footprint* of cities, which he defines as the land required to supply them with food and timber products, and to absorb their CO_2 output via areas of growing vegetation. I have examined the footprint of London, which also happens to be the city that started it all: the 'mother of mega-cities'. Today London's total footprint, following Rees's definition, extends to around 125 times its surface area of 159,000 hectares (see Appendix 1). With 12 per cent of Britain's population, London requires the equivalent of Britain's entire productive land.[6] In reality, this land, of course, stretches to far-flung places such as the wheat prairies of Kansas, the tea gardens of Assam, the forests of Scandinavia and Amazonia, and the copper mines of Zambia.

But large modern cities are not just defined by their resource use. They are also centres for investment banking and other financial services. When discussing urban sustainability we have to try to assess the financial impact of cities on the rest of the world.

A colleague of mine recently had the following experience: 'I attended a meeting typical of those which take place every day in the city of London. A group of Indonesian businessmen organised a lunch to raise £300 million to finance the clearing of a rainforest and the construction of a pulp paper plant. What struck me was how financial rationalism often overcomes common sense; that profit itself is seen as a good thing whatever the activity, whenever the occasion. What happened to the Indonesian rainforest was dependent upon financial decisions made over lunch that day. The financial benefits would come to institutions in London, Paris or New York. Very little, if any, of the financial benefits would go to the local people. Therefore, when thinking about the environmental impact of London, we have to consider the decisions of fund managers which affect the other side of the world. In essence, the rainforest may be geographically located in the Far East, but financially it might as well be located in London's Square Mile.'[7]

A crucial question for world cities such as London, New York or Tokyo is how they can reconcile their special status as global trading centres with the new requirement for sustainable development. Their own development was closely associated with gaining access to the world's resources. How can this be reconciled with creating a sustainable relationship with the global environment and also with the aspirations of people at the local level? Businesses in metropolitan centres certainly have the desire be sustainable in their own right. The question now is how the momentum for sustainable development can assure that people can lead lives of continuity and certainty, whilst also achieving compatibility with the living systems of the biosphere.

The metabolism of cities

Like other organisms, cities have a definable metabolism. The *metabolism* of most 'modern' cities is essentially linear, with resources flowing through the urban system without much concern about their origin and about the destination of wastes; inputs and outputs are considered as largely unrelated. Raw materials are extracted, combined and processed into consumer goods that end up as rubbish, which can't be beneficially reabsorbed into living nature. Fossil fuels are extracted from rock strata, refined and burned; their fumes are discharged into the atmosphere.

In distant forests, trees are felled for their timber or pulp, but all too often forests are not replenished. Similar processes apply to food: nutrients that are taken from the land as food is harvested, and not returned. Urban sewage systems usually have the function of collecting human wastes and separating them from people. Sewage is discharged into rivers and coastal waters downstream from population centres and is usually not returned to farmland. Today, coastal waters are enriched with both human sewage and toxic effluents, as well as the run-off of mineral fertiliser applied to farmland feeding cities. This open loop is not sustainable.

The linear metabolic system of most cities is profoundly different from Nature's circular metabolism, where every output by an organism is also an input, which renews and sustains the whole living environment. Planners designing urban systems should start by studying the ecology of natural systems. On a predominantly urban planet, cities will need to adopt circular metabolic systems to assure the long-term viability of the rural environments on which they depend. Outputs will also need to be inputs into the production system, with routine recycling of paper, metals, plastic and glass, and the conversion of organic materials into compost, returning plant nutrients to keep farmland productive.

The *local* effects of urban use of resources of cities should also be better understood. Cities accumulate large amounts of materials within them. Vienna with 1.6 million inhabitants, every day increases its actual weight by some 25,000 tonnes.[8] Much of this is relatively inert material, such as concrete and tarmac. Other materials, such as heavy metals, have discernible environmental effects: they gradually leach from the roofs of buildings and from water pipes into the local environment. Nitrates, phosphates or chlorinated hydrocarbons accumulate in the urban environment and build up in water courses and soils, with as yet uncertain consequences for future inhabitants.

The critical question today, as humanity moves to full urbanisation, is whether living standards in our cities can be maintained whilst curbing their local and global environmental impacts. To answer this question it helps to draw up balance sheets comparing urban resource flows (see Appendix 2). It is becoming apparent that similar-sized cities supply their needs with a greatly varying throughput of resources. Most large cities have been studied in considerable detail and in many cases it won't be very difficult to compare their use of resources. The critical point is that cities and their people could massively reduce their throughput of resources, maintaining a good standard of living whilst creating much needed local jobs in the process.

Are solutions possible?

It seems unlikely that the planet can accommodate an urbanised humanity that routinely draws its resources from a distant hinterland. Can cities therefore transform themselves into sustainable, self-regulating systems – not only in their internal functioning, but also in their relationships with the outside world?

An answer to this question may be critical to the future well-being of the biosphere, as well as of humanity. Maintaining stable linkages with the world around them is a completely new task for city politicians, administrators, business people and people at large. Yet there is little doubt that the world's major environmental problems will only be solved through new ways of conceptualising and running our cities, and the way we lead our urban lives.

Today we have the historic opportunity to implement technical and organisational measures for sustainable urban development, arising from agreements signed by the international community at UN conferences in the 1990s. Agenda 21 and its prescriptions for solving global environmental problems at the local level are well known. Building on Agenda 21, the Habitat Agenda, signed by 180 nations at the recent Habitat II conference in Istanbul, will also strongly influence the way we run cities. It states:

> Human settlements shall be planned, developed and improved in a manner that takes full account of sustainable development principles and all their components, as set out in Agenda 21... We need to respect the carrying capacity of ecosystems and preservation of opportunities for future generations. Production, consumption and transport should be managed in ways that protect and conserve the stock of resources while drawing upon them. Science and technology have a crucial role in shaping sustainable human settlements and sustaining the ecosystems they depend upon.[9]

What, then, is a sustainable city? Here is a provisional definition: A 'sustainable city' is a city that works so that all its citizens are able to meet their own needs without endangering the well-being of the natural world or the living conditions of other people, now or in the future.

This definition concentrates the mind on fundamentals. In the first instance the emphasis is on *people and their needs for long-term survival.* Human needs include good-quality air and water, healthy food and good housing; they also encompass quality education, a vibrant culture, good health care, satisfying employment or occupation, and the sharing of wealth; as well as factors such as safety in public places, supportive relationships, equal opportunities and freedom of expression; and meeting the special needs of the young, the old or the disabled. In a sustainable city, we have to ask: *Are all its citizens able to meet these needs?*

Conditions for sustainable development

Given that the physiology of modern cities is currently characterised by their routine use of fossil fuels to power production, commerce, transport and water supplies, as well as domestic comfort, a major issue for urban sustainability is whether *renewable* energy technologies and increased energy efficiency may be able to reduce this dependence.

22

London, for instance, with seven million people, uses twenty million tonnes of oil equivalent per year, or two supertankers a week, and discharges some sixty million tonnes of CO_2. Its *per capita* energy consumption is amongst the highest in Europe, yet the know-how exists to bring down these figures by between 30 and 50 per cent, without affecting living standards, whilst creating tens of thousands of jobs in the coming decades.[7]

To make them more sustainable, cities today require a whole range of new resource-efficient technologies, such as combined heat-and-power systems, heat pumps, fuel cells and photovoltaic modules. In the near future, enormous reductions in fossil fuel use can be achieved by the use of photovoltaics. According to calculations by BP, London could supply most of its current summer electricity consumption from photovoltaic modules on the roofs and walls of its buildings.[10] This technology is still expensive, but large-scale production will massively reduce unit costs.

Looking back, the physiology of towns and cities was defined by muscle power. Early cities, such as Ur in Mesopotamia some 3,500 years ago, were themselves centres of food production. One author conjures up an image of Ur: 'Most of the people we pass in the streets would be farmers, market gardeners, herdsmen and fishermen and correspondingly many of the goods transported in carts would be food products. However, some of the farmers could have had other roles as well: carpenters, smiths, potters, stone-cutters, basket-makers, leather-workers, wool-spinners, baker and brewers are all recorded, as are merchants and what we might call the 'civil service' of the temple community – the priests and the scribes.'[11]

Dense concentration of people was the norm in cities throughout history, particularly in those that were surrounded by defensive walls. Many cities in history adopted symbiotic relationships with their local hinterland to ensure their continuation. This applies to medieval cities with their concentric rings of market gardens, forests, orchards, farm and grazing land. Chinese cities have long practised the return of night soil onto local farmland as a way of assuring sustained yields of foodstuffs.[12] Even today most Chinese cities administer their own adjacent areas of farmland and, until recently, many were largely self-sufficient in food.[13] Beijing, now a city of over ten million people, still administers its own adjacent farmland extending to an area the size of Belgium.

A major effect of the routine use of fossil-fuel-based technologies was for cities to replace this density with urban sprawl. Motor transport has caused many cities to stop relying on resources from their local regions and to become dependent on an increasingly global hinterland.

However, some modern cities have made circularity and resource efficiency a top priority. Cities right across Europe are installing waste recycling and composting equipment. Austrian, Swiss, Danish and French cities have taken the lead. In German towns and cities, at this point in time, dozens of composting plants are under construction. In the developing world, cities often have very high rates of waste reuse and recycling, even with rudimentary waste management systems, simply because poverty is a major spur to using waste materials efficiently.[14]

Today we can argue that, given the reality of a vast human population, cities could be beneficial for the global environment.[15] The very density of human life in cities creates the potential for energy efficiency in home heating as well as in transport. Waste management can be more efficiently organised in densely inhabited areas. And urban agriculture, too, if well developed, could make a significant contribution to feeding cities and providing people with livelihoods.

Urban food growing is certainly common in the late twentieth century and not just in poorer countries – a new book published by UNDP proves the point:

> The 1980 US census found that urban metropolitan areas produced 30% of the dollar value of US agricultural production. By 1990, this figure had increased to 40%. Singapore is fully self-reliant in meat and produces 25% of its vegetable needs. Bamako, Mali, is self-sufficient in vegetables and produces half or more of the chickens it consumes. Dar-es-Salaam, one of the world's the fastest growing large cities, now has 67% of families engaged in farming compared with 18% in 1967. 65% of Moscow families are involved in food production compared with 20% in 1970. There are 80,000 community gardeners on municipal land in Berlin with a waiting list of 16,000.[16]

Of course, urban agriculture is not the only aspect of greening urban spaces. Cities also need park landscapes and spaces for wildlife. In fact, suburban gardens in the UK have been found to contain a greater variety of wildlife than surrounding farmland. This aspect of cities is crucial for nature conservation and every effort should be made to support urban wildlife conservation.

Policies for sustainability

Today we have a great opportunity to develop a whole new range of environmentally friendly technologies for use in our cities. Efficient energy systems are now available for urban buildings, including combined heat-and-power generators, with fuel cells and photovoltaic modules waiting in the wings. New concepts of architectural design allow us to greatly improve the energy performance and to reduce the environmental impact of materials use in buildings. Also, waste-recycling technologies for small and large, rich and poor cities, can facilitate greater efficiency in the urban use of resources. Transport technologies, too, are due for a major overhaul. Fuel-efficient low-emission vehicles are at a very advanced stage of development. In US cities, rapid urban transit systems are starting to reappear even where people had come to depend almost exclusively on private transport.

With some 75 per cent of the population in the north of the USA living in cities, and with cities using most of the world's resources, it is critically important to develop new policies for the sustainability of those cities – social, economic and environmental. This means, above all else, *self-financing investment in end-use efficiency – reducing resource use whilst simultaneously generating urban jobs and business opportunities.*

Using Agenda 21 and the Habitat Agenda as the basis, we have the opportunity to refocus investment from *resource extraction* to *resource conservation* and recycling, with a great many employment and business opportunities. Whilst a policy based on high *resource productivity* would reduce employment in mining, much of it abroad, it would enhance job creation in end-use efficiency – in the building trade, in environmental technology industries and in the electronics sector – in places where they are most needed: in our cities.

Policies proposed here aim to create synergies between various business sectors: the waste outputs of cities can be a basis for new business ventures. Energy efficiency, so far tackled half-heartedly, should be given top priority. Government can do a great deal to facilitate sustainable urban development by using legislation, regulations and budgetary signals to initiate change.

Smart cities

Cities are centres of communication and new electronic systems have dramatically enhanced that role. Information technologies have given cities a global reach as never before, and particularly in further extending the financial power of urban institutions. The daily money-go-round from Tokyo to London and on to New York and Los Angeles is the most striking example of this: '... the new economy is organised around global networks of capital, management, and information, whose access to technological know-how is at the roots of productivity and competitiveness.'[17] But will this power ever be exercised with a sense of responsibility appropriate to an *urban age*? If this is the global network society, who controls its ever-growing power?

The global economic and environmental reach of cities today needs to be matched with communication systems that monitor new impacts. We need early warning systems that enable city people to ring alarm bells as soon as new, unacceptable developments occur, whether it is the dumping of toxic waste or the transfer of environmentally undesirable technologies from one city or territory to another. Much more needs to be done to ensure processes by which cities monitor and ameliorate their impact on the biosphere. I would like to postulate that modern cities could develop *cultural feedback systems*, responding to the challenge of achieving sustainability by limiting urban resource consumption and waste output through technological and organisational measures.

The impact of city people on ever remoter areas needs to be matched with appropriate monitoring. As it is, environmental awareness is often very well developed in cities and most environmental organisations are based there. It is vital that the awareness of the impact of cities themselves on the global environment is better understood and that policies are developed and implemented accordingly.

It is of critical importance to recognise the great inherent creativity of city people in solving problems. But people need a good knowledge base. For this purpose, the most important thing is the collection and dissemination of best practices to assure that people in cities worldwide actually are informed about existing projects. That would be an indication that cities were becoming *smart* in the best sense of the word.

The legacy of Habitat II

The Habitat II Conference in Istanbul in 1996, organised by the United Nations Centre for Human Settlements, made a great deal of the fact that cities, more often than not, are considered places where problems are concentrated. However, in reality, people wherever they are seek to improve their situation wherever possible. This information is now available via the World Wide Web[18] and through direct contacts with urban groups all over the world. Exchange programmes for disseminating this information are now reaching even some of the poorest urban communities.

There are five lessons that emerged out of Habitat II[19]:

1 *The power of the good examples.* There are fascinating initiatives throughout the world's cities. Habitat and its partners have helped groups from around the world to prepare reports and to make films about their own activities. It is also undertaking the dissemination

of best practices. This process will deepen our understanding of urban challenges and opportunities so that realistic steps can be taken at local, national and international levels to develop new partnerships for solving problems and enriching the life of cities.

2 *Complexity of issues.* The contributions Habitat received also illustrated just how complex modern cities are. In this context, obstacles to successful implementation must be analysed and effective processes for implementing projects identified. In situations of rapid urban growth it is particularly important for the development of urban infrastructure problems to be overcome.

3 *Local level action has large-scale repercussions.* Implementation must be tailored very closely to local situations. We then have to ask: how applicable are best practices outside their own regions? For urban best practice to be transferable from one city to another, implementation must be closely tailored to local situations. It is particularly important to establish under what circumstances and with what types of partners successful projects have materialised.

4 *Exchanges take place between peer groups in different cities.* The sharing of best practice between cities is an essential tool for sustainable urban development. Once outside interest in a project has been established, site visits are of critical importance. By learning from example, local transformation can lead to global change.

5 *Changing the way urban institutions work.* The power of allowing people direct access to best practice examples through a dynamic process of decentralised co-operation has become very apparent. The material collected under the Habitat 'best practice initiative' is a gold mine for the world's cities and its dissemination will be of paramount importance for all the potential partners concerned.

By 2020, more than a billion and a half people in the world's cities could face life- and health-threatening environments unless we create a revolution in urban problem solving. We could also see ever greater impacts by cities on the global environment. We need a new global partnership between national governments and local communities, between the public and private sectors. The sustainable development of cities is becoming a priority challenge for the international community.

Cultural development

With the majority of the world now copying Western development patterns, we need to formulate new cultural priorities. Cultural development is a critical aspect of sustainable urban development, giving cities the chance to realise their full potential as centres of creativity, education and communication. Cities are centres of knowledge and today this also means knowledge of the world and our impact on it. Reducing urban impacts is as much an issue of education and of information dissemination as of the better uses of technology.

Ultimately, that cannot be done without changing the value systems underpinning our urban lifestyles. Initiatives to that effect are now in evidence all over the world. In many cities there is growing awareness that the urban superorganism can become a sustainable, self-regulating system through appropriate cultural processes. In the end, it is only a profound change of attitudes that can bring the deeper transformations that will make cities truly sustainable.

We need to revive the vision of the city as a place of culture and creativity, of conviviality and above all else of sedentary living. As I have suggested, currently cities are not centres of *civilisation* but *mobilisation* of people and goods. A calmer, serener vision of cities is needed to help them fulfil their true potential as places not just of the body but of the spirit. Great cities of the past were above all else places of beauty, with their great public spaces, their magnificent bridges and the rising spires of their religious buildings.

Eco-friendly urban development could well become the greatest challenge of the twenty-first century, not only for human self-interest, but also for the sake of a sustainable relationship between cities and the biosphere on which humanity crucially depends. Cities accommodate half the world's population on just 2 per cent of the world's land surface. Given our ever-growing numbers it is critically important to utilise the potential of urban density as a basis for sustainability.

Cities for a new millennium will be energy and resource efficient, people friendly and culturally rich, with active democracies assuring the best uses of human energies. In northern mega-cities prudent inward investment will contribute significantly to achieving higher levels of employment. In cities in the south, significant investment in infrastructure will make a vast difference to health and living conditions.

Thought has created the unstable world in which we now live – manifested in mega-technology, mega-cities, global power structures and vast environmental impacts. Practical visions and working examples of innovative, alternative systems urgently need to be implemented in cities all over the world. City people the world over have a crucial responsibility for implementing such a process.

It is clear that IUCN can play a key role in this process. With member organisations active all over the world, IUCN can help create the new awareness that cities and their people have a vital role to play in establishing sustainable relationships between cities and the biosphere. This will be one of the greatest challenges of the twenty-first century.

Appendix 1: London's ecological footprint

London's footprint	

7,000,000 people
Surface area: 158,000 ha
Area required for food production: 1.2 ha per person: 8,400,000 ha
Forest area required by London for wood products: 768,000 ha
Land area that would be required for carbon sequestration = fuel production:
   1.5 ha per person: 10,500,000 ha
Total London footprint: 19,700,000 ha = 125 times London's surface area
Britain's productive land: 21,000,000 ha
Britain's surface area: 24,400,000 ha

Compiled by H. Girardet (1996).

Appendix 2: the metabolism of Greater London, population 7,000,000

	Tonnes per year
1. Inputs	
Total tonnes of fuel, oil equivalent	20,000,000
Oxygen	40,000,000
Water	1,002,000,000
Food	2,400,000
Timber	1,200,000
Paper	2,200,000
Plastics	2,100,000
Glass	360,000
Cement	1,940,000
Bricks, blocks, sand and tarmac	36,000,000
Metals (total)	1,200,000
2. Wastes	
CO_2	60,000,000
SO_2	400,000
NO_x	280,000
Wet, digested sewage sludge	7,500,000
Industrial and demolition wastes	11,400,000
Household, civic and commercial wastes	900,000

Compiled by H. Girardet (1995 and 1996); sources available.

Notes

1 Extracted summary of facts from: Satterthwaite, D. (1996) *An Urbanising World: The Second Global Report on Human Settlements*, Oxford: Oxford University Press.
2 *State of the World 1997* (1997) Worldwatch Institute, London: Earthscan.
3 Environmental Investigation Agency, London.
4 Fritjof Capra (1996) *The Web of Life*, London: HarperCollins.
5 Mathis Wackernagel and William Rees (1996) *Our Ecological Footprint*, Gabriola Island, BC: New Society.
6 Herbert Girardet (1996) *Getting London in Shape for 2000*, London: London First (unpublished).
7 Mark Campanale, personal communication.
8 Prof. Paul Brunner, TU, Vienna, personal communication.
9 *The Habitat Agenda* (1996), New York: UN.
10 Scott, R. BP Solar, personal communication.
11 Whitehouse, R. (1977) *The First Cities*, Oxford: Phaidon.
12 King, F.H. (1911) *Farmers of Forty Centuries*, Emmaus: Rodal Press.
13 Sit, V. (ed.) (1988) *Chinese Cities: The Growth of the Metropolis since 1949*, Oxford: Oxford University Press.
14 *Warmer Bulletin*, Summer 1995.
15 Gilbert, R. (1996) in Richard Gilbert, Don Stevenson and Herbert Girardet, *Making Cities Work: The Role of Local Authorities in the Urban Environment*, London: Earthscan.
16 *Urban Agriculture* (1996), New York: UNDP.
17 Castells, M. (1996) *The Network Society*, Oxford: Blackwells.
18 On http://www.bestpractices.org
19 Quoted in: Girardet, H. (1996) *The Gaia Atlas of Cities*, 2nd edn, London: Gaia Books.

3

BUILDING ETHICS INTO THE BUILT ENVIRONMENT

John Whitelegg

Introduction

We live in a dirty, stressful, polluted world. Liverpool has levels of air pollution that frequently breach World Health Organization thresholds. Calcutta has levels of air pollution that exceed the same thresholds by one and sometimes two orders of magnitude. Every child attending a primary school in urban Britain experiences noise levels that damage the cardiovascular system and impair learning skills. The built environment is a powerful determinant of who gains and who loses in this distribution and redistribution of positives and negatives. This is not surprising and is also not a particularly useful insight. What is surprising and insightful is the realisation that we have a total design failure on our hands. The built environment does not take account of the needs of children or the elderly, it does not produce intrinsically healthy environments (indoors and outdoors) and it has evolved in a manner that has obliterated place distinctiveness and place identity.

John Adams at University College, London, has explored some of these issues through thought experiments. He asks interviewees to express a preference between two different worlds. Would they prefer to live in a dirty, dangerous world or one where air and noise quality is high and streets are well used by pedestrians with high levels of security for everyone. He has not yet discovered a subset of respondents opting for the first of these two choices. This small experiment is worth pondering on for a few moments. The vast majority of our urban environments are dirty and dangerous. The danger is multifaceted and interlinked. Traffic danger deters local residents from using their streets. They are afraid of the danger, particularly when lorries are present and they will avoid using the street or road as social space. This 'people-reduction' effect then feeds into danger of another kind, so-called 'stranger danger'. The transformation of social space into an increasingly narrow kind of circulation space (motorised traffic) has opened up ecological niches for danger. This process is well recognised by local residents and by those most directly affected. It produces unattractive places and it destroys one of the foundations of social interaction. From an ethical perspective we are witnessing a transformation that penalises those without a voice (e.g. children), rewards those with higher levels of material wealth (e.g. car drivers) and reorganises the built environment with no reference to any process of debate or consensus building with local residents.

This transformation can be characterised as the 'boiling frog' syndrome (an extremely unethical metaphor). If a frog is placed in a pan of cold water and heated up slowly it will not notice the dramatic transformation of its environment into something that is unpleasant (at first) and then fatal. If, on the other hand, the frog is put directly into a pan of boiling water it will react violently and leap out (hopefully). The highly unpleasant environment is the same in both cases. In the case of the human subject and the built environment we are in more trouble than the frog. Every aspect of our daily lives is refracted to represent the joys of the rising water temperature. Car ownership and use deliver freedom and mobility (but not congestion, pollution, cancer, concrete car parks and cities dedicated to the movement of vehicles and not people); roads are improved (never just widened); cars are made safer (but only for those inside the car); vehicle exhaust emissions are cleaner than 'city air' (but are never used to provide 'clean air' in the offices of vehicle manufacturers). Our planning and development systems are still delivering large, land-greedy, energy-wasting leisure, recreational and retail facilities, at the same time as our urban communities wither and die because of lack of facilities and lack of attractiveness. A walk around Preston, Wigan or Warrington (or any town in NW England) reveals the extent to which dirty, dangerous environments have been designed and implemented and social space exterminated. This adds its own pressures on developments in the countryside in the form of new housing areas and new tourism/leisure facilities. The rural dweller needs more vehicles and more road space and the conditions on many rural roads are as bad or worse (no pedestrian facilities) than roads in urban areas. The new rural dweller who has left an urban area in search of a better life in a rural area purchases this better life at the cost of much increased fossil fuel consumption and vehicle emissions. Depending on geography, this additional health-damaging pollution burden will be 'dumped' on poorer communities through which the long-distance commuter will often travel. The ethical dimension underlying 'dumping' is a strong one but is made stronger still by the extent to which taxation revenues are used to encourage the dumping. I will return later to some issues surrounding economics, taxation and public expenditure from an ethical perspective. In the remainder of this chapter, I will examine the ethical issues raised by some recent project work (Heathrow Airport Terminal 5, Lancaster Local Plan, Calcutta's flyover project), identify four principal dimensions of ethical considerations in the built environment (place identity, empowering local residents, the economics of ethics and professional ethics) and make preliminary suggestions on how to build ethics into the design of the built environment.

Ethical issues: a case study approach

Some 70–80 per cent of Europe's population live in urban (depending on the definition of urban) areas. The vast majority of the remainder have a lifestyle that revolves around the urban. They commute to a large urban centre (or its edge), shop on a regular basis in cities, fly several times a year or simply consume a rich diet of social and cultural products that are created in cities. Our urban way of life is centred on the built environment. We live, work, shop and play in its buildings. We depend on its large-scale medical facilities for health care and we travel increasingly often and on increasingly lengthy journeys by motorised transport to connect all these things. This transport alone can account for 30–40 per cent of the surface area (roads, car parks, etc.) of our urban areas and has a profound effect on shaping the nature of our interactions with place and with each other.

In most discussions of the built environment it is assumed that there is a very large fixed stock of buildings, roads, etc. and a small annual 'turnover' measured in demolition and new build. This is correct in terms of dwellings, where new build cannot compete with the historic legacy of millions of dwellings from the Victorian, Edwardian and inter-war periods of suburban expansion. It may not be true of other important elements of the built environment. The wholesale conversion of retailing from a small-scale activity to a large-scale industrial activity has been matched by the wholesale conversion of hospitals from the locally based facility they once were to the very large (and fewer) industrial activities they now are. Similar processes have taken place with the decline of employment in cities (witness the large-scale urban dereliction in former mills and factories in the north of England) and its replacement by the growth of business parks and land-greedy, low-density developments on the edge of cities. Employment in the city of London which was very recently characterised by commuter trips with a 90 per cent plus public transport bias has now been replaced by commuter trips to business parks on the M25 corridor with 90 per cent plus car bias.

It is important to recognise the speed and thoroughness of these changes. They have reorganised almost every aspect of everyday life, they have been 'purchased' at enormous expense, both financially and environmentally, and they have not been subjected to any collective discussion about costs and benefits or alternative scenarios. A fundamental reorganisation of choices has been imposed on a population that has not been involved in defining the landscape of possible choices. At the very least, this degree of imposition has a strong ethical dimension and one that is reinforced when the landscape of choice imposes severe burdens on some sections of the community and confers gains on others.

Notwithstanding the speed and thoroughness of these changes, more is on the way. The process of conversion or transformation of the built environment is not yet complete and is also shifting into a global phase reflecting the globalisation of the economy which has been a feature of the last 20 years or so. The nature of these shifts can be seen in a small number of recent development proposals:

- Heathrow Airport Terminal 5
- Lancaster Local Plan
- Calcutta flyover project.

Heathrow Airport Terminal 5

The public inquiry into the proposal to build a fifth terminal (T5) at Heathrow (LHR) has just ended. It was the longest ever in British planning history and may well be the last ever inquiry of this kind. The proposal is to expand LHR from a capacity of fifty million passengers per annum (mppa) to 80 mppa. The fifth terminal would be bigger than the present capacity of Frankfurt or Schiphol Amsterdam airports. It would add to noise, local air pollution and greenhouse gas emissions. It would have a particularly damaging effect on the lives of 250,000 residents of west London (Hounslow and Hillingdon). Evidence was presented at the inquiry showing the extent to which the increased noise levels would damage the learning ability of primary school children in those areas and add to the national inventory of greenhouse gases at a time when the UK is committed to reducing these gases. The arguments in favour of T5 are economic. Over 50,000 jobs would be created, many more would be protected and London would retain its role as a global economic centre. Without T5 the growth would happen anyway but would be located in Paris, Frankfurt or Amsterdam. There is no disagreement about the anticipated growth in aviation and the need for increased capacity on a 'business as usual' model. There is a huge disagreement about the extent to which this demand should be met/encouraged. The arguments surrounding this disagreement are ethical. Should we turn off the supply of aviation facilities so that demand is restrained? Do we accept a situation in which only the rich can fly? How do we give real significance to the residents of west London in their demands for a quality environment? Do we really *need* green beans to be grown in Nicaragua and flowers to be grown in Chad. Do we really *need* these commodities to be flown in to meet consumer demand? Do we accept the damage done by aviation to the atmosphere (with all its difficult to quantify risks) as a price worth paying for our holiday flights? Do we accept the consequences of climate change attributable to aviation as a price worth paying for the benefits of aviation, when that price includes the (possible) loss of land and agricultural production in Bangladesh and many other countries? Who are *we* in all these questions?

Lancaster Local Plan

The UK planning system has a number of admirable features that have been designed to encourage community participation in decision-making and forward thinking about the development of a specific local area ten years into the future. This is the local plan system which has at its centre the local plan inquiry. In practice the local plan process (especially the inquiry) is adversarial with a local authority pressing its viewpoint and supported by barristers all paid out of public funds whose function it is to attack local residents, community groups and others who present an alternative viewpoint, or simply disagree with the vision of the local authority. The Lancaster Local Plan contains a proposal to build approximately 1,000 new houses to the south of the city on 'greenfield' sites that in previous plans have been protected as well-defined urban edges of landscape character, reflecting well-established planning concern to stop sprawl. The 1,000 new houses are justified by the local authority as part of the 4.4 million new homes that central government has deemed necessary to meet future demand in England and Wales. As in the case of aviation, a clear political principle of 'predict and provide' has been elevated to the ranks of scientific orthodoxy with very little scope for challenge. Residents and community groups in Lancaster have strongly opposed the housing plan. The arguments against are that it will generate thousands of extra car trips per day on roads that are already congested, it will fuel the demand for new road construction and it will destroy a valuable and valued tract of countryside that currently provides a clear marker to the edge of Lancaster. More fundamentally, the opponents of the plan argue that there is no need to take greenfield sites. Lancaster and its adjacent urban area of Morecambe is provided with ample reserves of 'brownfield' sites (i.e. land that has had a previous industrial, commercial or residential use, but that is now redundant). House prices are very low in Morecambe (typically £25,000 for a four-bedroomed terraced house) and they are very difficult to sell. There is a strong ethical character to this debate. First, the process itself is fundamentally flawed. Residents and community groups are effectively in a battle with the local authority. They have no resources and no legal representation and they are attacked by legal representatives on the other side of the argument who are paid for out of public funds. Second, the detailed arguments themselves are ethical. A valued landscape is under threat because of an argument that new homes are needed to satisfy market demand, which cannot be satisfied by the existing stock. As the existing stock of brownfield sites and dwellings can meet (numerically) the predicted demand, the argument reduces to one of preference. The planning system can operate in favour of accumulating derelict land and vacant properties whilst at the same time destroying landscape, or it can work to reuse and conserve by making maximum use of existing stocks of dwellings and brownfield sites. The pseudo-scientific arguments about household size twenty years into the future cannot disguise that a choice has to be made between two very clear alternatives. There are at least two visions of an urban future for Lancaster and the choice can be informed by an ethical discussion.

Calcutta flyover project

Calcutta is a city with fourteen million inhabitants and significant problems of poverty, slum dwellings, disease, unemployment and underemployment. Its industrial and traffic-related pollution put the city in the top five polluted cities of the world. It is a compact city with generous amounts of open green space, parks, water and trees. It has an excellent public transport system in its trams, buses, underground and rickshaws. It has very high levels of use of non-motorised transport especially walking and rickshaws, though low levels of use of cycling. The state government of West Bengal, responsible for the city, has decided that urgent action is needed to solve transport problems, particularly traffic congestion. Its solutions are supported by the World Bank, US multinational companies, the Japanese government and transport professionals. They are opposed by very active community groups and a number of transport professionals in India and in Europe. The solutions include:

- abolishing rickshaws on the argument that slow-moving, human-powered vehicles cause traffic congestion and on the argument that it is degrading for people to run along the streets pulling other people behind them in a hand-pulled rickshaw;
- closing several sections of the tram system, which is now very old and starved of investment even for daily repair and servicing, and replacing this street running system with an elevated high-technology monorail system. A feasibility study into this project is currently being funded by the US government;
- building fourteen new flyovers with Japanese international aid to relieve traffic congestion at the main intersections (e.g. Gariahat in south Calcutta).

The Calcutta transport debate is crucial on a global scale. Indian cities in general, but Calcutta in particular, still have the potential to deliver very high-quality urban living experiences with very low demands on energy and resources (a small ecological footprint). The outcome of the transport debate in Calcutta will be a choice of alternative futures for that city. It can go in the direction of high levels of motorisation and associated infrastructure provision or it can go in the direction of high-quality non-motorised provision and collective transport. Less than 0.5 million residents of Calcutta own a vehicle and the likelihood is that this total will remain low by European standards if (and only if) the city chooses to move in the direction of developing high-quality accessibility and alternatives to the car. The flyover project represents a very clear choice in favour of the car. It is funded and is going ahead.

From an ethical perspective there are a number of issues in play at the same time. The transport plans in Calcutta will damage the interests of the poor and very poor (e.g. depriving 250,000 rickshaw workers of an income). The plans for the tram system will remove a transport option that is well used by women and children. Trams are currently very cheap and are largely stress free in contrast to the experiences available on grossly overcrowded and aggressively driven buses. The new (proposed) monorail system will replace the tram system with an expensive alternative. The US consultancy developing the plan has already indicated that fares would have to be much higher than on the current tram system in order to generate an acceptable rate of return on the investment. This will put journeys by tram/monorail out of the reach of women and children. It will replace a street level system with an elevated system specifically to make more room for cars on the streets. The transport plans of the State government ignore the interests of women, children, the poor, rickshaw workers and non-car drivers. The plans are encouraged by global financial and commercial interests with a wish to encourage vehicle ownership and use in India. The ethical dimension is made more complicated still by the very clear view in Calcutta, and in India, that these commercial interests represent welcome opportunities for development and modernisation and make available to Indians what Europeans and North Americans have enjoyed for the last fifty years. To put a different viewpoint is regarded as intrusive, neo-imperialistic and selfish. The climate change debate raises similarly profound ethical issues. Are European countries desperately trying to prevent climate change through restrictions on fossil fuel use to protect themselves when their current levels of prosperity have resulted from that selfsame fossil fuel use? The future of Calcutta and by extension many Third World 'mega-cities' depends on the quality of a global ethical debate about choices and alternative futures.

Identifying ethical dimensions in the built environment

The case studies have revealed a dense web of ethical considerations that have a striking and undervalued relevance to our understanding of the built environment and its future development. The need to develop this source of insight and understanding is urgent as the pace of transformation of the built environment accelerates globally. The case studies are drawn from a wide range of locations and cultural circumstances and yet point very clearly to a small number of key dimensions in the ethical debate. No claim is made that these dimensions are definitive, exhaustive or even the most important. They are:

- place identity
- empowering local residents/communities
- the economics of ethics or the ethics of economics
- professional ethics.

Place identity

Much has been written about place identity and its significance, but this is not the place to rehearse the arguments in any detail. In many ways it should not be necessary to have to make any arguments at all since place, place identity, the meaning of place and the processes through which human use gives place a rich, multilayered significance, are valued by most cultures and most periods in history. *Place is under attack.* In contemporary Europe, it is not possible to defend any places on any historical, social, religious or environmental grounds. In Germany, national sites of environmental significance are made into roads. The UK has contributed Twyford Down to the sad catalogue of sites that have enormous place significance, but not enough to prevent huge rock cuttings and new motorway lanes. In Israel the 300-km-long trans-Israeli highway will destroy thirty sites that are mentioned by name in the Bible and bits of Nazareth and Bethlehem had to go to make room for the millions of car-based millennium visitors. More important, every local plan in England, development proposal, landfill site proposal and housing development spell out how unimportant the landscape is. Language has been subverted to support the argument for more concrete and more asphalt. Sites with outstanding geomorphological significance, settlement history and importance to the local population today, for walking the dog or taking the children on a bike ride, are described as 'of no particular significance', 'appropriate in morphology to absorb the development successfully' or of 'poor landscape value'. Language and meaning have also been subverted in the case of 'NIMBY' ('not in my back yard') and 'NIMBYISM'. Local people defending local places are now afraid to assert their rights to defend place because of the negative associations that have been given to this term. The ethical challenge here is to assert the importance of the meaning of landscape to local people, to recognise the spiritual and the emotional attachments that support people in their daily lives and to eliminate the 'ethnic-cleansing' approach to landscape that is deemed untidy, inconvenient or disposable.

Empowering local residents

When Swiss voters were asked in a national referendum in 1997 whether or not they wanted to ban lorries that were in transit (using Switzerland as a corridor rather than a destination), they voted for the ban. Local communities throughout the Alpine region had been vociferous about the need to put their quality of life (and the Alpine environment) above the needs of goods in transit from Germany to Italy. The European Union objected strongly and is still trying to get the ban reversed, even though the ban will not come into force until 2007. Meanwhile, the Swiss are investing millions of dollars in building new rail transit facilities that can carry the lorries on the back of trains through Switzerland.

In 1996 the city of Amsterdam asked its voters to accept or reject a proposal to convert the city into a 'car-free' city. This would not be taken literally, but would involve taking road space away from cars and giving it to bicycles and pedestrians on selected streets, reducing car parking in and near the centre and investing in new tram lines. The vote went in favour of 'car-free' (only by a narrow majority) and it is now being implemented.

Both examples could be contrasted with recent UK experiences, where the idea of local/national referenda has very little support. Both raise important issues about resolving and balancing the needs, desires and preferences of local areas (e.g. an Alpine valley with 30,000 lorries per day passing through) with the 'greater good' of the EU economy and its preference for shipping large quantities of potatoes from northern Germany to Italy and large quantities of potatoes from Italy to northern Germany. The 'greater good' argument will lead to the acceptance by government of the Heathrow Terminal 5 development regardless of the wishes of 250,000 local residents. An ethical debate is urgently needed to sharpen our understanding and appreciation of the importance of meeting local aspirations and of the inadequacies associated with the 'greater good' argument.

The economics of ethics or the ethics of economics

There is a problem with economics and it is probably beyond the insights of ethics to correct this problem. In 1876 and 1877 3.5 million Indians died in the Mysore Presidency famine. The British government both in London and at the Indian HQ in Calcutta were deeply committed to *laissez faire* economic policies. They were convinced that intervention was wrong. Food was available, the mechanisms for controlling prices and moving food into the famine areas were available, but nothing was done until it was too late. An economic ideology had remained intact and survived a threat to its integrity. In late twentieth-century Britain, these economic ideologies are alive and well. Bus deregulation has resulted in a 25 per cent loss of bus passengers outside London and rail privatisation has resulted in over one million complaints. This has been registered as a success and the same economic logic is now to be applied to the London underground. Conclusions about the success or otherwise of deregulation and privatisation in terms of their effect on the built environment and on different user groups are not relevant to the pursuit of the same economic logic.

In the UK, private transport is heavily subsidised by all taxpayers, including those who do not own or use cars. Aviation fuel is not taxed, but other forms of transport fuel are taxed. Local transport in the form of walking and cycling receives very little financial support from the government, but airports and the Channel Tunnel Rail Link (high-speed and non-local) receive huge amounts of public funds. The world of economics leads to the conclusion that greenfield sites are cheaper to develop than brownfield sites and that investments in high-quality, long-lasting environmentally efficient buildings cannot proceed if the initial cost is higher than a low-quality alternative. Some 75 per cent of our journeys are less than 5 miles in length, but 95 per cent of the funding in transport supports long-distance (>50 miles), high-speed transport and discriminates against low-speed, local transport. Most journeys undertaken by the poor, children, the elderly and women are local and yet these journeys are underrepresented in government funding. Is this an unethical policy?

Professional ethics

Should landscape architects, quantity surveyors, architects, road engineers and planners adopt a code of ethics that guarantees human rights, outlaws the kind of bullying that goes on at public inquiries and requires a high level of respect for landscape, place and local attachment to place? Whilst there is a very clear ethical dimension to professional behaviour, there are also a number of grey areas where the ethics of professional involvement might clash with the democratic institutions directing the political choice process.

Ian McHarg had no difficulty in clarifying his own distinctive view of the role of professionals in the destruction of American cities by US highway engineers when he delivered a lecture to this group in 1966:

> I welcome the opportunity to describe the ecological planning method for highway route selection…but, first, I have to reveal my loathing for you and your kind. If you all had a fatal paroxysm, I would find it difficult to mobilise a single tear. You have been engaged in an onslaught against the American environment, you have dismembered, dissected and destroyed significant areas of American cities. Your depredations must end. There is no reason that the American public should pay so dearly to have their environments attacked by such insensitive bullies.
>
> (McHarg 1966)

He would have had no difficulty generalising from his engineers to the councillors, barristers, planners and engineers who have devoted so much time, energy and cash to the destruction of environment, landscape, place and participative democracy in the UK and in major highway projects such as the Birmingham Northern Relief Road.

Conclusion

This is a new and exciting area. The conclusions in this chapter should be regarded as preliminary and will come into much sharper focus as the discussion of ethics and the built environment proceeds, but a number of milestones are already emerging:

- There is a strong ethical dimension to the workings of the built environment and this dimension is currently underdeveloped or completely absent.
- The built environment is now the dominant environment in which people live in the developed world and is becoming so in the developing world. Its transformation along industrial and consumerist lines is creating future inequalities, inequities, social injustice, loss of community, loss of place identity and loss of a spiritual dimension to life. All of these issues are ethical issues, as is the absence of an ethical perspective from the built environment agenda itself.
- Globalisation of the economy and human experience is taking built environment issues into a new dimension where an ethical perspective is more important still. What are the global ethics of dominant lifestyles, mass consumerism, mass motorisation and climate change? Just as biodiversity in plant and animal worlds is an ethical issue, so 'eco-diversity' in the built environment world is an ethical issue. Is it really acceptable that we all consume the same mass-produced products from the same multinational corporations, carried around the world by lorry and aircraft with every place looking like every other place and no place for community/spiritual/alternative lifestyles?
- Professions do have a responsibility in these matters. How can professional ethics work towards building ethics into the built environment?

A final anecdote might help to give focus to the discussion. After years of campaigning for traffic calming on a busy residential street in Lancaster (Ullswater Road), the local authority finally agreed to proceed. They designed a scheme and put it to the residents as a consultation document. The residents replied and their views were ignored. The construction work began and the street was closed to traffic so that humps, bumps and chicanes could be built. During this period of genuine traffic calming, neighbours appeared on the streets and chatted to each other, children played safely on the street and the character of the street changed completely. Then the construction work finished and the street was once again opened to traffic bringing to an end the accidental creation of place and community. That evening the children appeared once again on the street and replaced all the barriers closing the street to traffic. This was a short-lived expression of 'child-centred' management of the built environment and within a couple of hours the barriers were removed, the traffic restored and 'normal' life resumed (i.e. no children, no community activity on the street and the reinstatement of noise and pollution).

Reference

McHarg, I.L. (1996) *A Quest for Life: an Autobiography*, Chichester: Wiley.

4

GREEN BUILDING

Establishing principles

Tom Woolley

Introduction

One of our tasks when we produce the *Green Building Digest and Green Building Handbook* (Woolley *et al.* 1997) is to distinguish between what is genuinely beneficial to the environment and what might be called 'greenwash'. Many products are presented as being environmentally friendly without any commonly accepted criteria having been established to ensure that this is the case. Many organisations now include 'enviro speak' in their marketing, words like *environmental, ecological* and *sustainable* are inevitably being devalued in the same way that the word *community* once was. Establishing a basis for environmental assessment in buildings involves consideration of ethical principles.

Greenwash

Despite recognition that environmental issues are important in construction, this has not led to any significant changes in practice. Quarries are still running; toxic waste is still being burned to produce cement; dioxin by-products from PVC manufacture are still being accumulated; waste materials are still being dumped in landfill sites. Hardwood timber is still being imported from Latin America and the Far East, where forests are being clear felled and burned. The main difference is that the manufacturers and distributors will *tell* you that their materials are environmentally friendly. In other words, the green agenda creates a marketing opportunity. Some environmental legislation has been introduced, mainly in Europe, which has led to the reduction of volatile organic compounds and solvents in paint, for instance (*Green Building Digest* 1999). Some companies have introduced environmental management procedures. Others have adopted some form of environmental labelling. However, without fundamental changes in the way the industry operates, these forms of marketing are likely to amount to little more than greenwash.

Consumer awareness of green building issues?

The average consumer is likely to become fairly bemused when confronted by the various systems of eco or environmental labelling. Most timber merchants will tell you that *all* their timber is environmentally friendly or from well-managed forests when a bit of questioning may establish that they do not even know the source of the timber. The public has already been convinced that water-based paints are the last word in technological development, in that simply lowering the odours of the paints makes them environmentally friendly. There has been a huge switch to the use of laminated timber flooring as a result of an awareness of the health problems associated with carpets from dust mites and so on, but little is said about the emissions from toxic glues and varnishes from the timber laminates (*Green Building Digest* 1997). Scares about GM foods and other environmental problems have impacted strongly with the public, but there is little awareness about the damage done to the environment and our health by building and building materials. Even many environmentalists and environmental organisations, in my experience, do not attach a high priority or are relatively ignorant of such issues.

Establishing principles

If we are to provide an authoritative source of information for people who want to be environmentally responsible when they design, commission or build buildings, we need to have both a methodology and a set of principles that will underpin any claims that we make. So far this has happened in a largely pragmatic way without much debate as there are, as yet, no commonly accepted standards. Such principles also have to be defensible as they may be attacked by trade associations defending their products and those companies who would not appreciate it if their product was maligned.

There are two main aspects to deal with. One is to establish a framework for green construction, to identify the main areas of concern such as energy efficiency, embodied energy, resource depletion, extraction and manufacturing pollution and emissions, the impact on health and waste and disposal issues. The other issue to is establish criteria at a more detailed level that make it possible to say whether one product is more environmentally friendly than another by identifying risks to health and the environment.

Social and ethical context

Such a framework can be found in the introductory chapter to the first *Green Building Handbook* (Woolley *et al.* 1997), so this chapter concentrates on the societal and ethical context. It is necessary to examine how society, as a whole, perceives the issue of sustainable construction and to ask why the issues of green building have failed to make much of an impact on public consciousness when compared with public concerns over food, medical and pollution issues. We spend most of our lives in buildings – working and sleeping. Buildings and the construction industry make the largest contribution to CO_2 emissions and pollution and waste in general, yet the general public fail to recognise the impact that buildings and building materials have on our health and the environment.

There are a number of arguments that can be used to help people become more aware of these issues. They can be presented in terms of *self-interest* and *ethical* positions. First, in terms of self-interest, will it cost more or will it save money? Will it benefit my health and those working on the building? Second, from an ethical standpoint, is the client concerned about the broader impact on the environment of their choices? If people choose dolphin-friendly tuna, then are there 'dolphin-friendly' building materials? We need to examine both the self-interest and the ethical reasons for producing greener buildings.

Green self-interest and costs

There is no need at all for environmentally responsible buildings to cost more than conventional buildings, indeed they can be potentially cheaper. Unfortunately, providing products that are green labelled is seen as an added value by most producers and a way of increasing profits, as they exploit a niche market. We pay more for organic food, so why not for sustainably managed timber? Builders normally tender higher when faced with unfamiliar materials or construction systems. An organic paint based on linseed oil rather than a more toxic and synthetic, petrochemical solvent will cost more today, but only because the organic paint is sold in much smaller quantities and has to be imported from Holland or Germany (*Green Building Digest* 1999). As the volume of natural and sustainable materials increases, so their price will come down. Using locally sourced timber or second-hand materials can increase labour costs but can also save money. Cost should not be a major barrier to sustainable practices.

Self-interest and energy efficiency

While the initial capital costs of green buildings may sometimes be higher, buildings which are very energy efficient can save a client money, in terms of heating and running costs, in a relatively short space of time. The technology of zero-energy buildings is simple and easy to achieve and, even in rehabilitation or conversion, low energy running costs can be achieved (DETR 1998a). Despite this, it is surprisingly hard to convince even intelligent clients to spend a little bit extra on insulation and other simple measures that will lead to vastly reduced electricity and heating bills. Estate agents and developers will tell you that energy efficiency doesn't sell houses!

However, let us assume that a client does want an energy-efficient house. This can be achieved quite easily, but often using materials which, in themselves, use a lot of energy to produce and have damaging effects on the environment. So having won the first battle you are immediately faced with another which has environmental and ethical implications.

Conventional insulation materials such as extruded polystyrene or UPVC windows use a lot of energy to produce and potentially cause a great deal of damage to the environment, using up petrochemical products and creating toxic waste by-products (Howard *et al.* 1998). Yet these are first-choice materials for people who want energy-efficient houses. The energy efficiency industry, which has grown up recently, barely addresses these issues and seems only interested in the ends, not the means. When I rang the Energy Saving Trust and asked them to send me information on the embodied energy of insulation materials they told me that they had totally ignored the issue of embodied energy (Energy Saving Trust 1999).

Unfortunately, energy efficiency often leads to hotter houses rather than a reduction in energy usage. We work in overheated offices and shops, travel in overheated cars, expect to come home to overheated, draft-free houses, where all means of ventilation have been blocked up. This has health implications as well as energy waste. Many people assume that 'green building' is simply increasing insulation, but it is a much more complex issue.

The self-interest of healthy buildings

The health reasons for building green is one of the most compelling self-interest arguments, but these are often invisible and difficult to promote. True, toxic paints smell and induce headaches, but these subside and are quickly forgotten about. The risks from sawing up MDF are largely to the joiners, not the householders. It is not easy to compile convincing evidence on health issues because either no research has been done or the research has been published only in obscure academic journals (*Indoor Air* 1996). Sometimes the evidence of damage to our health is there, but conclusions are not drawn by researchers, many of whom are largely being funded by industry.

If you believe there is a conspiracy of multinational giants to poison the environment with GM foods, to gain control of all seed production, then it is easy to believe that the evidence on toxic and dangerous building materials is being suppressed. The *Green Building Digest* has been criticised by the manufacturers for suggesting that there might be some problems with various materials. They are not keen for it to be widely known that many building materials emit radon and gamma-radiation. It is argued that the radiation emitted by such materials as blocks and bricks is much lower than that caused by naturally occurring radon and thus the cancer risk from such radiation is extremely low. However, there is a wide variety of scientific opinions on what is a safe level of radiation and in some areas, where the natural radon level is low, that emitted by building materials can be higher. In Italy concrete is made from aggregates that have very high levels of radiation, capable of setting off a nuclear alert in a NATO base (Cherubini and Aumento 1995).

A list of toxic substances currently commonly found in building materials in Laura Zeiher's book *The Ecology of Architecture* runs to nearly 800 entries. She also claims that there are over fifty carcinogenic agents and nearly 200 'possibly carcinogenic' (Zeiher 1996). There is little doubt that the more highly sealed and energy efficient a house becomes, the greater the exposure to a cocktail of toxic chemicals from building materials, even, if singly, the levels of emission are quite low. A study at the Building Research Establishment (BRE) identified 254 toxic substances emitted in a study of new houses built on the BRE site (Crump *et al.* 1997). Apart from concern about carcinogens in building materials, many health effects of modern building materials are linked to asthma. There has been a significant increase in childhood asthma in recent years and the causes have not yet been identified (Kuehni *et al.* 1998). While little research has been carried out on the links between indoor air quality and asthma, many of the toxic materials used in building cause occupational asthma in the factories where they are produced.

Apart from chemicals causing asthma, many carcinogenic materials, chemical pesticides and toxic timber treatment chemicals, such as copper chrome arsenic, are freely used in buildings. Toxic emissions from timber preservatives, such as lindane, can be at a sufficiently high level to be absorbed by clothes and washed into the sewers via washing machines, in high enough concentrations to poison rivers near sewage outfalls. The amount not absorbed by clothes and other fabrics goes into the lungs (Harper *et al.* 1977).

According to Hans Van Weenan of the UN Environment programme in the Netherlands, a television programme on the effects of solvents in paints on the nervous systems of painters and decorators jammed the switchboard of the TV company and hugely boosted the sales of natural, solvent-free paints (Van Weenan 1999). Such is the impact of the indoor built environment on our health. It is surprising that there is not more concern from the public for a greener environment. Unfortunately, however, most people are largely ignorant of these problems.

Broader environmental impact – the ethical case

Apart from the effect of building materials and products on our health, they also have a wider environmental impact. If a material pollutes the inside of a house, it is also likely to be polluting the wider environment. The source of materials is important. Many architects specify tropical hardwoods with little concern about where they come from, or how the forests in Third World countries are being managed (Long 1999). To change such a policy requires a principled decision by client, builder and specifier and a certain amount of openness from the supplier.

It is relatively easy to find statistics that show that the construction industry is one of the largest destroyers of the natural environment. Most building materials today are synthetic and are derived either from the petrochemicals industry or are harvested from natural sources that cannot be replaced. Even small reductions in the vast consumption of resources would significantly reduce our negative impact on the planet. The UK government's consultation document, *Opportunities for Change*, lists highly significant figures (DETR 1998b):

- 300 million tonnes of quarried material per year in the UK;
- energy use in buildings accounts for 50 per cent of CO_2 emissions;
- consumption of 6 tonnes of material per person per year.

While the environmental impact of buildings and the construction industry is slowly being recognised, very little is being done to establish standards to say what is acceptable. Some efforts are being made to introduce *eco-labelling* and assessment systems, but the UK wound up the 'independent' eco- labelling board and have absorbed it into the DETR (ECO-DESIGN 1998). Only the Forest Stewardship Council scheme has any real credibility internationally (Forest Stewardship Council). Blue

Angel and Nordic Swan are German and Scandinavian (respectively) eco-labelling systems for consumer products. They are largely applied to items such as refrigerators and dishwashers to indicate their energy consumption and other environmental factors such as recyclability, packaging, etc. However, such schemes are in their infancy (Nordic Swan).

Even where attempts are being made to establish environmental criteria or 'green purchasing policies' there is usually little input from environmental organisations or consumers on what standards should be set. We are in danger of being presented with a set of simplistic judgements about materials and products where the underlying rationale is unclear, relatively pragmatic and not subject to public scrutiny, decided by a new breed of unaccountable environmental technocrats. Steps to establish environmental policies have to be welcomed as they are steps in the right direction, but there is a lack of open and ethical debate, which would help to establish green standards with real teeth from mere greenwash.

One of the best documents to emerge recently has been produced by the UK Greening Government Team in the Department of Environment, Transport and the Regions: *Towards More Sustainable Construction – Green Guide for Managers on the Government Estate* (DETR 1999a). If applied it would set a progressive standard for any specification policy. It contains a 'Green Code for Architecture' which sets out very clear principles that would go a long way to safeguarding the environment. However, there is very little evidence of this getting through to the day-to-day business of architects working on public sector projects.

The Building Research Establishment has also established a methodology for formulating environmental profiles for building materials. They plan to offer a database of products which have environmental profiles that can be accessed through the Internet (BRE 1999). This initiative has been supported by most of the trade associations in the construction industry and claims to establish a 'level playing field' for information about the relative environmental impacts of different design options. This is an ambitious aim and it is too early to see whether it has been achieved. It will be important to review the criteria being applied. As Trinius explains, 'valuation principles' are highly significant in environmental assessment:

> By definition, valuation is related to other ethical values in society...
> A valuation method, of course, faces the risk of only being regarded as valid by those who understand and share the represented valuation principle as being reasonable and relevant.
>
> (Trinius 1998)

Such an environmental profiling system has existed in Sweden for several years. The Swedish Ecocycle Council for the Building Sector has established a very clear and useful *pro forma* for *Building Products Declarations* (Swedish Ecocycle Council for the Building Sector 1998). Such declarations would be extremely useful if they were widely available but less than 20 per cent of buildings materials companies in Sweden have prepared such declarations to date (Ewander 1999).

Two key publications which provide guidance on the greenness of building materials have adopted simple classification systems so that the specifier is presented with A, B or C or 1, 2 or 3 classifications. However, with such limited information we are reliant on the judgement of the researchers and the more obscure the assumptions which underlie the classification information. For instance, in the BRE guide to the environmental impact of materials, there is a classification into three categories of A, B and C, though it does break this down into a series of headings (Howard *et al.* 1998). The use of such a classification leads to arguments as to whether a particular material should be A, B or C. The plastics industry, for example, was unhappy at the treatment of PVCu in the guide and apparently put pressure on the BRE to include the following statement: 'It should be noted that the toxicity aspects are contested by the PVC industry and designers are advised to take note of the industry's guidance as well as that of environmental groups in judging this issue.'

While the BRE guide gives some indication of the possible risks of PVCu, it does not make a more explicit and unequivocal comment as is found in a Greenpeace report (Greenpeace 1998): 'The production and disposal of PVCu windows leads to the release of highly poisonous chemicals which threaten the environment and human health.'

There is a wide spectrum of views on the environmental properties of materials, and judgements cannot simply be taken as technical or scientific. Ethical value judgements and political outlooks also play a part. Unless there is a completely independent assessment of these issues, we must take those driven by industry with a hint of suspicion.

Construction industry attitudes

By and large, the construction industry has been slow to respond to the environmental agenda, although this is largely reflecting the low priority attached to environmental issues in UK society as a whole. Further afield in Europe, alternative environmentally friendly and ecological materials represent between 5 and 15 per cent of the construction sector (Konig 1998), but this is not the case in the UK. Most of the non-toxic paints which are derived from plants and other natural materials are manufactured in Germany and the Netherlands, as are products from natural materials such as wool insulation, clay plasters. Virtually all the materials stocked by the first ecological builders' merchant in the UK, Construction Resources, near London Bridge in London, are imported from Germany and Holland.

While the Labour government has been quick to draw attention to environmental issues in the construction industry (DETR 1998b), the consultation exercise yielded a very poor response and there was negligible debate and discussion on the issues in the trade press (DETR 1998c). Only 250 responses were received for the whole of the UK! While other topics have involved high-powered committees chaired by key industry figures, such as Egan (DETR 1998d) and the Urban Task Force, chaired by Lord Rogers (DETR 1999b), this has not been the case with sustainability.

The construction industry is unlikely to do much about environmental issues without legislation. Government reports such as 'Egan' have been largely concerned in moving the industry on to a more 'efficient' and technocratic basis, emphasising the business efficiency of large multinational companies and the use of prefabrication and high-tech construction methods. This will further undermine the viability of a local and craft-based industry, which would be preferable in environmental terms. The word sustainability only appears once in the whole of the Egan report.

Pressure is on for more housing development in the countryside on greenfield sites. The Labour government has given way frequently to the demands of developers following public enquiries. Even in a small area like Northern Ireland, the government talks of the need for 200,000 new houses in the next ten to twenty years (DoE 1998). This will lead to greater consumption of materials and energy and unless there is a significant change in building regulations new houses will continue to be built with standards of insulation barely above primitive. The introduction of the Standard Assessment Procedure (SAP) into the Building regulations (BRECSU 1998) seems unlikely to greatly improve energy standards, as it allows designers to trade off other measures against insulation levels. The Home Energy Conservation Act is a very weak tool in tackling energy efficiency.

Some construction industry companies and professionals have adopted environmental management systems and standards. Grants and subsidies are available to encourage companies to sign up to these schemes, but they are largely concerned with procedures and documentation rather than the environmental impact of the activities they are carrying out (EMSI 1999). Fundamental changes in attitudes and the adoption of ethical principles will be necessary before the construction industry really begins to seriously consider environmental issues.

The environmental movement

It might be expected that environmental organisations would have taken a lead in campaigning for sustainable construction, but few take more than a passing interest in the subject of building. Most environmental organisations emphasise protecting the natural environment, and a recent study showed that many did little to change the environment in their own offices (Devaney and Lyons 1998). There is some evidence that the bigger environmental organisations tend to ignore groups such as the Ecological Design Association (EDA) and the Association of Environment Conscious Builders (AECB) when campaigning on issues to do with construction. For example, Greenpeace, Friends of the Earth and the World Wide Fund for Nature decided to tackle the specification of uncertified timber by architects, as revealed by Building Design.

> The campaign – details of which remain secret but could involve direct action against major construction projects … (said) Architects don't give a damn about the origin of the wood they specify…the aesthetic qualities are all they look for.
>
> (Long 1999).

However, they didn't get a group of architects, already active on this issue together, and try to work out the best way of getting the message across. Not surprisingly the 'campaign' has fizzled out.

Organisations like the AECB and EDA have done a tremendous job in raising the profile of green design and building, but within the ranks of green practitioners there is a wide range of views on how to achieve environmentally friendly buildings. These vary from scientific, through pragmatist, to New Age mysticism. The credibility of green practice is put at risk by those who promote design principles that are based on belief and superstition, rather than rational methods. The fashion for 'feng shui' is one example of this (Woolley 1998). While there is nothing inherently wrong with a plurality of views and positions, some terms like 'breathing walls,' 'dynamic insulation', 'feng shui', 'building biology' assume the status of holy cows that cannot be questioned. Many reputable books include references to 'feng shui' and other mystical practices presented on an equal basis with other more rational and scientific concepts (Baggs and Baggs 1996; Borer and Harris 1998; Pearson 1989). Such ideas, based on religious and spiritual belief systems, instead of being advanced as an ethical position are mistakenly presented as scientific principles or practical tools.

The way forward?

Criticism of the environmental movement is rarely welcomed as it is claimed to give succour to our enemies! We shouldn't 'rock the boat', as something is better than nothing is the usual argument. This is a dangerous approach and yet I hear it frequently. An energy-efficient house is not environmentally friendly, but it's better than nothing. Environmental profiling provides good marketing for materials manufacturers without them really changing anything, but at least it's better than nothing. This is a dangerous argument because it glosses over the need to establish clear principles and ground rules that are subject to real open and public debate about what is acceptable to protect the environment and what is not. We are a long way off from establishing such a debate, and unless there is a stronger concern for ethical principles in this area of work we will not see progress towards a genuinely sustainable way of creating our environment.

References and bibliography

Building for a Future. Magazine of the Association of Environment Conscious Builders: Nant-y-Garreg, Saron, Llandysul Carmarthenshire SA44 5EJ.

Baggs, S. and Baggs, J. (1996) *The Healthy House Book*, London: Thames and Hudson.

Blue Angel <www.umwelt bundesamt.de>

Borer, P. and Harris, C. (1998) *The Whole House Book,* Machynlleth: The Centre for Alternative Technology.

BRE (1999) The UK Building Research Establishment has recently launched various publications and CDs to promote an environmental profiling system. These are available on subscription from the BRE.

BRECSU (1998) *The Government's Standard Assessment Procedure for the Energy Rating of Dwellings,* Watford: BRE-BRECSU.

Building Research Establishment (1999) *Methodology for Environmental Profiles*, London: BRE.

Cherubini, G. and Aumento, F. (1995) 'Additional Radon Emissions from Building Materials used in Geographically High Radon Risk Zones.' *Healthy Buildings 95,* Conference Proceedings M. Maroni (ed.), Milan.

Crump, D.R., Squire, R.W. and Chuck, W.F.Y. (1997) 'Sources and Concentrations of Formaldehyde and Other VOCs in 4 Newly Built Houses' *Indoor and Built Environment* 6: 44–55.

DoE (1998) *Shaping Our Future,* Belfast: Department of the Environment, Northern Ireland.

DETR (1998a) *Building a Sustainable Future, Homes for an Autonomous Community,* London: BRECSU/DETR Best Practice General Information Report No. 53.

DETR (1998b) *Opportunities for Change.* Consultation Paper on a UK Strategy for Sustainable Construction, Norwich: Department of Environment Transport and the Regions, HMSO.

DETR (1998c) *Opportunities for Change – Analysis of Responses* November 1998, Circular Letter from Department of Environment, Transport and the Regions, London.

DETR (1998d) *Rethinking Construction – Report of Government Task Force,* London: Department of Environment, Transport and the Regions.

DETR (1999a) *Towards More Sustainable Construction – Green Guide for Managers on the Government Estate,* London: Department of Environment, Transport and the Regions SDU/99/1, March 1999.

DETR (1999b) *Report of the Urban Task Force* London: Department of the Environment, Transport and the Regions.

Devaney, D. and Lyons, C. (1998) *Whether Environmental Organisations Consider Environmental issues in their Own Premises,* MSc in Environmental Engineering, Queens University, Belfast.

ECO-DESIGN (1998) 'Eco Labelling Board to be wound up.' *Eco-Design* vi(3): 3. [The Ecological Design Association The British School, Slad Road, Stroud Glos. GL5 1QW.]

EMSI (1999) *What is an Environmental Management System? EMSI* web site – <www.aspexint.com>

Energy Saving Trust (1999) Telephone enquiry in which member of staff stated that the issue of embodied energy was totally ignored. *Energy Saving Trust* web site www.est.org.uk

Ewander, H. (1999) Swedish Ecocycle Council and Building Products Declarations.

Forest Stewardship Council can be contacted via Avenida Hidalgo 502, 68000 Oaxaca, Mexico.

Green Building Digest (1998) 'Adhesives', *Green Building Digest,* No. 17, Belfast.

Green Building Digest (1999) 'Interior Decoration', *Green Building Digest,* No. 19, Belfast.

Greenpeace (1998) 'Look Out – Implementing Solutions', *Briefing Note 1 – Installing New Windows.* London: Greenpeace.

Harper, D., Smith, R. and Gotto, D. (1977) 'BHC Residues of Domestic Origin: A significant Factor in the Pollution of Freshwater in Northern Ireland', *Environmental Pollution* No. 12.

Howard, N., Shiers, D. and Sinclair, N. (1998) *The Green Guide to Specification* Garston, Watford: Building Research Establishment, Report 351.

Indoor Air 96 (1996) Proceedings of the 7th International Conference on Indoor Air Quality and Climate, Nagoya, Japan.

Konig, H. (1998) Talk at official opening of Construction Resources, Great Guildford Street, London, April 1998.

Kuehni, C.E., Brooke, A.M. and Silverman, M. (1998) *Change in Prevalence of Pre-school Wheeze in Leicestershire: Two surveys 8 years apart*, Leicester: University Department of Child Health.

Long, K. (1999) 'Identifying Your Sources' *Building Design* March, p. 6.

Nordic Swan <www.sis.se/miljo/ecolabel/htm>

Pearson, D. (1989) *The Natural House Book*, London: Gaia Books.

Swedish Ecocycle Council for the Building Sector (1998) *Building Products Declarations*, Stockholm: Swedish Building Centre.

Talbott, J. (1993) *Simply Build Green*, Findhorn: Findhorn Press.

Trinius, W. (1998) *Environmental Assessment – Implementation in the Building Sector.* Licentiate of Engineering Thesis, Stockholm: Kungliga Tekniska Hogskolan.

Van Weenan, H. (1999) 'Environmentally Superior Products'. Lecture, given at Environmentally Superior Products Conference – Enterprise Ireland, 31 March, Dublin.

Woolley, T. (1998) 'Green Architecture – Man Myth or Magic', *Environments By Design* 2(2): 127–37.

Woolley, T., Kimmins, S. and Harrison, R. (1997) *The Green Building Handbook*, London: E &FN Spon.

Zeiher, L. (1996) *The Ecology of Architecture*, New York: Whitney Library of Design.

5

BUILDING, GLOBAL
WARMING AND ETHICS

Terry Williamson and Antony Radford

Introduction

The Union of International Architects' World Congress of Architects meeting in Chicago in June 1993 following the lead given by the Rio Declaration on the Environment and Development the previous year declared 'We commit ourselves, as members of the world's architectural and building-design professions, individually and through our professional organisations, to: Place environmental and social sustainability at the core of our practice and professional responsibilities ...'.

In amplifying this proclamation at a more local level, the Royal Australian Institute of Architects, in 1995, released its Environment Policy which

> ...reaffirms the responsibility of the architectural profession to contribute to the quality and sustainability of the natural and built environment... Such a commitment will contribute to preserving and restoring the ecological processes on which life depends, thereby providing the opportunity to maintain or improve the quality of life for current and future generations, and maintain the intrinsic values of the natural environment...
>
> (Royal Australian Institute of Architects 1995)

The policy goes on to give various principles directed at maintaining and restoring biodiversity, minimising the consumption of resources, minimising pollution of air, soil and water, maximising health, safety and comfort of building users.

If ethics deals with the standards by which human actions can be judged right or wrong, appropriate or inappropriate, then the notion of a 'sustainable' architecture expressed in these statements is fundamentally an ethical issue. But what is the link between sustainable building as an ethical issue and building design as a pragmatic activity? How can the ethical positions held by different architects (and their design team colleagues and clients) be reconciled? Can designers and designs that do not conform to the principles be judged unethical?

These are not easy questions to answer, so in order to tease out some of the issues, a practical example is considered here, 'global warming'. This issue is often found at the heart of sustainable design recommendations that are concerned with reducing energy consumption and carbon dioxide (CO_2) emissions.

From the point of view of on-the-job architects, design decisions addressing the global warming subject will be conditioned by the knowledge (or lack of knowledge) they have concerning, among other issues, the science of global warming, the politics of global warming and the available specific design advice. There follows an outline of some of the information that conscientious architects may gather on these topics to help inform their decision-making.

Knowledge of global warming

The science

The makeup of the Earth's atmosphere is a principal factor in establishing the planet's temperature, and this, in turn, sets the conditions for all life on Earth. Without the heat-trapping properties of so-called 'greenhouse gases', which make up only a small fraction of the Earth's atmosphere, the average surface temperature of the Earth would be around minus 16 °C. The greenhouse gases are those gases in the atmosphere, such as water vapour (H_2O), CO_2, tropospheric ozone, nitrous oxide (N_2O) and methane (CH_4), that are transparent to solar radiation, but opaque to longwave radiation. Their action is similar to that of glass in a greenhouse. The main greenhouse gases are H_2O, CO_2, CH_4, N_2O and halocarbons (such as CFC-11 and CFC-12). With the exception of halocarbons, most greenhouse gases occur naturally. Water vapour is by far the most common, with an atmospheric concentration of nearly 1 per cent, compared with less than 0.04 per cent for CO_2. Concentrations of other greenhouse gases are a fraction of that for carbon dioxide. Figure 5.1 shows the estimated contribution of the various greenhouse gases to global warming.

Scientists first reliably determined that concentrations of CO_2 in the atmosphere were increasing in the late 1950s. Measurements of CH_4,

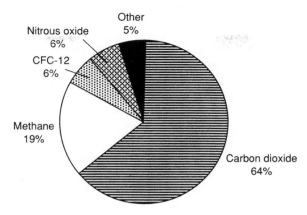

Figure 5.1 Calculated greenhouse warming effects of the different greenhouse gases (Houghton *et al.* 1996).

N_2O and other gases began in the late 1970s, and increasing concentrations were observed. In studies of the consequences of increasing greenhouse concentrations using computer-based simulation techniques, most models show an increase in the average temperature of the Earth. It is hypothesised that these temperature increases may lead to changes in the weather and in the level of the oceans around the world. In turn, these changes may prove disruptive to current patterns of land use and human settlement, as well as to existing ecosystems. Data, based mainly on surface temperature measurements at meteorological stations, seem to support the simulation models and show a temperature increase of around 0.5 °C over the twentieth century. Most of this increase, however, occurred in the period 1920–40. However, data collected over the last 20 years from high-altitude measurements appear to show a slight decrease in the temperature over the period. Some scientists argue that the surface temperature measurements are in error for several reasons, the principal being the 'heat island effect' in populated areas.

Long-run records using samples of 'fossil air' trapped in the ice of Greenland and the Antarctic have been used to study atmospheric carbon dioxide and methane concentrations. The results appear to indicate that concentrations of both these gases in the Earth's atmosphere stand at historically high levels. This growth in the concentration has occurred largely in the past 200 years, and especially since 1940. The timing of the growth in concentrations imply that the prime source for the growth in CO_2 concentrations is the combustion of fossil fuels, especially in the northern hemisphere. The computer models developed to study climate predict that there is a causal relationship between atmospheric CO_2

concentration and average global temperature. Increases in CO_2 cause the temperature of the globe to increase. The earlier simulations showed that if atmospheric CO_2 continued to increase, by the year 2100 the Earth will heat up by 8 °C. The current models predict about 1–4 °C warming by the year 2100. Despite this evidence, scientists seem to agree that it is difficult to determine unambiguously whether or not global warming is actually taking place, or whether the observed temperature variations are periodic fluctuations that will eventually reverse themselves. It is even more difficult to determine the consequences of global warming on the Earth's climate and how this may affect natural ecosystems and the human economy.

A report by the Environmental Health Center of the US National Safety Council would seem to provide a good summary of the current state of knowledge.

> ...are scientists certain that natural greenhouse warming is a real effect? The answer is: 'Yes, there is strong scientific consensus on that one.' Are scientists certain of how much human-induced change to the atmosphere will cause how much warming over what period of time? The answers to those questions are: 'No.' ... What matters more from the perspective of humans is not the greenhouse gases themselves, but the climate change that scientists believe will eventually come if humans continue indefinitely to increase greenhouse gas concentrations. But climate prediction and finite details of the greenhouse effect, timing, and scope are by no means an exact science...
>
> (Environmental Health Center, National Safety Council 1997)

Our on-the-job designers may, however, be confused when they compare this somewhat cautious statement with the normative statements made by many leading the debate for action on climate change, '...climate change is now being effected by human interference. Since the industrial revolution, we have been using the sky as a waste unit ...'[1]

The international politics

By the mid-1980s, the global warming issue entered the arena of global politics. Matthew Paterson (1996) gives an account of negotiations concerning the framing of the UN Convention of Climate Change. In 1988, an Intergovernmental Panel on Climate Change (IPCC) was established by the World Meteorological Organization and the United Nations Environment Programme, to examine available scientific research on climate change, and to provide scientific advice to policy makers. Their work included studies into sea level rise, precipitation levels, surface temperature, mid-latitude continental dryness (droughts), response of ecosystems and the incidence of severe storms. In late 1990, and following a resolution of the Second World Climate Change Conference, which had the first IPCC report available for consideration, the UN established the Intergovernmental Negotiation Committee for a Framework Convention on Climate Change (INC). By 1990, many of the industrialised countries had already put in place unilateral undertakings ostensibly aimed at reducing greenhouse gas emissions. Some saw these as pre-emptive moves to set the international agenda against more severe international treaty measures urged by environmental groups.

The Convention after considerable negotiation was opened for signature at The Earth Summit in Rio de Janeiro in June 1992. The main objective of this United Nations Framework Convention on Climate Change (UNFCCC) was to '...achieve...stabilisation of the greenhouse gas concentrations in the atmosphere at a level that would prevent dangerous anthropogenic interference with the climate system.'

Shortly after ratification of the Convention, it became apparent that major greenhouse gas-emitting nations such as the United States and Japan would not meet the voluntary stabilisation targets by 2000. A number of other important questions were also raised in the international arena:

- How can the international community strike the necessary balance between expanding the pace of economic development and the resultant higher energy use, and responding adequately to concerns about climate change?
- How can nations gradually, but substantially, reduce their emissions of greenhouse gases without stalling their economies?
- How can the burden of protecting the climate be shared equitably among nations?

In December 1997, nations came together to address these questions and to complete negotiations of the Kyoto Protocol, which as a follow-on to the original climate treaty, marks the first international attempt to place legally binding limits on greenhouse gas emissions from developed countries. Under the Kyoto Protocol, the countries listed in 'Annex B of the agreement' shall: '...individually or jointly, ensure that their aggregate anthropogenic carbon dioxide equivalent emissions of the greenhouse gases do not exceed their assigned amounts, calculated pursuant to their quantified emission limitation and reduction commitments...in the commitment period 2008 to 2012.' (Kyoto Protocol 1997: Article 3).

By 2005, countries are expected to have made demonstrable progress in achieving their commitments under the Protocol.[2] Countries in transition to a market economy are allowed some flexibility in achieving their targets. All countries must take steps to formulate national and regional programmes to improve local emissions of greenhouse gas emissions and sinks that remove these gases from the atmosphere. In addition, all countries are committed to formulate, publish and update climate change mitigation and adaptation measures, and to co-operate in promotion and transfer of environmentally sound technologies and in scientific and technical research on the climate system.

However, scenarios produced by the Inter-governmental Panel on Climate Change suggest that global emission and concentrations of greenhouse gases will continue to rise even with implementation of the Kyoto Protocol (IPCC 1995). Our on-the-job architect who comes across literature from environmental groups might find this point emphasised.

> Even if the developed countries do manage to reduce their emissions by the promised 5% below 1990 levels, by 2012, the projected rise in emissions from the growing economies of the developing world will more than cancel this out. Even if the Kyoto Protocol is followed to the letter, figures produced by the US Department of Energy point to a global rise in emissions of 30% by the year 2010— quite the opposite of what is needed to combat climate change. What is needed is a safe global limit on emissions, and much larger reductions by industrialized countries.
>
> (EarthAction 1998)

As well as setting down emission commitments for Annex I countries, the Kyoto Protocol establishes, certain 'flexibility mechanisms' that may be used in reaching emission targets. These mechanisms are:

1 joint implementation among UNFCCC Annex I parties (Article 4);
2 the Clean Development Mechanism (CDM), which permits investors to earn 'certified emission reduction' units for emission reduction projects in developing countries (Article 12);
3 emissions trading among UNFCCC Annex I countries (Article 6).

No details for the implementation of these mechanisms were established at Kyoto. These were intended for resolution at the follow-up meeting in Buenos Aires held in November 1998. At this meeting however there were deep divisions, particularly between developed and developing countries, and the most that could be achieved was a procedural decision to establish a work programme for addressing the numerous unresolved issues. As of mid-1999, few countries had in fact ratified the Kyoto Protocol, meaning that nations are not subject to its commitments. The US Administration, in particular, has indicated that, until developing countries make commitments to 'meaningful participation' in greenhouse gas limitations, it will not submit the Protocol to the Senate for consent. Without US ratification, the Protocol is likely never to come into force.

The reasons and motives

The policies, both international and national, that have developed on climate change are essentially based on the 'best guess' assumptions found in the scientific and technical work reviewed by the IPCC.[3] Scientists with opposing views on climate change argue that the evidence reviewed by the IPCC was selected to achieve a predetermined response. The architect with access to the Internet would discover that the sceptics of global warming and dissidents of the IPCC findings have embraced this medium to air their opinions.[4] Many draw parallels with the influential, yet highly criticised, study undertaken by the Club of Rome (Meadows et al. 1972) in the early 1970s which, using computer models, predicted a global catastrophe early in the next millennium: 'If the present growth trends in world population, industrialisation, pollution, food production, and resource depletion continue unchanged, the limits to growth on this planet will be reached sometime within the next 100 years' (Meadows et al. 1972: 23).

Others suggest it is another example of what the American journalist and satirist Henry Louis Mencken is quoted as saying: 'The whole aim of practical politics is to keep the populace alarmed – and hence clamorous to be led to safety – by menacing it with an endless series of hobgoblins, all of them imaginary.'[5]

Our architects seeking information may begin to think that global warming is the 'Puck of a mid-1990s dream'. They will find that some argue that it is a conspiracy by developing countries to slow the growth of the industrial countries.[6] Others will suggest it is an excuse for these developing countries to procure funds from the developed countries. Still others will imply it is an excuse for radical environmentalists to push for a reduction of economic growth, an issue promoted by scientists in order to receive government and/or industry research funding, or an issue fostered by the nuclear industry as a way of promoting their fuel source as 'clean and responsible'. These and many other explanations have been put forward to account for the relatively sudden rise of global warming as an issue in both domestic and international politics.[7]

Different ethical positions

At least in 'official' Australian government publications, the application of the *precautionary principle* embedded in the aim of the UNFCCC is the reason given for the unprecedented scale of international and national actions on global warming.[8] Under the *precautionary principle*, if there is any doubt about the long-term environmental effect of an action, decisions should always err on the side of caution, where ecological assets are at risk. In this view of the environment, the only response is to play safe, including preserving the components of our existing environment so as not to deprive future generations of a possible benefit. This view is derived essentially from an ecological conception of the world that sees biotic organisms and abiotic elements as integral parts of an ecosystem. Potential global warning must be slowed down or stopped in order to protect the ecosystem. The notion of sustainability is founded in the same ethic, but the on-the-job designer is likely to know that architecture traditionally operates primarily in a utilitarian ethic that sees the environment as a resource, generally hostile to humans, something to be controlled and dominated for the self-interest humans. This concept of the environment in fact forms part of the way architecture is defined, for example:

> Architecture is the art and the technique of building, employed to fulfill the practical and expressive requirements of civilized people…with it, [man] has not only a defense against the natural environment but also the benefits of a human environment, a prerequisite for and a symbol of the development of civilized institutions… The natural environment is at once a hindrance and a help, and the architect seeks both to invite its aid and to repel its attacks. To make buildings habitable and comfortable, he must control the effects of heat, cold, light, air, moisture, and dryness and foresee destructive potentialities such as fire, earthquake, flood, and disease.
>
> (*Encyclopaedia Britannica* 1998)

Human needs, wants and interests are taken as the basis of the norms that determine conduct in relation to the provision of buildings. Actions are confined in a pragmatic way to those which can be derived from acquired knowledge and experience, that is, from the point of view of the cognitive human. Value may be assigned to ecosystems, future generations, etc. providing reciprocity where a present individual's or society's interests can be demonstrated. Once this reciprocity is determined, a moral or ethical position could be seen to be established (one has a duty to act for the present good). The concepts of cost/benefit analysis or risk management assessment and evaluation are inherent to this approach and these techniques are taught as a basic part of the education of architects. The actions taken are said to be 'logically' derived; environmental action is initiated and resources devoted to that pursuit because there is a perception of net benefits being achieved. No inherent value is assigned to ecological systems outside the instrumental value they have to humans. The *precautionary principle* does not have a place here because it is invoked when uncertainty exists. Speculation as such is eliminated in risk/reward analysis because events are assigned a probability and a course of action chosen from a number of alternatives according to the likely net benefits. The failure to consider courses of action, apart from imposing a reduction in CO_2 emissions, is a criticism often levelled at the recommendations of the IPCC.

The building design problem

Understandably, our on-the-job architects may be somewhat confused about how to proceed in an ethical way. Let us assume that she makes a decision to be 'responsible' by embracing the *precautionary principle* approach, following the UIA Charter and adopting design practices which it is hoped will reduce greenhouse gas (particularly CO_2) emissions.

To this end, several 'technical' objectives could be addressed, either explicitly or implicitly. These are likely to include

- reducing the capital or embodied energy of the building materials;
- reducing fossil fuel (operational) energy use, for heating, cooling, lighting, hot water, etc. (or a goal of low energy use in general because reticulated energy may involve nuclear energy).

Both these goals are of course linked to social and economic questions, such as internal thermal comfort, as well as the initial and operating costs. Although aspects of these goals are covered in certain jurisdictions by mandatory provisions, for example thermal insulation requirements, many fall to the architect to deal with within the context of designing, for example the choice of particular building materials and products. The on-the-job designer is therefore likely to seek authoritative design advice that deals with these issues. Such a situation immediately raises the question: Is the design advice relevant or in error? Two examples are now considered.

The 'no worries' design advice

All too often, design advice does not deal with the problem at hand in a holistic manner, despite rhetoric to the contrary. In terms of general design advice, an architect in France, for example, hearing statements from Électricité de France (EDF), could naturally assume electric heating is an answer to the global warming issue.

> L'utilisation de l'énergie électrique n'etraîne par elle-même aucune pollution sur les milieux naturels. Elle possède toutes les caractéristiques d'un écoproduit.[9]

Electricity generated by nuclear power and promoted as a 'clean' energy source denies the many environmental issues associated with its use, such as the possibility (probability) of catastrophic accidents, short- and long-term pollution, not to mention mining on Aboriginal sacred lands and national parks in Australia.[10]

Design accreditation

In many places around the world, design advice for dwellings may be found in the form of an energy-rating scheme. In Australia, the publicity says that the Nationwide House Energy Rating Scheme (NatHERS)[11] will

> ...give houses a rating of up to five stars, according to their design, heating and cooling energy requirements. The scheme will reduce *household energy use* and *greenhouse gas emissions* by providing information on the design and selection of cost-effective energy-efficient housing[12] (our italics).

> (*Innovation* 1997)

The methodology adopted in NatHERS is, however, limited to assessing the general performance of the exterior envelope of a dwelling based on the sum of the heating and cooling *loads* (that is, excluding a consideration of plant efficiencies and fuel types) for an assumed use pattern and a defined climate (Cassell and Ballinger 1996). The scheme does *not* and *cannot* address directly the issues as stated of energy use, greenhouse gas emissions or cost-effectiveness. Attempting to maximise the rating points with this scheme will often lead a designer to the use of materials (e.g. bricks) with high-embodied energy. The overall effect may, particularly in the more temperate climates, be to increase the net or life-cycle energy consumption and CO_2 emission. A recent Australian study (Olweny and Williamson 1998) illustrates this point. Figure 5.2 taken from this study shows the estimated life-cycle CO_2 emission for various building construction and heating/cooling plant options.[13] These results can be compared with the design ranking for the same construction options produced by NatHERS. As shown in Figure 5.3, ordering the designs with NatHERS, because it deals with only part of the issue (energy load), achieves a very different ranking. The 'best' of these construction forms according to the NatHERS ranking may (depending on the choice of heating/cooling plant) result in over 25 per cent more predicted life-cycle CO_2 emission than another option. The well-meaning designer

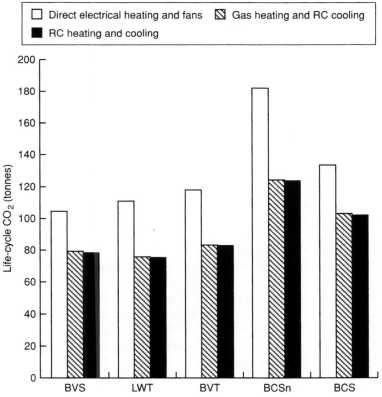

Figure 5.2 Estimated total life-cycle CO_2 emissions for various construction and plant options, Sydney (Olweny and Williamson 1998). Construction options: BVS, brick veneer walls, concrete slab floor; LWT, lightweight timber construction, timber floor; BVT, brick veneer walls, timber floor; BCSn, brick cavity walls (no insulation), concrete slab floor; BCS, brick cavity walls (with insulation), concrete slab floor; RC, reverse cycle.

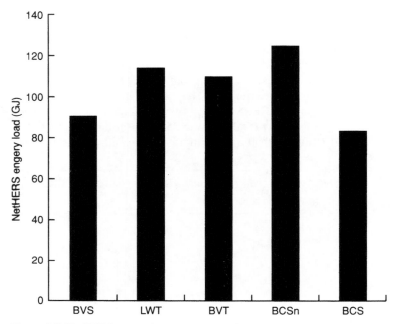

Figure 5.3 NatHERS energy load assessments for various construction and plant options, Sydney (Olweny and Williamson 1998).

following inadequate design advice may inadvertently and unduly be contributing to global warming.

Although we have highlighted NatHERS, any building accreditation methodology that concentrates on operational (site) energy alone could give equally misleading results if minimum life-cycle CO_2 emission is a main end.

Even the designer who understands the pitfalls and limitations of certain design advice may have trouble finding better information. For example, obtaining information on embodied energy and manufacturing CO_2 emission is often difficult for particular (or even generic) building products because they are often retained in propriety databases and only accessed with expensive computer software[14]. Must a designer use such authoritative information to evaluate proposed designs or can knowledge acquired from experience or even intuition be relied upon? The answer here is that probably conventional design understandings cannot be relied upon to get 'correct' answers and that analysis that is more precise is necessary. This however raises another dilemma. Given that sustainability is just one of the many issues that the architect will need to consider, the time factor becomes an important point in determining how thoroughly or otherwise each goal can be addressed. Designers operating in the present commercial environment, where designing for sustainability is considered as an individual responsibility, may find themselves at a financial disadvantage and without clients prepared to pay for their services.

Discussion

What, finally, have our responsible architects discovered? We have calls to adopt a design end (reducing greenhouse gas emission) which, although covered by an International Convention, is based to some extent on speculative scientific reasoning. We have views that suggest that proper risk analysis may lead to alternative courses of action. We have public authority and government-backed design advice that is demonstrably irrelevant and incorrect if this particular end is to be met. None of this however answers the question about how an ethical architect ought to act.

At the surface, the ethical question appears to be a binary issue, to adopt sustainable building design practices or not. But, just below this binary surface lurks the real problem – how? Even accepting the *precautionary principle* as a basis, that it is better to assume than reject global warming, individual architects who embrace this principle face at least three difficulties in dealing with CO_2 emissions:

- how to establish appropriate emission targets for their buildings and, at the same time, deal with conflicting ends;
- inadequate design guidance on how to deal with the technical problems;
- the likely cost implications which often puts this mode of operation at a financial disadvantage for both self and client.

The first issue is somewhat difficult, because consensus on design protocols has yet to be established. Perhaps eventually countries committed to greenhouse gas reductions will need to promulgate regulations in this area to control building designs.[15] But because the individual country commitments for the reduction of greenhouse gasses under the Kyoto Protocol vary, what does this imply for the architect at present operating internationally? Is it sufficient to simply reflect the values and objectives of the different countries? The advice that can be given appears weak. One pragmatic approach to the issue for an architect seeking to act ethically on the global warming issue is to focus, within the financial and functional constraints, on design options that maximise local content and renewable energy use. The second problem is caused in part by simplistic (and sometimes officially endorsed) models that confuse ends. The ethical architect may well seek to use the 'best' available information, but there is much apparently authoritative advice around which is not well founded. Can the designer who follows the NatHERS ranking be said to be acting ethically? As well as ethics for designers, we must include in the debate the ethics of design information givers. The third problem is familiar from another field in which ethical stances are important, the protection of buildings of cultural heritage value. In both cases, the benefits flow to the community as a whole, whereas the costs are born by the building owner. In the case of 'heritage' buildings, many countries have developed a range of incentives as well as penalties to make 'acting in the community's interests' less onerous. Both incentives and penalties reflect the society's objectives.

Having failed to discover an unequivocal position on what constitutes sustainable design in connection with the global warming issue our responsible architects are most likely to conclude that to act ethically really means taking individual responsibility for the future consequences of their design decisions.

Notes

1 From a speech by Sir Crispin Tickell (former UK Ambassador to the UN and author of *Climate Change and World Affairs*) at a climate conference London. Reported in *The Independent*, 17 March 1999.

2 National commitments of Annex I countries for greenhouse gas emissions by 2012. Percentage change from 1990 levels. Australia +8 per cent; Bulgaria* –8 per cent; Canada –6 per cent; Croatia* –5 per cent; Czech Republic* –8 per cent; Estonia* –8 per cent; European Union –8 per cent (Austria, Belgium, Denmark, Finland, France, Germany, Greece, Ireland, Italy, Luxembourg, Netherlands, Portugal, Spain, Sweden, UK); Hungary* –6 per cent; Iceland +10 per cent; Japan –6 per cent; Latvia* –8 per cent; Liechtenstein –8 per cent; Lithuania* –8 per cent; Monaco –8 per cent; New Zealand 0 per cent; Norway +1 per cent; Poland* –6 per cent; Romania* –8 per cent; Russian Federation* 0 per cent; Slovakia* –8 per cent; Slovenia* –8 per cent; Switzerland –8 per cent; Ukraine* 0 per cent; USA –7 per cent. An asterisk indicates countries that are undergoing the process of transition to a market economy.

3 'Ability to quantify the human influence on global climate is currently limited because the expected signal is still emerging from the noise of natural variability and because there are uncertainties in key factors. These include the magnitude and patterns of long-term natural variability and the time-evolving pattern of forcing by, and response to, changes in concentrations of greenhouse gases and aerosols, and land surface changes. Nevertheless, the balance of evidence suggests that there is a discernible human influence on global climate.' (UNFCCC 1996: 8).

4 See, for example, Science and Environmental Policy Project, a group lead by Professor Fred Singer, Online. http://www.sepp.org/ (June 1999); Douglas Hoyt, Greenhouse Warming: Fact, Hypothesis, or Myth?, Online. http://users.erols.com/dhoyt1/index.html (May 1999); John Daly, Still Waiting for the Greenhouse? Online. http://www.vision.net.au/~daly (June 1999).

5 Reproduced from Favourite Quotes: H.L. Mencken, Online. Available HTTP: http://www.geocities.com/Athens/Delphi/7248/mencken.html (May 1999).

6 See Consumer Alert/Cooler Heads Coalition (1998) as an example of a pressure group arguing against the introduction of CO_2 emission controls.

7 See Paterson (1996: 1–2) for the several arguments advanced to explain the rapid interest in 'global warming' as a political issue.

8 For example, Dr Colin Grant (1998), Deputy CEO, Australian Greenhouse Office, in an article says, 'The only prudent course of action available to the world is to start now on the huge task of reducing greenhouse gas emissions.'

9 Quoted from an interview with M. Christian Sulle, Environment and Marketing, EDF, in Le Magazine de la Construction (May 1993) 54: 7, 'The use of electricity does not have any pollution effects of itself on the natural environment. It [electricity] possesses all the characteristics of an eco-product.'

10 Approximately 76 per cent of electricity in France is generated from nuclear power.

11 The Nationwide House Energy Rating Scheme (NatHERS) was announced initially by the Council of Australian Governments in a National Greenhouse Response Strategy during 1992, for implementation in 1994. In November 1997, the Prime Minister in a major statement on Greenhouse Strategy, announced key measures such as 'expanding NatHERS by including a minimum energy performance requirement for new housing and extensions to improve energy efficiency'. As of mid-1999, the national scheme had still not been launched; however, many local authorities, particularly in New South Wales, had referenced the Scheme in energy-efficient planning guidelines making it the de facto standard.

12 Quoted from Innovation (1997) 'The Nationwide Home Energy Rating Scheme', 12: 24 (A newsletter of CSIRO, Division of Building, Construction and Engineering). Information attributed to the Commonwealth Department of Primary Industries and Energy, Energy Efficiency Branch, Canberra.

13 The life-cycle CO_2 emission represents the total over a fifty-year period. A full fuel cycle emission coefficient was used to convert fuel consumption calculated with the EnCom2 software into CO_2 emissions. Embodied energy is estimated according to the method of Pullen (1995).

14 For example, Eco-Indicator 98, A product life-cycle assessment computer tool and databases. Amersfoort, The Netherlands: PRé Consultants (May 1999). It costs approximately 2,800 Euros.

15 Although many countries have regulations concerned with reducing energy consumption, these do not necessarily equate with low CO_2 emission. Most standards deal only with minimising the operational site energy use.

Bibliography

Cassell, D. J. and Ballinger, J. A. (1996) 'The Development and Capabilities of the Nationwide House Energy Rating Scheme', in *Proceedings of Conference – Second National Energy Efficient Building and Planning Seminar*, Wollongong: Paraclete Building Consultants, pp. 1–6.

Consumer Alert/Cooler Heads Coalition (1998) *Global Warming in Brief*, Online. http://www.globalwarming.org/brief/index.htm (June 1999).

EarthAction (1998) *From Kyoto to Buenos Aires*. Online. http://www.oneworld.org/earthaction/en/Recent/98–09-ClCh/kyoto.html (June 1999).

Encyclopaedia Britannica (1998) 'The Art of Architecture', CD 98 Multimedia Edition.

Environmental Health Center, National Safety Council (1997) 'Understanding the Science, How Warm? How Fast? Scientific Consensus and Debate', in *Reporting on Climate Change*, Ch. 4, Washington, DC: Environmental Health Center, The National Safety Council. Online. http://nsc.org/ehc/guidebks/climtoc.htm (June 1999).

Grant, C. (1998) 'Climate Change – An Issue of Concern', *Greenhouse News* 1(4): 3.

Houghton, J.T., Meira Filho L.G., Callander, B.A., Harris, N., Kattenberg, A. and Maskell, K. (eds) (1996) *Climate Change 1995: The Science of Climate Change*, Cambridge: Cambridge University Press (The Intergovernmental Panel on Climate Change, in collaboration with the World Meteorological Organization and the United Nations Environment Programme).

IPCC (1995) *Intergovernmental Panel on Climate Change – Second Assessment Report*, Geneva: World Meteorological Organization/United Nations Environment Programme.

Meadows, D. H., Meadows, D. L., Randers, J. and Behrens III, W.W. (1972) *The Limits to Growth*, Washington DC: Potomac Associates.

Olweny, M.R.O. and Williamson,T.J. (eds) (1998) *Environmentally Responsible Housing for Australia*, Adelaide: School of Architecture, Landscape Architecture and Urban Design, The University of Adelaide.

Paterson, M. (1996) *Global Warming and Global Politics*, London: Routledge.

Pullen, S. (1995) *Embodied Energy of Building Materials*, Unpublished Master of Building Science Thesis, Adelaide: The University of Adelaide.

RAIA (1995) *Environment Policy*, Canberra: Royal Australian Institute of Architects.

UNFCCC (1996) *Scientific Assessments: Consideration of the Second Assessment Report of the Intergovernmental Panel on Climate Change*, Geneva: Report for COP2-FCCC/CP/1996/5/Add.1.

6

CONTESTED CONSTRUCTIONS

The competing logics of
green buildings and ethics

Simon Guy and Graham Farmer

Introduction

Today, as Deyan Sudjic has pointed out, 'for any architect not to profess passionate commitment to 'green' buildings is professional suicide' (Sudjic 1996: 7). Within the mainstream of architectural discourse, the ecological imperative is portrayed and perceived as a shared problem in urgent need of addressing through a united effort, constituting 'actors as joint members of a new and all inclusive risk community' (Hajer 1995: 14). However, beyond this apparent consensus of concern and widening embrace of green design principles 'the designation "green" is extremely wide ranging, encompassing many viewpoints and open to broad interpretation' (Cook and Golton 1994: 677). In this sense the environmental conflict has changed. As Hajer and others have suggested, it has become discursive (Hajer 1995; Hannigan 1995). It no longer simply focuses on the question of whether there is an environmental crisis with competing actors pro and con. Instead the debate around green buildings can be visualised as a landscape of often fragmented, contradictory and competing values and interests. It has become a site of conflicting interpretations in which a complex set of actors participates in a continuous process of defining and redefining the meaning of the environmental problem itself. This chapter attempts to open up an analytical pathway through these issues by examining the competing logics of green building. It highlights the conceptual challenge of defining what we mean by calling a building 'green' and outlines an interpretative framework for understanding the green architecture debate by uncovering and untangling the underlying assumptions, values and normative commitments involved in the process of design and their resulting embodiment in built form.

What makes a building green? A conventional view

Any attempt to understand and analyse green buildings is immediately confronted by the complexity and scope of environmental issues that are potentially relevant to buildings (Curwell and Cooper 1998). This apparent complexity is further compounded by the fact that many of the adverse environmental effects are not directly experienced. Instead they are revealed in a growing body of scientific data highlighting the environmental impact of buildings, ranging from fossil fuel and resource use through to the health of building occupants. Scientific analysis therefore tends to occupy a central position in conventional methods for categorising, understanding and assessing the greenness of buildings. The dominant approaches are characterised by *performance threshold* models, which assess the impact of a building against a range of criteria, which can be directly measured and weighted. Such realist interpretations of green buildings tend towards generalised frameworks of assessment that are based on a common and verifiable set of criteria and targets on environmental performance.[1] In this sense, the debate around green buildings revolves around differently configured technical structures that can be judged through the exchange and comparison of objective findings. These techniques presuppose a degree of agreement on what defines sustainable building, and that certain types of technology and development can be shown to be more sustainable than others. In the field of environmental policy, these ideas are characterised by a consensual, top-down view of environmental and technological change in which a 'progressive process of innovation mitigates the adverse effects of development' (Blowers 1997: 853).

Green buildings as social constructions

Whilst the technical performance threshold approach to understanding green buildings has brought undoubted benefits in terms of highlighting the broad range of environmental issues relevant to buildings, it also tends to detract from a situated, contextualised and social understanding of the environmental problem. As Hajer points out, to analyse environmental questions in terms of 'quasi-technical decision-making on well defined physical issues misses the essentially social questions that are implicated in these debates' (Hajer 1995: 18). The analytical framework of social constructivist theory has demonstrated the contingent and multidirectional character of environmental concerns, which are both time and space specific and are shaped by a particular image and interpretation of Nature. The same approach and 'logic can be applied to technology and to sustainable architecture. In other words, there is interpretative flexibility attached to any artefact: It might be designed in another way' (Moore 1997: 23), i.e. the concept of sustainable building is fundamentally a social construct and, in order to understand green buildings more fully, we have to account for the social structuring of both the identification of environmental problems and their resulting embodiment in built forms. Understanding the concept of a green building as a social construct does not seek to deny that there are serious environmental problems in urgent need of addressing or that the wide range of built responses are not valid, ethically, socially, commercially or technically, in their own terms. The premise is that individuals, groups and institutions embody widely differing perceptions of what environmental innovation is about. We have only to think of the tensions and inter-linkages between the various contributors to the green building debate to spot the opportunity for contestation: Prince Charles, Energy Efficiency Office, Friends of the Earth, British Council of Offices, Royal Institute of British Architects, Centre for Alternative Technology, Building Research Establishment, etc. Each of these actors and institutions possesses a particular way of visualising the nature of the environmental problem which becomes reflected in differing commitments and design approaches. From this perspective, we begin to view green buildings as a social representation of differing ecological and ethical values, or material embodiments of the logics that make up the green buildings debate. In this sense, logic, with Hajer, is 'here defined as a specific ensemble of ideas, concepts, and categorisations that are produced, reproduced, and transformed in a particular set of practices and through which meaning is given to physical and social realities' (Hajer 1995: 44).

The competing logics of green buildings and ethics

Our analysis is based on studies of completed buildings and an extensive literature review of books, articles and reports covering issues related to 'environmental', 'ecological' or 'green' buildings, resulting in a typology of six logics, which are illustrated in Table 6.1.

The logics are not meant to be in any way exclusive, they rarely surface in isolation. That is, in the design of any particular development logics may collide, merge or co-inhabit in debates about form, design and specification. The main point is that the 'environmental problematique is hardly ever discussed in its full complexity'. Rather, 'environmental logic tends to be dominated by specific emblems: issues that dominate the perception of the ecological dilemma' (Hajer 1995: 19–20). Emblematic issues are indicative of the way in which differing notions

Table 6.1 The six competing logics of green buildings

Logic	Ecological	Smart	Aesthetic	Symbolic	Comfort	Community
Emblematic issue	Sustainability	Efficiency	New millennium	Authenticity	Sick buildings	Democracy
Ethical concerns	Eco-centric	Futurity	Building form	Identity	Wholeness	Equity
Building image	Polluter	Asset	Iconic	Harmonious	Healthy	Home
Risk	Planetary survival	Market survival	Identity	Cultural life	Individual	Alienation
Life-cycle	Inter-generational	Business cycle	Design fashion	Evolutionary	Daily	Generational
Rhetoric	Holistic	Commercial	Architectural	Experiential	Medical	Societal
Design strategy	Reduce footprint	Reduce energy	Express Nature	Contextual	Living building	Create identity
Scale	Decentralised	Urban	Gestural	Human	Climate specific	Centralised
Space	Functional	Flexible	Organic, fluid	Situational	Tactile, sensory	Individual
Mobility	Ban cars	Virtual travel	Hide car parking	Pedestrian	Lessen car use	Minimise trips
Networks	Autonomous	Integrated	Reveal networks	Regional	Diminish intensity	Locally managed
Technology	Renewable, appropriate	Hi-tech, intelligent	Pragmatic, soft	Local, low-tech	Passive, non-toxic	Flexible, participatory
Evaluation	Truth to Nature	Cost–benefit, quantitative	Transformative value	Truth to place	Well-being, qualitative	Social cohesion

The table is based on research funded by the ESRC under the Global Environmental Change Programme Phase 4. The authors wish to acknowledge the work of Suzie Osborn in conducting the literature reviews leading to its production.

of the 'environment' have been broken up and reinterpreted by development actors as they pursue design strategies. Emblems represent differing forms of environmental value and are generated through distinct, though often related, sources of environmental concern, with their own history and constituency of advocates within architectural discourse. These differing concerns encourage particular development and design priorities, which encompass a broad range of issues with differing emphases on technique, aesthetics and social responsibilities.

Green building as technique – the ecological and smart logics

Conventional opinion tends to draw marked distinctions between the *ecological* and *smart* approaches based on differing technological stances represented by what Pepper has termed 'eco-centric environmentalists' and 'technocentric environmentalists' (Pepper 1984). In the case of buildings what is common to both approaches is an emphasis on technique and the framing of concerns relating to building as a process of both production and resource consumption.

The ecological approach stems from a particular view of Nature generated from an ecology systems-based conception, requiring a holistic framework of analysis. It is a natural sciences-based view, which emphasises the dynamic interaction between the living and the non-living as a community of interdependent parts. The green design problem conceived from this perspective leads to images of buildings which emphasise the negative impacts of built form. Here we have visions of cities out of control, buildings greedily utilising non-renewable resources and causing pollution to spiral. The perception of buildings is that they are of a form of 'pure consumption' (Rees 1992).

> Each building is an act against nature; it directly makes some proportion of the Earth's surface organically sterile by covering it over, rendering that area of soil incapable of producing those natural resources that require the interaction between soil, sun and water. As a result, in ecological terms, a building is a parasite.
>
> (Curwell and Cooper 1998: 24)

The emblematic issue here is sustainability and ethical judgements stem from an ecological view of knowledge which respects the moral standing of non-human entities, necessarily extending beyond anthropocentric concerns to encompass a moral concern for the integrity of the natural world. Our responsibilities are conceived as a kind of management ethic which dictates the human use of the Earth, determined by 'limits' which come from within Nature itself. The role of designers is to reduce the environmental impact of buildings and, it is argued, that nothing less than planetary survival is at stake. Approaches to building tend to draw directly on analogies from ecological systems as living, closed, cyclical processes, which oppose the linear, open systems of conventional building. Design strategies revolve around small-scale, decentralised, autonomous techniques which emphasise the reuse and recycling of building material and the reduction of dependency on infrastructure services of water, energy and waste through the use of appropriate technologies. There is an emphasis throughout on the use of renewable building materials and technology. The overall aim of the ecological approach is to reduce the ecological footprint of the building and what is required to achieve this is 'a paradigm shift in society from mechanistic to holistic systems-based conception of reality' (Pearson 1991: 69).

In contrast to the ecological logic with its emphasis on a radical reconfiguration of values, the *smart* approach represents a belief in incremental, techno-economic change and that science and technology can provide the solutions to environmental problems. In the field of environmental policy, these ideas have been expressed in terms of 'ecological modernisation' which 'indicates the possibility of overcoming the environmental crisis without leaving the path of modernisation' (Spaargaren and Mol 1992: 334). In this logic, environmental concerns are not the predominant issue but are wrapped up within wider organisational innovations. As Cook and Golton (1994) put it, 'technocentrics recognise the existence of environmental problems and want to solve them through management of the environment' putting their trust in 'objective analysis and a rational scientific method' (Cook and Golton 1994: 677). Here the emblematic issue is efficiency, and concerns are mainly for the global environmental problems of climate change and non-renewable resource depletion. Ethical responsibilities are generated around the concept of futurity and our responsibilities to future generations in maintaining both the stability and the resource richness of the globe. The design strategy is adaptive, but based on recognisably modern, usually high-technology, buildings. Here, there is an emphasis on urban development, which is softened by the creation and use of 'intelligent' technologies. The rhetoric of the smart approach tends to be purely quantitative; the success of the design approach is expressed in the numerical reduction of building energy consumption and material embodied energy and in concepts such as life-cycle flexibility and cost–benefit analysis. This approach, whilst borrowing much of its symbolic language from ecology, puts its faith in the potential and possibilities of technological development as a panacea for our environmental ills:

> Technology will offer us more control rather than less. The buildings of the future will be more like robots than temples...Future architecture will be animated by a holistic ecological view of the globe. Non-mechanical, it will be fluid, seamless and self regulating, programmed by electronic and bio-technical means to interact with the user and the environment.
>
> (Rogers 1991: 59)

Green building as appropriate form – the aesthetic and symbolic logics

In opposition to approaches that are based on technique, with their emphasis on a functional approach founded on environmental science, the *aesthetic* and *symbolic* logics are generated through discourses which emphasise the role of architecture as symbolic of societal values, as a visual art which is essentially aesthetic in appeal and experiential in quality.

The aesthetic logic tends towards a future-oriented 'new age' view, and the emblematic issue is how to represent the epoch shift of the new millennium. Our ethical responsibility is in creating a new architectural iconography that has transformative value in altering our consciousness of Nature. So, having overcome the 'influences of Modernist orthodoxy' with its association of energy-intensive growth for growth's sake, the challenge for green architecture is to 'identify a new language in the building arts' (Wines 1993: 23). For Wines, 'green architecture needs to go beyond just the current catalogue of environmental control techniques' and create architectural forms where both function and image celebrate the environmental message:

> From an aesthetic standpoint, the objective is to look at the fusion of structure and landscape as a kind of interactive biographical dialogue, that, when translated into visual imagery, describes the natural origins in nature. The entire direction in design suggests the development of a new paradigm in the building arts that is based on ecological models.
>
> (Wines 1997:33)

The role of green buildings is therefore not simply to reduce the energy consumption or the ecological footprint of buildings, but to inspire and convey an increasing identification with Nature and the non-human world. Design strategies aim to break away from strictly Cartesian interpretations of architecture, often resulting in crystalline, chaotic or spatially complex forms with a distinct lack of formal hierarchies. The use of organic forms is intended to reflect both the image of Nature and to deepen our experiential understanding of it. The prime concern, at the threshold of the millennium, is to create a new architectural language. According to John Farmer, this requires acceptance of design approaches not conventionally associated with environmental issues:

> In the apparently chaotic, in fact complexly organised forms of Deconstructivist buildings there is, as well as ruing over the human situation, an opening up away from the pressure of the Western tradition...Because of the disordered (by Cartesian criteria) warping and twisting they open up pragmatic, transient ways of making space. The forms seem meaningful, as if in making a transition between two mutually exclusive orders.
>
> (Farmer 1996: 176)

Rather than postulating a universal, radical change of attitudes, the *symbolic* logic emphasises a fundamental reorientation of values to engage with both environmental and cultural concerns. The emblematic issue here is authenticity and the notion that truly sustainable buildings need to relate more fully to the concept of locality and place. Our ethical responsibilities are to resist the phenomenon of universalisation prevalent in modern culture. As Frampton suggests, 'sustaining any kind of authentic culture in the future will depend ultimately on our capacity to generate vital forms of regional culture' (Frampton 1985: 314). The assumption is that current technologically based sustainable architectural approaches and design methodologies often fail to coincide with the cultural values of a particular place or people. According to Ujam and Stevenson (1996) this means:

> Refuting the concern of certain 'green' architects with 'green' but culturally unsustainable technical fixes situated within existing building typologies...Without cultural awareness, any attempt to create a more sustainable environment is likely to falter as it encounters but fails to recognise very deeply structured personal responses to particular places that will tend to override shallow environmentalism.
>
> (Ujam and Stevenson 1996: 47–8)

The approach emphasises de-centralisation and there is concern with the characteristics of regions or 'bio-regions', which are conceived as the basic geographical unit of a small-scale ecological society. It draws inspiration from indigenous and vernacular building strategies which are seen as indicative of ways in which culture adapts to the limitations of a particular environment. As John Farmer points out:

> The designers who had looked at the work of the anthropologists and the traditional buildings of the developing world were not overtly aiming at green design in terms of energy efficiency or precise climatic modification. For them the attraction was the holistic nature of traditional building in which physical, spiritual and environmental need were integrated within the greater context of social groups and structures.
>
> (Farmer 1996: 173)

Contemporary architecture should therefore seek a greater understanding of local culture if it is to be sustainable. The design approach of the symbolic logic stems from a phenomenological concern with the deeply rooted identities that determine the qualitative experience of place and there is an emphasis on cultural continuity as embodied in traditional settlement patterns and building typologies.

Green building as social concern – the comfort and community logics

These approaches highlight the social dimensions of green architecture as expressed in notions such as 'quality of life', 'social justice' and 'democracy'. Both logics promote social responsibilities with a differing emphasis on either the individual or collective. They share a humanist emphasis based on the assumption that our duties to present generations generally outweigh those to future generations.

The *comfort* logic is primarily concerned with effects of the environment on the quality of individual health and tends to focus on the work environment, where the concept of 'sick buildings' is becoming a familiar emblematic issue. Our ethical responsibilities are therefore to ensure the well-being of individual building occupants. As the Vales put it, 'awareness of a range of indoor pollutants…has turned the designers' attention to the need for healthy buildings, non-hazardous to builders and users alike' (Vale and Vale 1991: 114–15). Here the image of buildings as a technological barrier to the hostile, natural world that allows people to live and work in otherwise uninhabitable places has been transformed

(Guy and Shove 1994). Instead, we have a new image of buildings as potentially hostile environments themselves, in which individuals are put at daily risk from a variety of hazards. This logic utilises a medical rhetoric to focus attention on the adverse impacts and causes of stress that engender health problems, chemical, physical and psychological. Critics utilising this logic point out that in our working environments many people spend their lives in artificial conditions, effectively cut off from the outside world. This isolation from Nature is being increasingly challenged by building occupiers, who now desire more control over their internal environments and, as a result, new design principles of 'environmental diversity are emerging' (Hawkes 1996: 18). This approach envisages 'spaces in which environmental uniformity is replaced by variations, within limits, which maintain, in the occupant, a sense of dynamics of the natural climate, of the proper condition of mankind' (Hawkes 1996). Here, there is an emphasis on notions such as the 'living' building, the use of natural, non-toxic materials and on tactile spatial qualities. What we need is an architecture that can 'honour the senses' (Pearson 1991: 68).

> Witness the growth of a new awareness known as building biology which combines healthy building with ecological and spiritual sensitivity. It also recognises the senses as guardians of our health. The pleasant scent of the building and its materials is as important as their visual impact. Paints that smell unappetising cannot be good for you.
>
> (Pearson 1991: 69)

Whilst the comfort logic generally addresses the internal environment of buildings as healthy or otherwise places to live and work, it also reflects wider concerns about environmental pollution. By linking health to issues such as the quality of air, water and urban space, 'sick buildings' become indicative of a far wider malaise, highlighting our aspirations for a better quality of life and control over our immediate surroundings.

Rather than focusing primarily on the individual, the *community* logic addresses the emblematic issue of democracy or the creation of buildings that embody and express the notion of community. This logic derives from a notion of building as home and seeks to challenge the feelings of alienation attached to many examples of modern architecture. The logic is exemplified by Dick Russell's suggestion that 'we need a building metaphor that somehow encapsulates the idea of co-operative community, of a responsibility toward the Earth and each other that we have abandoned' (Russell 1993: 20). Here, ethical concerns stem from the creation of buildings that have the potential to help us forge a sense of individual and collective identity. The design approach aims to express the organic formation of society with links to the natural locality within which communities are developed. Through this, we will become more aware of our impact on the environment. Thus, we have a notion here that 'sustainable architecture is a social process which will require the full participation of its human beneficiaries' (Clarke 1992: 4). The strategy deriving from this logic is then as much social as technical and aesthetic and prioritises 'involving the community most closely affected by the development in its planning and execution' (Clarke 1992: 2). The aim throughout is to construct appropriate, flexible and participatory buildings which serve the needs of occupiers without impacting on the environment unnecessarily by using renewable, recycled and wherever possible local materials. As the Vales put it,

> The requirement that a building shall remain relevant and functional for as long as possible is an important consideration for green architecture. One way to achieve longevity and avoid demolition is to design buildings that are capable of adapting to the users' changing needs.
>
> (Vale and Vale 1991: 116)

Mixing modes of home, work, leisure and welfare is also a feature of the creation of viable eco-communities, and the central argument of this logic is that the 'formation or training of the community at all levels, on the basis of their needs, is thus the foundation of sustainable development' (Clarke 1992: 4).

Green buildings as social expressions of competing green values

Our brief survey of the contemporary ecological architecture debate has highlighted that there can be no simple or single definition of what constitutes green building or ethical design. Instead, we have suggested that we have to understand alternative environmental approaches and values in terms of competing 'logics' of innovation which emerge from particular 'emblematic issues'; sustainability, efficiency, aesthetics, health, authenticity and communitarian concerns. Following Hajer, these discursive ethical and design 'strategies have to be understood in their own social and cognitive context' (Hajer 1995: 21). This means rejecting any notion of green buildings as merely differently configured technical structures which can be more or less better designed relative to an external definition of accepted environmental standards. Rather, we should view green buildings as social expressions of competing green values and, in accepting this, we will begin to identify more clearly the relationship between the process of building design, ethical values and environmental issues. In understanding green buildings, we therefore have to be sensitive not only to the widely differing *motivations and commitments* of actors, but also to the *range of techniques* or technical innovations employed, the variety of *contexts and settings* in which development occurs and the *social processes* involved in the definition and redefinition of the nature of the environmental problem itself.

Conclusions – green buildings and the ethical challenge

A social constructivist approach to understanding green buildings could help in defining both a wider and fuller interpretation of the nature of the green design problem and may also contribute to developing contextual and socially based methods of ethical analysis. In placing the social setting of green values in the foreground of analysis, ethics become viewed not as static, universal concepts, but 'moral judgements are fundamentally social; as part of intricate cultural systems constructed within communities, they are built, refined, and transmitted through the process of communication and education' (Minteer 1998: 340). In the case of buildings, ethics become viewed as concepts that we test, qualify and reconstruct through an ongoing, dynamic process of design innovation. Further, a social accounting of moral positions may help to make ethical analysis more practically significant and would also more closely coincide with the context of real-life building and environmental decision-making processes which engage with a wide range of building types, located within differing ecological and human settings. The situational diversity and apparent complexity of the green design problem may demand 'that we entertain a pluralistic accounting of our moral positions' (Minteer 1998: 334). Recognising the contingency and value richness of the many niches of the moral community does not necessarily signal a retreat into a disabling fragmented relativism. Our analysis has hopefully demonstrated that the wide variety of design approaches can bring potential environmental benefits at a variety of scales. Importantly, in this relatively immature period in the transition to more sustainable buildings, by suspending the search for a true or incontestable, consensual definition of green buildings and environmental ethics, we potentially become more sensitive to the range of possible logics of innovation which may surface in new buildings. We must still hold open the possibility 'of raising awareness of all the issues that can be considered' (Cook and Golton 1994: 684). This is a point further reinforced in a refreshingly pragmatic manner by John Farmer:

> Only man can decide what are to be the social, ethical and cultural green values. It may be that some materials and methods assumed to be green would fail searching evaluation and other less obvious possibilities succeed. It is probable that no absolute or universal solutions are possible. It may be a question of steering in the right direction.
>
> (Farmer 1996: 185)

Finally, the future direction and success of green building strategies will inevitably rely on our abilities as moral citizens to engage in an open process of negotiation, criticism and debate. We therefore cannot ignore the ways in which particular logics of environmental innovation take root in development practices. This means accepting that 'architecture is part of the conflicting and contradictory struggle of differing forces, interest groups and movements' (Borden and Dunster 1995: 4) and therefore contingent on the particular logic of those development actors with the power to implement their chosen design strategy. The real benefit of social constructivist analysis may lie in its ability to demonstrate how the power relations amongst competing interests are revealed to be the primary context for decision-making and this suggests an important future direction in research. Such research may help to identify those societal actors with most influence over decision-making and enable various professional actors to recognise their own position and role in the provision of more sustainable lifestyles. However, this may only be possible if, according to Hajer (1995), 'ecological politics could shed its prevailing techno-corporatist format and create open structures to determine what sort of nature and society we really want' (Hajer 1995: 294).

Note

1 The Building Research Establishment Environmental Assessment Method, or BREEAM (BRE: 1990), categorises a variety of building types against a range of approximately eighteen performance criteria organised to three scales: global, local and indoor.

References and bibliography

Blowers, A. (1997) 'Environmental Policy: Ecological Modernisation or the Risk Society?', *Urban Studies*, 34(5–6): 845–71.

Bordon, I. and Dunster, D. (eds) (1995) *Architecture and the Sites of History,* London: Butterworth Architecture.

Clarke, T. (1992*)* 'Building for Sustainability', *Institute of Advanced Architectural Studies Report,* University of York.

Cook, Sara J. and Golton, Bryn L. (1994) 'Sustainable Development Concepts and Practice in the Built Environment – A UK Perspective', *Sustainable Construction,* CIB TG 16, 6–9 Nov: 677–85.

Curwell, S. and Cooper, I. (1998) 'The implications of urban sustainability', *Building Research and Information,* 26(1): 17–28.

Farmer, J. (1996) *Green shift: Towards a Green Sensibility in Architecture,* London: WWF.

Frampton, K. (1985) *Modern Architecture: A Critical History,* London: Thames and Hudson.

Guy, S. and Shove, E. (1994) 'From Shelter to Machine: Remodelling Buildings for a Changing Environment', *Proceedings of the World Congress of Sociology,* Biederfeld, Germany, July.

Hajer, M. (1995) *The Politics of Environmental Discourse: Ecological Modernization and the Policy Process,* Oxford: Oxford University Press.

Hannigam, J. (1995) *Environmental Sociology: A Social Constructivist Perspective,* London: Routledge.

Hawkes, D. (1996) *The Environmental Tradition: Studies in the Architecture of the Environment,* London: E&FN Spon.

Minteer, B.A. (1998) 'No Experience Necessary? Foundationalism and the Retreat from Culture in Environmental Ethics', *Environmental Values* 7: 333–48.

Moore, S.A. (1997) 'Technology and the Politics of Sustainability at Blueprint Demonstration Farm', *Journal of Architectural Education,* 51(1): 23–31.

Pearson, D. (1991) 'Making Sense of Architecture', *The Architectural Review* 1136: 68–70.

Pepper, D. (1984) *The Roots of Modern Environmentalism,* London: Routledge.

Rees, W. (1992) 'Ecological Footprints and Appropriate Carrying Capacity: What Urban Economics Leaves Out', *Environment and Urbanisation* 4(2): 121–30.

Rees, W. and Wackernagel, M. (1996) *Our Ecological Footprint,* Canada: New Society Publishers.

Rogers, R. (1991) *Architecture: A Modern View,* London: Thames and Hudson.

Russell, D. (1993) 'Ecologically Sound Architecture gains ground', *The Amicus Journal,* Summer: 14–20.

Spaargaren, G. and Mol, A.J.P. (1992) 'Sociology, Environment and Modernity: Ecological Modernisation as a Theory of Social Change', *Society and Natural Resources,* 5: 323–44.

Sudjic, D. (1996) 'A House in the Country', *The Guardian,* 2 June: 7.

Ujam, F. and Stevenson, F. (1996) 'Structuring Sustainability', *Alt'ing,* March: 45–9.

Vale, B. and Vale, R. (1991) *Green Architecture. Design for a Sustainable Future,* London: Thames and Hudson.

Vale, B. and Vale, R. (1996) 'Urban Design: The Challenge of Sustainability', *Journal of Urban Design* 1(2): 141–2.

Wines, J. (1993) 'Architecture in the Age of Ecology', *The Amicus Journal*, Summer: 22–3.

Wines, J. (1997) 'Passages: The Fusion of Architecture and Landscape in the Recent Work of SITE', *Architectural Design*, 67: 32–33.

Part II

BUILDING WITH GREATER SENSITIVITY TO PEOPLE(S) AND PLACES

7

SOCIAL INCLUSION AND THE SUSTAINABLE CITY

Roger Talbot and Gian Carlo Magnoli

From the perspective of practical politics, the sustainability age is only in its second decade. Before publication of the report of the World Commission for Environment and Development, the Brundtland Commission, in 1987 (World Commission for Environment and Development 1987) it was difficult to identify any official social, economic or indeed environmental policies that recognised sustainable development as a significant policy objective. Since the publication of Agenda 21 following the United Nations Conference on Environment and Development, the Earth Summit, in 1992 (Halpern 1992), it is difficult to identify government policy statements that do not.

In such a new and rapidly changing policy arena, it is not surprising to discover a high proportion of myths, conflicts and contradictions and very few certainties. The principal aims of this contribution are, firstly, to separate mythology from reality and, secondly, to offer a values-based framework that can help to resolve some of the conflicts and build upon some of the certainties at a local level. An empirical point of reference for the construction of such a framework is provided by the innovative sustainable development agenda being followed by the city of Edinburgh (City of Edinburgh Council 1998).

There are four myths that need to be dispelled, to clear space for more objective analysis. The first is that the global environmental crisis is not as serious as doom-mongers would suggest and that, with the application of human ingenuity, growth economics and a few technical fixes, we will manage to muddle through without having to change the fundamentals of the existing system. It is and we will not! (Clayton and Radcliffe 1994).

The second myth is that the Earth's natural systems as a whole will eventually collapse under the pressure of human actions. Even when our very future is at stake, we retain the capacity to delude ourselves about our own importance and significance. Human life-support systems and social cohesion will break down to destroy us long before the Earth itself is threatened (Lovelock 1979).

The third myth is that consumerism is the root cause of environmental problems, of inequities between the rich and poor nations and of social exclusion within even the most developed societies. Feeling fashionably guilty may make one feel better but it is not our lifestyle *per se* which is the issue but the 1 per cent efficiency with which capitalism converts natural resources into useful, sustainable products and life-supporting services (Hawken 1993).

The global industrial 'system' is less of a system and more of a collection of linear flows. It draws upon a fixed stock of non-renewable materials and fossil energy from Nature, processes them for economic value and dumps the residue back into Nature. It is an operation of supreme inefficiency that inevitably consumes and degrades the very resource base upon which it depends, straining the limits of the Earth's carrying capacity (Wackernagel and Rees 1996).

The fourth myth is that the solutions to our problems lie in a shift away from polluted, congested, stressful city-living to some alternative, non-urban form of human settlement.

It is true that *present* forms of urban development are clearly and unequivocally unsustainable. It is true that the urban environment represents humanity's most intensively serviced and managed system and that cities are models of inefficiency. Occupying less than 2 per cent of the Earth's surface area, they appropriate some 75 per cent of its resources, most from less-developed countries. It is true that most of the wasteful and polluting by-products of urban life are simply dumped back unmoderated into the biosystem, threatening the health of the global life-support systems (Girardet 1992).

All this is undeniable, but so is the fact that we live in an inevitably urbanising world. The new millennium will open with 50 per cent of a growing global population living in cities. Cities and city-regions are already home to 80 per cent of Europe's population. Globally, the urban population is growing at a rate of a quarter of a million people per day – a new London every month. The conclusion of Habitat II was that the trend towards increasing and accelerating urbanisation is in all practical senses irreversible and, in policy terms, must be treated as given (United Nations Conference on Human Settlements 1996).

On the basis of such a reality check, it is simply not possible to envisage a future that is not rooted in urban living. For the great mass of the human population, cities are, and will remain, the only game in town. We will not meet the challenge of sustainable development unless and until we learn how to plan, build and live equitably within the sustainable city. This is the first of the new certainties of sustainability.

A further certainty, deduced from the laws of ecology and thermodynamics, is that we must first imagine, then learn, how to implement and finally execute a future free from fossil fuels. Since renewable energy sources will not be able to meet the projected demand and nuclear power presents unacceptable risk, the alternative has to be massive reductions in the throughputs of energy and materials through the world's economic and industrial systems (Lovins 1977).

If we are to maintain quality of life for the fortunate few and increase the quality of life to acceptable levels for the aspiring many, then our only choice is to make order-of-magnitude improvements in system efficiency. If we simultaneously seek to do so on an ethical basis by applying the equity principle across both developed and developing nations (Carley and Spapens 1998), then we are faced with achieving rapid reductions in urban resource use in the richest countries of the world of some 80–90 per cent (Ekins 1992). This effectively means that the sustainable cities of the near future must operate as systems, continuously recycling energy and matter, drawn from local sources and processed without waste.

We are presented here with an intriguing paradox. The city is, in respect to global environment problems, both culprit and victim. Cities are where the resource usage and inefficiencies are highest and where the adverse effects on vulnerable populations are most severe. The built environment of our cities represents a massive capital investment that, if we make mistakes, commits us irrevocably to long-term patterns of resource use, waste emissions and environmental degradation.

At the same time, the city is the principal locus for change, presenting the greatest opportunity for improving performance and offering the major concentration of essential human resources in terms of vision, information and knowledge. Building more sustainably offers solutions, which are simultaneously environmentally responsible, economically viable and socially beneficial – the three touchstones of sustainable development.

Governments generally have been slow to recognise the critical role of the built environment in delivering the sustainable development agenda (Talbot 1998). They have been even slower at recognising that the sustainability agenda is constantly evolving. Whilst achieving massive efficiency gains in the way we plan, design, construct and operate buildings must remain a primary objective of policy, it is now becoming clear that the ultimate barriers to change are neither technical nor economic, but social.

Offering economic or technical 'solutions' that are insensitive to issues of equity and inclusion is no longer an option. Increasingly powerful forces now successfully oppose such actions by companies and by governments on ethical grounds. This is a lesson being slowly, and often painfully, learned by big business in confronting the social values agenda. Without diminishing the ethical case for 'right actions', we want to add a second level of argument – that inequity and exclusion simply do not make ecological sense. It is a fundamental presumption of Agenda 21 that sustainable development is only possible if it is built by, through and with the commitment of local communities (Halpern 1992). Any action or policy that causes social division and threatens social cohesion weakens the capacity of a community to work together to solve its own problems, to build towards a collective social sustainability and to ensure the effective functioning of life-supporting ecosystems

In the context of urban development, sustainability is then seen to lie at the nexus of ethics and ecology – at the conjunction, in particular, of concerns with social inclusion and concerns with improving the eco-efficiency of the city (von Weizsacker *et al.* 1997).

For policy makers, even in an era of so called *joined-up* government, the mutual incompatibility of social division and urban sustainability seems not to be fully understood, or where understood, not translated into effective policy (Talbot 1998). The ability of central and local government to solve the problems of sustainability on behalf of communities appears strictly limited. As a consequence, communities will need to become increasingly sustaining by their own efforts.

The significance of the challenge of building urban communities that are simultaneously resource-efficient, ecologically sound and inclusive is reflected in the identification by Medard Gable of the nine most critical values for a desirable future world. Such a world, in Gable's view, will need to be abundant, regenerative, dependable, safe, appropriate, equitable, flexible, efficient and open-minded, and locally controlled (Gable 1995: 15).

This further assertion of the critical interdependency between ecological sustainability and inclusion is reinforced yet again by both Bookchin (1985) and Capra (1996).

Bookchin writes of the essential need for a decentralised, revitalised sense of community, in which people can recover control over their destinies and in which 'participation' refers to a sense of being part of Nature as well as part of a humanly scaled society (Bookchin 1985: 8).

In Capra's view, we need to recognise that most of our existing social and economic structures are fundamentally anti-ecological and to change our thinking to embrace the idea that human communities are complex adaptive systems, in which the emphasis must be upon connectedness, relationships and context – the very antithesis of exclusion (Capra 1996).

Both take the argument further – Bookchin from an essentially ethical perspective, Capra from an essentially ecological one – by emphasising the importance of learning.

Bookchin argues that politics must be educative and 'not simply oriented towards winning elections'. It should provide a 'curriculum for creating real citizenship' and 'presupposes a sense of civic virtue, a vital community life and a rich, creative and supportive collectivity' (Bookchin 1985: 8).

Capra argues that achieving sustainability will depend upon our ability to understand the key concepts of ecology and to apply these to fields as disparate as education, management, politics and building. Capra identifies these key principles of ecology as interdependence, networks, recycling, feedback, partnership, flexibility and diversity. He argues that whilst we cannot learn everything about human values from ecosystems, what we can learn from them is how to live sustainably.

Bookchin and Capra are agreed, from their different perspectives, that sustainable communities will need to possess the culture-specific knowledge and the capacity to manage and utilise their resources in ways that are analogous to those of natural, ecological systems. Such communities will need to learn new ways of thinking, new values, a new system of ethics, a new understanding of their connection to Nature and a new capability to act individually and collectively in a sustainable manner. In essence they need to become *learning communities*.

In the view of the authors, *community learning* will be the predominant tool of self-reliance and the basis of a new unifying approach towards planning and building sustainable, inclusive communities.

The lessons of evolution tell us that learning is a fundamental life force. It is the mechanism by which life forms and whole ecosystems control energy and information. Learning communities will be communities educated in the essentials of sustainable development and environmental stewardship and be equipped to monitor and evaluate their own environmental performance. This means developing systematic feedback mechanisms that allow both the social and the ecological consequences of individual and collective actions and interventions to be better understood and accounted for in decision taking.

Community learning is a process for ensuring that informed decisions for social change are based on the fullest possible public participation and the most effective use of local expertise and knowledge. Design and planning for sustainable communities need to be firmly grounded in the details of place. Traditional local knowledge, which is place and culture-specific, is a critical asset, which needs to be acknowledged, preserved, restored and utilised.

Learning communities will be those able to adapt their social structures, their cultural values and their patterns of resource utilisation in response to the complex and interrelated environmental, social and economic problems of sustainability. By learning to think systemically communities can come to see that they are not exempt from Nature but are an integral part of it. They need to learn from ecology and recognise the connectivity between their lives and actions and the systems and cycles of Nature. Above all they need to learn the limits which this places on human activity.

In part, the 'art and practice' of community learning have their parallels in the concepts, objectives and methods of organisational learning as shaped and applied by Peter Senge (Senge 1990). Some useful lessons can be learned from Senge's exposition of the characteristics of learning organisations in which he argues that the most powerful learning comes from direct experience. This is so-called 'single-loop' learning resulting from direct trial and error – taking an action, seeing the consequences of that action then taking a new and a different action as a result. Of fundamental concern in the context of urban sustainability, however, is what happens when we can no longer directly observe the consequences of our actions, when the direct feedback loop is missing? What happens if the consequences of our actions are in the distant future or in a distant part of the larger system within which we operate? It then becomes impossible to learn from direct experience and we must look instead at the processes of 'double-loop' learning in which the learner is encouraged to understand the overall context for their learning. This is the essence of systems thinking and is the type of learning we need in order to deal with the complexities and interrelationships of sustainability.

A key issue is not our ability to generate new information but our inability to disseminate it effectively. Knowledge often does not get to the people who most need it in a form they can most use it. Learning communities will need to develop and utilise the communication skills and networks to be able to share their learning experiences and maximise the opportunity for the exchange of information, knowledge and culture. Such a requirement demands practical instruments in the form of information services, feedback loops and decentralised representative structures to guide and support decision-making by new partnerships and networks of individuals, groups, companies, planners and policy makers within the community.

Direct empirical support for our belief in the value of community learning as a tool for empowering communities, for embracing both the ecological and ethical dimensions of sustainable development and for helping to build a community's capacity to deliver the urban sustainability agenda, has been gained from recent experiences in the city of Edinburgh (City of Edinburgh 1998).

Edinburgh is regarded as one of the finest – and most liveable – cities in Europe, with a superb natural and built environment and a high quality of life for many of its citizens. Recognition that, in a changing world, such a position could not be taken for granted played a major part in policy developments in the city following local government reorganisation in 1996.

Edinburgh, with a population of around 450,000, is the main service centre for south-eastern Scotland. Many people from the Forth basin and the Scottish Borders work and shop in the city, extending the total travel to work area population to around one million. The resident population is predicted to grow by approximately 15,000 by the year 2006, against the trend in Scotland as a whole.

Edinburgh has a service-based economy, which is growing faster at the present time than the United Kingdom economy generally. Banking, finance and tourism are its most important components. A knowledge-based economy, centred around the activities of the three universities, is also highly significant. The city is also the seat of government in Scotland and 1999 saw the return of a Scottish Parliament to Edinburgh after almost 300 years.

The Old and the New Towns of Edinburgh have been declared a World Heritage Site as a measure of their international architectural and historic significance. Future development in the city will be required to preserve and enhance the culturally important city centre.

Edinburgh has a history of innovation in urban planning and design, exemplified by the work of Craig, Adam and Geddes. The high density and compact nature of Edinburgh, and its development around a number of strong, distinctive communities, created a city which followed many of the principles now associated with sustainable urban development.

Many recent developments, however, have diminished the sustainability of the city. The city has great natural advantages that are not being properly utilised. Existing policies are either not leading the city towards sustainability or are actually leading it away.

The high-density, compact city that is crucial to achieving sustainable development is being undermined by urban sprawl and edge of town developments. Planning controls are weak and fail to ensure the fullest possible participation by the wider community. Overall there is a lack of a strategic framework for managing development in the city-region and integrating it with public transport services and communities.

There remain unacceptable gaps between the wealthy and the poor in the community, manifest in terms of employment, health, crime and opportunities in life. Homelessness is high and there is poverty and other forms of social exclusion throughout the city.

There is no existing long-term approach to the sustainable economic development of the city. There is a lack of support for indigenous and smaller businesses.

There are serious barriers to many people in the city gaining the necessary skills, training and employment to allow them to contribute fully within the community and a lack of ability for those in peripheral estates to access capital and other resources that they require to take advantage of opportunities.

The city has poor air quality, a high level of casualties amongst children and a high level of growth in car ownership. The transport system in the city is disjointed and lacking co-ordination.

As a city, Edinburgh over-consumes its share of resources and fails to manage the waste it produces in a sustainable manner. Many organisations – including leading businesses and universities – have yet to set firm targets for improving the efficiency of resource use. There is room for major improvements in energy efficiency in the housing, commerce and transport sectors.

Major developments or redevelopments taking place in the city have yet to convince that planning rhetoric about sustainable development will be turned into reality.

Critically, there is a lack of leadership, real vision and real champions of sustainability at the highest levels and a collective failure to grasp the opportunities that a sustainable Edinburgh could offer.

Recognising these problems during its policy reviews in 1996 and 1997, the new City of Edinburgh Council took the innovative step of promoting the establishment of an independent civic Commission on Sustainable Development. The role of the Commission was to help the city give practical expression to the concept of sustainable development for politicians, planners and citizens alike and to propose a unifying policy framework for progressing the city's sustainable development agenda on the basis of consensus.

The Commission, the first of its kind in the United Kingdom, was officially launched in January 1997. Fourteen Commissioners were selected on the basis of their experience and knowledge of sustainable development in all its different aspects. Commissioners were drawn from business, the Universities, non-governmental organisations, local government and other public institutions, the trade unions and community groups.

Over a period of twelve months, the Commission conducted the most extensive and inclusive public consultation exercise ever carried out on behalf of a local authority in Scotland. The Commission gathered evidence from all sectors of the community and structured its findings under seven main headings:

- Inequality and Social Exclusion
- Economic Development
- Transport and Air Quality
- Waste Management and Resource Use
- Land Use Planning and Management
- Energy and Global Climate Change
- Quality of the Neighbourhood

A key finding of the Commission was that Edinburgh – despite its image – was a city with a high level of social exclusion and that such a condition presented a major barrier to sustainability. The Commission concluded that progress towards ecological and economic sustainability for the city would ultimately depend upon solving the problem of social exclusion. It recommended that the city – in the interest of all its citizens, not just those excluded – should move towards a more inclusive structure, which ensured that the conditions of poverty, poor health, inadequate housing and unemployment that blight areas of the city are reduced, and that all in the community are given a say in the future direction of their city. The positive response of the City of Edinburgh Council to this recommendation has been to establish a second Commission to undertake a more in-depth study of social exclusion within the city.

A critical part of the work of the Commission on Sustainable Development was an envisioning exercise. The Commission envisaged a sustainable Edinburgh as:

An *ecologically sound* city
- which was organised on ecological principles
- where the basic resources of air, land and water are clean and free of pollution and where use of both renewable and non-renewable resources are kept within sustainable limits
- which values its existing building stock and seeks to make the best use of what it has

An *inclusive* city
- where everyone has equal access to opportunities, where people are integrated into their community and are fully aware of both their rights and their responsibilities
- in which the planning and development processes are as transparent

and as accountable as possible

A *learning* city
- where high-quality education is available to all citizens
- which has developed and maintains effective and open structures for accessing and sharing an extensive knowledge and resource base
- which has promoted and facilitated a high-level understanding of sustainability principles and practices
- which sees itself as a leader but is open to sharing its experiences, its ideas and its resources freely with others

A *prosperous* city
- where people can earn a livelihood that will provide for themselves and their dependants
- which recognises the importance of local sourcing of goods and services

A *connected* city
- with exemplary methods of communication
- where there is a partnership approach to research that ensures the benefits of innovation are widely applied
- characterised by the lack of institutional barriers not the presence of them
- in which the network rather than the hierarchy is the dominant organisational structure

An *efficiently and effectively managed* city
- where the integration and co-operation of different groups within the city reduces duplication of tasks and strengthens the overall positive impact of policies

A *compact* city
- where there is a high density of population living within easy access of services, leisure facilities and greenspace. Such a criterion is based upon the belief that high urban density leads to energy efficiency and to support for an effective integrated transport system.

Such a vision embodies key principles about the interdependency of ecological soundness and inclusiveness and about the duality of ethics and ecology. It reinforces the concept of the 'learning city' as a necessary pre-condition for urban sustainability. The conclusions of the Commission on Sustainable Development for the City of Edinburgh lend weight to our contention that community learning offers a practical and highly cost-effective approach to empowering communities through knowledge and helping to build the capacity for sustainable urban development.

References

Bookchin, M. (1985) 'Visions', *Environmental Action* (Special Issue).

Capra, Fritjof (1996) *The Web of Life: A New Synthesis of Mind and Matter*, London: HarperCollins.

Carley, M. and Spapens, P. (1998) *Sharing the World: Sustainable Living and Global Equity in the 21st Century*, London: Earthscan.

City of Edinburgh Council (1998) *The Lord Provost's Commission on Sustainable Development for the City of Edinburgh*, Edinburgh: City of Edinburgh Council.

Clayton, A. and Radcliffe, N. (1994) *Sustainability: A Systems Approach*, London: Institute for Policy Analysis and Development for the World Wide Fund for Nature.

Ekins, P. (1992) *The Gaia Atlas of Green Economic*, New York: Anchor Books, Doubleday.

Gable, M. (1985) 'Visions', *Environmental Action* (Special Issue).

Girardet, H. (1992) *The Gaia Atlas of Cities, New Directions for Sustainable Urban Living*, London: Gaia Books.

Halpern, S. (1992) *United Nations Conference on Environment and Development: Process and Documentation*, Providence, RI: Academic Council for the United Nations System (ACUNS).

Hawken, P. (1993) *The Ecology of Commerce: How Business Can Save the Planet*, London: Weidenfeld and Nicolson.

Lovelock, J. (1979) *Gaia*, Oxford: Oxford University Press.

Lovins, A. (1977) *Soft Energy Paths*, New York: Harper & Row.

Senge, P. (1990) *The Fifth Discipline: The Art and Practice of the Learning Organisation*, London: Random House.

Talbot, R. (1998) *Sustainable Construction: A Scottish Perspective*, Edinburgh: The Scottish Office.

United Nations Conference on Human Settlements (1996) *The Habitat Agenda*, New York: United Nations.

von Weizsackjer, E., Lovins, A. and Lovins, H. (1997) *Factor Four; Doubling Wealth, Halving Resource Use*, London: Earthscan.

Wackernagel, M. and Rees, W. (1996) *Our Ecological Footprint: Reducing Human Impact on the Earth*, Philadelphia, PA: New Society Publishers.

World Commission for Environment and Development. (1987) *Our Common Future*, New York: Oxford University Press.

8

TRANSFORMATIVE ARCHITECTURE

A synthesis of ecological and participatory design

Bob Fowles

Introduction

There is, emerging amongst some architects, a new way of thinking about how the built environment can be created. It embodies an ecological awareness, a systems understanding or holism and it incorporates participatory procedures. Together, these present moral and ethical considerations as architects are challenged to absorb responsibilities beyond the building itself. The concept of sustainability has become both the focus and the goal of this new paradigm, which can be observed in a range of building types. When architects incorporate user and community participation in the design and development process, whilst at the same time embracing an ecological agenda, there evolves a strengthening of social sustainability as well as increasing sustainability in the physical environment.

The implications of incorporating participation reach beyond changes in the structure of the design process and the methods of construction, to altering the conventional relationship between the expert and the user. The architect also becomes the facilitator of change within the participants themselves in terms of personal and community transformation towards empowerment and ownership. With ecological design, architects are extending their brief into decision areas, which impact upon the health of people and the health of the planet. The extended implications of this synthesis, in terms of personal and community sustainability through the creative engagement of users with environmental and ecological issues, present new challenges to the architect as well as influencing the economic and spiritual well-being of the participants.

Systems, interdependence, interrelatedness

A major characteristic of the new thinking of the *green* movement is holism: the belief that things are interconnected, that each problem is part of a larger one, and that solutions to problems in one area can create problems for someone else to solve in another.

René Descartes (1596–1650), French philosopher and the father of scientism, distinguished between mind and matter, that the two were separate and fundamentally different. This Cartesian division had a profound effect on Western thought. It led to setting a higher value on mental than manual work. It also led to the belief that Nature worked according to mechanical laws and as such could be controlled and conquered. This was in complete contrast to the organic world view, which was still prevalent in the Middle Ages, and implied a value system conducive to ecological behaviour:

> The image of the earth as a living organism and nurturing mother served as a cultural constraint restricting the actions of human beings. One does not readily slay a mother, dig into her entrails for gold, or mutilate her body... As long as the earth was considered to be alive and sensitive, it could be considered a breach of human ethical behaviour to carry out destructive acts against it.
>
> (Merchant 1980)

This significant division between humankind and the natural world has led to the greatest heresy, the belief that *man is apart from Nature and not part of her.* Pre-Christian societies saw the Earth as Mother and worshipped Gaia, the Earth Goddess. The anthropocentric view of Christianity replaced the ecocentric world view, which for many societies was animistic and Nature-reverencing, as reflected in their shrines and sacred places in groves of trees, by wells or on mountain tops. Christianity as it spread suppressed these earlier religions, branding them as heresy.

As well as the separation of man from Nature, the separation of thinking from doing took place. By the time of the industrial revolution, the split was established. In manufacturing, with machines and buildings, the designing, i.e. the thinking, was done by white collar professionals in drawing offices, and the making, i.e. the manual work, by blue collar workers in factories. A division of labour was fundamental to the streamlining of the industrial production process; the whole was broken up into parts so that people became specialist at their particular task. The overview was to be the prerogative of the designer. But was this the case? In the design office a *division of thinking* got under way as specialists in one field or another become identified. No-one, in the end, had an overview. No-one was in a position to look at things holistically. The architect was regarded as the universal man, or rather regarded himself as such. However, at the formation of the profession in the 1880s the architects' principal concern was with silhouette, proportion and style of buildings, i.e. the aesthetics, and this became a specialism. This had the effect of divorcing the architect from much of the decision-making and from the *procedures of making* buildings. Everyone was becoming preoccupied with their particular task, solving problems within the confines of their own perceived world. The three legacies of Descartes, and of scientism, which have had such a deleterious impact upon the values and practice of architecture, may be summarised as the belief that man is separate from Nature; the separation of manual from mental work; and the following of a parts approach, as opposed to a holistic approach.

Hence the necessity for a paradigm shift to reverse and make good, in which designing for a sustainable future should adopt three principles:

1 Man is not separate from Nature, and man's activities, including the making of the built environment, must recognise and respect the processes of ecosystems: we must practice ecological design.
2 Manual and mental activities, theory and practice, designer and maker, etc. should be reintegrated: we should regard design as a social process.
3 A holistic approach that recognises interrelatedness and interdependence of all matter and all living things: we must adopt systems thinking.

It is James Lovelock's theory of Gaia that has allowed us to bridge between the pre-Christian intuitive respect for mother Earth and a modern scientific understanding of the interrelatedness of all life and the environment. 'The evolution of the species of organisms is not independent of the evolution of their material environment. Indeed the species and their environment are tightly coupled and evolve as a single system.' (Lovelock 1989). Humankind and its buildings are part of this evolution, the sacred value of which is emphasised in the Buddhist concept of Esho Funi, meaning *the oneness of self and environment*:

Life at each moment encompasses both body and spirit and both self and environment of all sentient beings in every condition of life, as well as insentient beings – plants, sky and earth, on down to the most minute particles of dust. Life at each moment permeates the universe and is revealed in all phenomena.

(Nicharin Dishonin, thirteenth century)

When participation meets ecology

The Declaration of Interdependence for a Sustainable Future by the UIA/ AIA World Congress of Architects, Chicago 1993, takes up the concepts of interrelatedness and interdependence: 'We are ecologically interdependent with the whole natural environment. We are socially, culturally, and economically interdependent with all of humanity. Sustainability, in the context of this interdependence, requires partnership, equity, and balance among all parties'.

Alongside the ecological and environmental components of sustainability, and significantly for the development of participation, an emphasis is placed on another fundamental component of sustainable design, i.e. the relationship between players in the process in the form of *partnership, equity and balance.*

With a few exceptions, participatory design and ecological design have evolved independently over the past two decades, but when these two are brought together in the design process, when they are really intertwined, when a synthesis of the two takes place, we begin to witness the characteristics of a new paradigm.

Participatory design

An influential role for tenants, employees and whole neighbourhoods in the design of a range of building types at different scales of the built environment is now taking place (Hatch 1984; Woolley 1989; Fowles 1997). Participatory procedures even extend user involvement into the construction and management of buildings.

A significant UK example of participatory design is for the Lambeth Community Care Centre, London (Lubbock *et al.* 1985). The result is a new prototype local care facility incorporating general practitioners together with a wide range of specialist services, twenty in-patient beds, thirty-five day centre places, facilities for local groups, etc. A self-formed client project team of fifteen persons including doctors, nurses and home helps held public meetings, carried out household surveys, had discussions with councillors, tenants' associations, etc., and produced a building brief. They then selected Edward Cullinan, Architects, with whom they worked to further develop the brief and generate a design. In total, 300 meetings were held, including thirty meetings between the architects and the client group before the design was frozen.

Different relationships between architect and user can be identified in participation. Fredrik Wulz in his 'scale of participation' (Wulz 1986) describes seven distinct relationships which he places between the poles of *expert autonomous* architecture and *user autonomous* architecture.

They are *representation* (the most passive form in which the architect has consideration for the wishes and personal needs of the user-client); *questionnary* (statistical gathering of the population's requirements); *regionalism* (sensitivity to the specific and cultural heritage within a geographic area); *dialogue* (often based on informal conversations between architect and users, with the architect reserving the right to make the final decisions); *alternative* (users are given alternative solutions from which to choose); *co-decision* (user-clients are in balance with the architect with regard to the degree of influence); and *self-decision* (the architect is called in as required).

If one accepts that the user can be brought into the process on a contributive basis, and face to face with the professional, then a number of questions arise: Can the parties actually reach a *partnership, equity and balance* in their relationship? What information or expertise can the user contribute which equates with that of the professional? In other words: Is it possible to find a *symmetry* in the relationship between the parties? The possibility of the two parties meeting mid-way is in fact recognised by Wulz at the level of *co-decision,* but what does this mean in practice?

At Lambeth, there was a clear model of the relationship between the architect and the user-client group: the client selected the architect then each contributed specific inputs to the process and influenced different aspects of the design. Each had influence and control over different aspects of both the process and the design. In design terms, the architect contributed the theme of country house party; the idea of the conservatory stairwell and its relation to the garden; and the sitting room and ward verandas. The client-group contributed the idea of corridors as places to commune and exercise; the functional zoning; and the detailed design of the garden. Additionally, many other features and detailed design ideas were the product of joint debate. Here we see users producing architectural design ideas, whereas more often in participatory design they offer their knowledge of how they do their job so the architects can design appropriate environments for them. At the end of this process, Cullinan observed 'Those who hold the pen have the power, but they should share the power'.

Horst Rittel (1972) had already suggested that users should be party to the process as it is the *knowledge* held by a wide range of people affected by a problem which should be utilised in seeking solutions to that problem. He claimed 'expertise does not reside solely in the professional, but in all those whose interests are affected by a design or planning problem' (Rittel 1972). In other words, Rittel saw gaps in the knowledge and expertise of the professionals, i.e. a degree of ignorance on their part, which can only be filled by other people, and succinctly emphasised this point by introducing the concept of a *symmetry of ignorance.*

The UIA Declaration followed on from Agenda 21, agreed by Heads of States at the Earth Summit in Rio de Janeiro 1992, emphasised the importance of involving whole populations in broad processes to achieve change. The rationale for this is simple: in a society with no common visions, only short-term decisions are made. Visions to be of value and to be realisable have to be shared by all, i.e. by experts and lay people. A non-participatory community, one that cannot join together to develop and share visions and their implementation, is inherently unsustainable.

Ecological design

The principles of ecological design in relation to architecture were initially explored during the 1970s in small experimental buildings, often single dwellings, and in *alternative* communities but are now becoming applied to larger buildings. One example is the Okohaus, in Frankfurt, Germany, by architects Joachim Eble and Sambeth (Goldner 1995). This is a 7,000-m^2 cultural and business centre, comprising offices, a printing works, conference/exhibition venue, restaurant, language school and health centre. A large glazed conservatory forms a light-flooded communication space with a climatic function related to a heating system, which includes solar gain and waste heat from the printing works. The roofs are intensively greened to reduce heat loss, increase sound insulation and to purify rainwater. Rainwater is filtered through reed-beds, stored and used for flushing toilets. Fresh air enters the conservatory, where plants and water fountains humidify it. Electric cables are shielded to reduce electromagnetic radiation. Rendering is with lime plasters, and mineral- or plant-based paints are used. Floors incorporating cork granules for insulation are finished with linoleum or softwood parquet with a natural resin-based sealant.

For the occupants, the building exudes an atmosphere of well-being through the presence of light, water, plants and the variety of activities that takes place, as well as overtly illustrating ways in which buildings can reduce their impact on the environment. Arising from this is the question of whether ecological design is simply a question of reducing impact, or can buildings be net contributors to environmental quality? A few buildings do give back energy to the national grid, but can they add to environmental quality in the broadest sense? What should we be aiming for? Where should we start?

Malcolm Wells (1981) asks if building design can be based on *life principles*. This, he says, is what wild land does. It creates pure air, creates pure water, stores rainwater, produces its own food, creates rich soil, uses solar energy, stores solar energy, creates silence, consumes its own wastes, maintains itself, matches nature's pace, provides wildlife habitat, moderates climate and weather, is beautiful and provides human habitat. He maintains that when we build, we do the opposite of these. We fail on every point except the last. We always provide human habitat whatever the cost. There is no reverence for life in the way we build. Autonomous buildings attempt to put the above into practice by aiming to design with no outside energy sources, using locally available, environmentally benign materials and recycling the waste of occupants.

A contemporary approach to design based on life principles and which contributes to an understanding of the holistic nature of ecological architecture is *baubiologie* or building-biology: the science of the holistic interactions and relationships between life-forms and the built environment. It aims to create a healthy living, working and cultural environment by methods which minimise the impact of a building on the health of people and on the health of the planet. Baubiologie regards the building as an organism with its surface being the third skin of the occupants. For the organism to be healthy, the skin should be allowed to function naturally: breathing, absorbing, protecting, insulating, regulating, communicating and allowing evaporation. Whereas the quality of the internal environment can be improved, for example by avoiding toxic chemicals and radioactive building materials and by the appropriate use of colour and lighting, the concept of baubiologie may be extended to consider the process by which materials and components are acquired for use in the building and the impact this may have on the health of the planet.

Transformative architecture

It should now be clear that when we speak of ecological architecture, we are no longer addressing the design of buildings as inert physical objects. Buildings are becoming biological extensions of ourselves, which live and breathe in response to climatic and local weather changes and they are adaptable to changes in human need and behaviour. Conscious participation in the processes of creating and using these buildings generates, for all concerned, a transformative environment. The following three examples are used to illustrate this approach.

ING Bank Headquarters, Amsterdam,
the Netherlands, formerly NMB Bank

The bank had a commitment to produce a high-quality and ecologically sound building. It claims to be one of the most energy-efficient office buildings in the world.

Energy efficiency is achieved by no wide spans in the structure; high insulation; heat gains from people, computers, lighting and sunlight; no air-conditioning; maximum use of natural lighting (workstations near windows, window to window maximum distance is 7 m, deflectors at tops of windows to place light in depth of building); computer-controlled sun blinds; access towers bring light in to filter down to the internal street; solar energy pre-heats air before it is drawn down into the building; waste heat is recycled.

The high quality of the internal environment is created by water flow-forms – pools and sculptures soothe, cool and oxygenate the air; planting improves air quality and creates a *natural* atmosphere; irregular non-institutional circulation routes; absence of 'imposing' rectilinear layout; domestic scale to the internal street and to the workspaces; everyone has the right of space next to a window which opens; all occupants have views out from their workplaces, many into gardens; internal street displays of local hand-crafted works including paintings, sculpture, stained glass, mirrors and textiles; soft coloured surfaces; night flushing of air through the building expels any contaminants.

The high quality of the external environment is created by the irregular form of the building, which gives domestic scale and allows daylight and sunshine into the mass of the building; the slope of walls deflects traffic noise; rainwater is collected, stored and filtered for internal flow-form use; the slope of walls at their base gives 'Earth-bound connection'; gardens help break down the barrier between 'outside and inside', 'life and work', 'Nature and artefact'. The brickwork traditions from the Amsterdam School help provide historical and cultural continuity with its architectural context.

Human resources were employed in the design and use of the building in the following ways: an elected employee committee selected the architect; there was democratic decision by the bank's 2,200 employees on where the building was to be sited; employees worked with the design team, which included acoustitions, landscapers, occupational therapists, artists, contractors, plus the more usual engineers and architect. In general, environmental control is in the hands of the users, and social criteria were used in the organisation of work spaces. Surveys reveal a high worker satisfaction with the building itself and there is very low absenteeism. Its occupants, and visitors, feel rejuvenated, positive and at ease in what is regarded as a truly healing environment.

The Diggers self-build housing at Brighton, England

The Diggers was completed in 1994 and is a twelve-unit, two-storey Segal Method project, with architects Architype Ltd.

Typical technology characteristics of Architype's self-build programme are timber construction – low embodied energy, simple bolt-together frames, Welsh-grown Douglas fir cladding, reducing transportation and supporting local (within the UK) industries; insulation is Warmcell recycled newsprint as part of a breathing wall construction; the avoidance of synthetic products such as rigid foam insulations, vinyl flooring, petrochemically based paints, stains and preservatives, all of which contain toxic chemicals which will outgas into a building and damage occupant health; south-facing conservatories for passive solar gain; natural ventilation; lobbies to prevent heat loss.

An emphasis on social criteria and participatory procedures aims to empower the self-builders giving them control over as many design and specification choices as possible, through communal and individual design sessions. Site training and the making of 1:20 scale models to help understand the construction, develops close relationships between self-builders, architects and the site manager prior to building. The numerous benefits that arise include the acquisition of building skills and self-confidence. A community is created and educated about environmental issues. Some may sell their assets to raise capital to start a business.

New headquarters for SGI-UK

SGI-UK is part of Soka Gakkai International, the worldwide lay organisation practising the Buddhism of Nicherin Daishonin. The new headquarters is nearing completion at Taplow Court in Buckinghamshire. The initial brief included a multifunctional butsuma/performance space to seat 500 people, conference facilities with accommodation, arts facilities, shop, restaurant and administrative offices. The requirements of each of these functions were examined and added to during the design participation process. A strategic framework for participation was sought which would be clear to understand, simple to implement, not greatly extend design time and cost, and which would take the process through from vision to detailed design. It aimed to maximise the involvement of the membership who, through their everyday professional lives, hold expertise to complement that of the architects and their consultants, and who, through their work with SGI, hold knowledge about the needs of the different activities of the organisation. The 6,000 members throughout the UK were provided with a range of opportunities to contribute, including regional and subject-based focus groups; two major design workshop events; and concluding with a public exhibition. The process took place between April and September 1997.

The buildings are designed with high levels of insulation, and with heavy thermal mass to reduce energy consumption for both heating and cooling. The main hall space has adiabatic ventilation and air cooling, with heat exchange on the extracted air. Ancillary spaces are all naturally ventilated by means of opening windows. Night purging is used to cool and cleanse the entire building. Materials are carefully selected, including home grown green oak cladding and structural elements, cedar shingles and recycled aluminium sheet roofing, recycled newspaper insulation, natural rubber flooring and wool carpets, organic paints and stains, and non-PVC wiring and cabling. All spaces are well lit with natural light and all artificial light is low energy. Grey-water is recycled to flush toilets and irrigate areas of green roofs.

The aim of Architype has been to transform the physical, psychological and spiritual needs of the users into built form, and to create an environment that will be healthy and pleasing. In addition, because of their direct involvement in the design process, a large number of people will feel a real sense of ownership of the buildings they use.

The healing transformation

The human mind makes its world by participating in its being. Our theories and models of the world are grounded in our experiential participation in what is present, in what is there. Therefore, the notion of participation must be central to the new world view... There is another important aspect of a participatory world view. It is not so much about the search for truth and knowledge as it is about healing. And above all, healing the alienation, the split that characterises modern experience... To heal means to make whole. We can only understand our world as a whole if we are part of it. As soon as we attempt to stand outside, we divide and separate. Making whole necessarily implies participation. One important characteristic of a participatory world view is that the individual person is restored to the circle of community and the human community to the context of the natural world. In a participatory world view, meaning and mystery are restored to human experience. The world is once again experienced as a sacred place.

(Reason 1998)

Although the three projects described are representative of a more inclusive approach to designing for sustainability and give some optimism for the future, there are considerable barriers to overcome. An analysis of seven of Europe's largest environmentally advanced new housing settlements (Fowles *et al.* 1994), which noted that many incorporated elements of user participation having a direct relationship with the emphasis on ecological design, commented:

> Although the reality of the global environmental crisis is now widely understood, the step from understanding to action is not easy. At the personal level, many people feel blocked and unable to take action to shape their lives in a more satisfying way. At the professional level many have quality ambitions which are frustrated by the narrow criteria applied in conventional projects.
>
> (Fowles *et al.* 1994)

However, it was also able to provide optimism. 'These projects represent initiatives which have released these two sources of energy and if more widely set up will tap a huge potential for action lying dormant in every community in village, town and city' (Fowles *et al.* 1994).

William McDonough's Hannover Principles (Zeiher 1996) indicate the way forward and suggests the widening ethical dimensions of the work of the new paradigm architect:

> Insist on rights of humanity and Nature to co-exist
> Recognise interdependence
> Respect relationships between spirit and matter
> Accept responsibility for the consequence of design
> Create safe objects of long-term value
> Eliminate the concept of waste
> Rely on natural energy flows
> Understand the limitations of design
> Seek constant improvement by the sharing of knowledge
>
> (Zeiher 1996)

Transformation to ownership

In a conventional planning and building process, the politicians, financiers, professionals and developers, i.e. the decision-makers, often work in isolation from the people and communities they serve, to the ultimate detriment of all parties. When participatory processes are initiated from the outset, with respect to contributions from all participants, frameworks for physical, social, economic and ecological change can be agreed by consensus. A common sense of ownership is established and action plans can be implemented in true partnership. Environmental change, to be more than superficial, depends upon such partnership.

Related to symmetry is the concept of *transparency*. This can be assured if information and process documentation is made available to participants. One consequence of transparency is participants developing a sense of *ownership* of the process. This will also be heightened if the creativity of people is realised from the start and their influence on the process identified and the benefit of their contribution acknowledged. The enabling architect should aim to realise objectives in a tangible form and ensure that all meetings have tangible outputs. It is important for participants to have a sense of achievement at regular intervals in the process. Confidence is likely to be gained and ultimately the sense of ownership of the process is likely to be translated into a sense of ownership of the building when it is occupied. The consequences of this for sustainability are immense. There are indications of pride being translated into greater care of buildings in a number of participatory estate regeneration projects.

From my personal experience, when people do participate in the creation of the environment, which they themselves will later inhabit, they begin to critically examine broader ecological aspects of building design. The experience of many participants indicates that the synthesis of participation with an ecological agenda results in a significant personal level of change within themselves. This personal transformation is one of the most beneficial outcomes of the participation process and is an important ingredient in contributing to sustainable communities. It is a spiritual outcome, and just as important as the creation of a socially responsible and ecologically sound architecture.

The architect's transformation

For many, the approach outlined remains a Utopian vision, and there are those who still argue against opening up the design process to all those affected by, or who have an interest in, the problem. Many hold the fear that the architect will abdicate responsibilities and expertise. However, there are an increasing number of architects who are realising that much is to be gained. One example of such a gain is from the work of architect Peter Hübner who joined with members of the Youth Club at Stuttgart-Wangen, in Germany, to design and build their own building:

We need have no fear that the architect's role will be lost in such a participative process – in some ways it becomes more vital. For without Hübner nothing would have happened at Wangen, and his is the most obvious shaping hand behind the project. Nonetheless he has taken the role of interpreter and co-ordinator rather than dictatorial designer, and has allowed the whole process to express itself without imposing too many of his own prejudices. It has been as much a voyage of discovery for him as for the other participants.

(Blundell Jones 1987)

References

Blundell Jones, P. (1987) 'Three Kinds of Participation: Kroll, Sulzer & Hubner', *Architectural Review* 1081: 60–76.

Fowles, R.A., Haas, D., Mehlmann, M., Shearer, K., Thomson, J. and von Zadow, A. (eds) (1994) *Building for Tomorrow: Report of the European Academy for the Urban Environment Workshop on Sustainable Settlements*, Berlin: EA.UE.

Fowles, R.A. (1997) 'Bibliography of Design Participation', *Social Aspects of Architecture Module*, Cardiff: Welsh School of Architecture.

Goldner, A. (1995) 'Eco-property development: Part 1' in *Eco Design*, Vol. III, No. 2, 'Part 2' in *Eco Design,* Vol. III, No. 3.

Hatch, R. (ed.) (1984) *The Scope of Social Architecture*, New York: Van Nostrand Rheinhold.

Lovelock, J. (1989) *The Ages of Gaia: A Biography of Our Living Earth,* Oxford: Oxford University Press.

Lubbock, J., Buchanan, P. and Aston, J. (1985) 'Lambeth Community Care Centre', *Architects Journal* 182: 60–103.

Merchant, C. (1980) *The Death of Nature,* New York: Harper & Row.

Nichiren Daishonin (thirteenth century) *Major Writings,* Vols 1–4, Tokyo: Nichiren Shoshu International Centre,

Reason, P. (1998) 'A Participatory World', *Resurgence* 186: 42–3.

Rittel, H. (1972) 'DMG 5th Anniversary Report', *Design Methods Group Occasional Paper* No. 1: 5–10.

Wells, M. (1981) *Gentle Architecture*, New York: McGraw-Hill.

Woolley, T. (1989) 'Design Participation Today: A Report on the State of the Art', ARCUK Report.

Wulz, F. (1986) 'The Concept of Participation', *Design Studies*, 7(3): 153–62.

Zeiher, L. (1996) *The Ecology of Architecture*, New York: Whitney Library of Design.

9

ETHICS AND VERNACULAR ARCHITECTURE

Paul Oliver

Those who are seriously concerned about the built environment, whether from a purely architectural viewpoint or with particular concern for its aesthetic, ecological, sustainable or other qualitative considerations, frequently use the perceived merits of vernacular architecture to further their arguments. Examples drawn from the Greek islands, or from the Middle East for instance, may be used to illustrate the beauty and simplicity of form, the structural and economic merits of materials such as earth, or the passive modification of the internal environment by wind-scoops. Sometimes the examples may be practically based, though more often they are employed to demonstrate intuitive responses to mankind's psychological needs for meaningful spaces, harmonious forms and human scale. There is a fair measure of self-gratification in this admiration of the vernacular aesthetic and an inclination to disregard those vernacular traditions that do not satisfy the criteria of the viewer, who is rarely an ordinary member of the culture that produced the buildings. Such criteria are generally ethical, the 'purity' of form, the 'truth to materials', the 'economy' of means being ascribed moral value.

Whether we can speak of the 'ethics of vernacular architecture' or even of the 'ethic' of a specific vernacular culture is a debatable issue and one which is seldom, if ever, addressed. Not least of the problems in any discussion of vernacular architecture is the definition of 'vernacular' and its application to building. Derived from the Latin, the term vernacular means 'the language of the slaves'. In Roman times, it was subsequently applied to the speech of the serfs and in English usage has referred more generally to the language of the people. Its application to architecture (or to building, the distinction is as imprecise) derives from the professional and historical discourse which resorts to a linguistic analogy. Writers and critics frequently refer to the 'grammar of architecture' or the 'vocabulary' and 'syntax' of a particular style or tradition. In this context to speak of 'vernacular architecture' as the 'architecture of the people' is not inappropriate. In the present discussion vernacular architecture is understood to mean the buildings *of* the people, built *by* the people. It does not refer to buildings designed and constructed by professional architects and builders *for* the people which, in suburban housing for instance, is considered as 'popular' architecture.

In Britain, we are accustomed to regarding vernacular architecture as the past traditions of predominately rural building, including farmhouses, barns and granaries, but also village churches and chapels, wind and water mills and, in specific regions, the workshops of craft industries. Houses, shops and premises of urban workers and artisans may also be included, as well as the boat sheds and other buildings of fishing communities. Specialists in the British traditions generally accept that they ended with the building of the railroads and the free movement of building materials, which brought about the demise of regional building. Such a determinist position has led to a concentration on the early history of those traditions and marginal attention to the cultural factors that influenced their foundation, development and continued use. Much of European vernacular study has a similarly retrospective view, but in Eastern Europe vernacular traditions have continued until recently, and in some instances still persist. When the focus of attention is shifted from the history of the buildings to their adaptation to meet changing uses and needs, it becomes apparent that vernacular architecture still constitutes a large proportion of the European, including British, domestic building stock.

Considered on a world scale, the picture is dramatically different. Bearing in mind that in broad statistical terms, all but a minute proportion of the billion people living in the Indian subcontinent dwell in vernacular buildings which they have inherited or have themselves constructed, it is evident that in any discussion of world housing the vernacular has to be seriously reckoned with. When the majority of the two billion Chinese who are similarly accommodated are added, close on half the world's population are included in the reckoning. If the dwellings, workplaces and places of worship of the peoples of Indonesia, Central Asia, the Middle East, sub-Saharan Africa, Latin America and not an inconsiderable proportion of the population of North America are also considered, it becomes apparent that somewhere above 80 per cent of the world's buildings, and possibly even 90 per cent of dwellings, are 'vernacular' in kind (Oliver 1997).

Seen from this perspective, not only does vernacular architecture constitute the majority of all domestic buildings, it is likely to remain so for most, if not all, of the twenty-first century. At the turn of the century the global population has reached six billion; predictions based on demographic trends indicate a global population of nine billion people by mid-century. Who is to build the houses that will be needed to accommodate the extra three billion, let alone replace or maintain the bulk of the existing housing stock? It seems inescapable that the peoples of cultures the world over will be obliged to build their own. Just as the inhabitants of the burgeoning peri-urban squatter settlements are self-built with the detritus and scrap materials of the cities by the occupants themselves, with no recognition or aid from national or city funds and resources, so the rapidly expanding millions, urban or rural, will find themselves in the same position.

In those countries whose wealth may grow and who recognise that their continued prosperity and political futures will depend on the well-being, health, occupations and accommodation of untold numbers of the general populace, measures may be taken to build mass housing for them. In view of their lack of concern for all but the wealthiest of clients, it seems unlikely that such housing will be initiated by multinationals and large construction companies, unless it can generate considerable profits or is subsidised by governments or other funding agencies. Whether low-cost housing (it will not be other than low-cost) is generated by governments, international charities or religious bodies, it raises important ethical issues. It can be argued that all people are entitled to fundamental services for their dwellings: water supply, disposal of waste including sewerage, provision of electricity, insulation or defence against extremes of weather as appropriate to the climate, rooms that ensure privacy, labour-saving devices within the kitchen, and so on.

A number of these ethically justified entitlements require technological solutions that may in themselves create problems elsewhere, such as the pollution risks arising from the nuclear generation of electricity, or the consumption of water that flushing systems for the disposal of human wastes can incur. This in turn leads to the problems of waste recycling, or composting on a massive scale. Land is inevitably consumed with housing, but the saving of land by the development of high-rise housing has often failed, further divorcing the occupants from the productive use of domestic farm plots. So it can also be argued that an ethically responsible approach to large-scale or 'mass' housing should give careful attention to the consumption of materials and the need to use renewable resources; that 'green' solutions to housing are essential for the survival of life on the planet.

Even if the problems and paradoxes that such ethical concerns for the housing of the world's poor can be resolved, the question arises as to who has the right, let alone the political will or the financial resources, to make and implement the design decisions necessary to meet these demands. Can they be made independently of the people who need to be housed? Can they in fact be effected without their active participation? Can the vernacular, the architecture of the people and built by the people be ignored, and can such rejection of the values and traditions of cultures, however large or small, be ethically justified? Mass housing, low-cost housing, community architecture, participatory building, however termed, and at whatever scale, the external 'solution to the housing problem' means intervention: intervention by the design decisions of those beyond and outside a culture, intervention through introduced technologies, intervention by builders, contractors, services engineers. Whatever the motivations and justifications – the settlement of space-consuming nomads, the rehousing of the poor believed to be living in inadequate shelters, the upgrading of urban squatter settlements, the relocation of ethnic, religious or other minorities, the provision of emergency shelter and housing for the victims of disasters – all such measures intervene (from *inter venire*: to come between). The ethics of intervention and their relevance to vernacular architecture are therefore of paramount importance in the vital issues of the ethics of building in the twenty-first century.

When considering the ethics of intervention in vernacular architecture it is necessary first to question whether there is a fundamental incompatibility in the very concept of 'the greater good'. Is ethics essentially a part of Western philosophy and, if so, what bearing does it have on the value systems of vernacular culture? For instance, many vernacular traditions have been used to illustrate particular architectural qualities of form, use of resources and environmental responsiveness, of which the Dogon of Mali are among the most frequently cited. Living on the *talus* or rock-fall of the Bandiagara escarpment, they are poised between the desert and more fertile lands. Their architecture has been the subject of both anthropological and architectural study; its structural forms and anthropomorphic symbolism much illustrated. But to speak of 'good design' being superior to 'bad design' in building would have little meaning for a people to whom the balance of the desirable and the undesirable is an essential aspect of life (Griaule and Dieterlen 1954). Similar concepts of maintaining a balance between stability and adversity are to be found among peoples across the world, ranging from the Pueblo cultures of the south-west United States to the Balinese of Indonesia.

Though generalisations about the nature of the world's cultures are fraught with problems and subject to numerous exceptions, it may be argued that, for the most part, the ethical issues in vernacular architecture are not abstracted by the cultures that produce it. Rather, they are part of the moral climate of the culture that may relate to ancestry and lineage, social and family structures, dependence on and nurturing of the environment, cultivation and the raising of livestock and other fundamental aspects of community life. In contexts that may vary with climate, topography, altitude, proximity to water, access to materials and many other factors, including those of accumulated knowledge and the transmission of skills, vernacular traditions have evolved to meet socio-cultural needs. They may range from transitory tented camps to compounds, from farm settlements to urban complexes; they may be built of animal products or moulded earth, wrought timber or dressed stone, grasses, palms and a variety of other natural and manufactured materials. Systems for modifying the climate – to protect from the weather, to promote air circulation, to cool or to insulate – will depend on prevailing climatic conditions. But these and innumerable other aspects of vernacular architecture traditions are special to the environmental and social circumstances of every culture, which accounts for their diversity and, in certain respects where conditions are comparable, their similarities.

Generating the commitment and responsibility necessary for the continuity of traditions and for development through them are the belief systems that unify distinct cultures. Often these may relate to the great, monotheistic religions such as Islam, wherein the rights of the community and of the individual with respect to building are enshrined in law. They may require rituals and customs from dedication to topping-out, through which the spirits of land and household are respected, worshipped and placated. Or they may guide or prescribe all stages in the layout and raising of buildings, as do the Hindu manuals of building, the *vastu sastras*, the *manasara* or the *lontars* (Chakrabarti 1997, Sulistayawati 1997). In many societies to be a member of a household or of an extended family may involve obligations in building, while in others guild systems may define the specialist roles and skills of craftsmen and builders. Whether obedience or default, observance or omission are matters of ethics within vernacular cultures may remain an open question in philosophical theory, but there is little doubt that interventionism in their building practices by alien groups, whatever their reasons, raises fundamental ethical issues.

Bearing in mind the complexity of environments, social life, building needs and processes, obligations and beliefs that give form and meaning to the vernacular architecture of countless cultures, one might wonder under what conditions, and by whom, intervention in vernacular architectural traditions can be justified. Yet there are many circumstances, from post-war resettlement to housing following natural disasters, when external intervention is necessitated, requested and even demanded. Over the past four decades scores of such occasions have arisen, when long-term housing needs have been anticipated and design solutions implemented after initial periods of temporary or emergency accommodation. The methods employed and the acceptability or otherwise of the resultant housing have afforded lessons in the ethics of intervention which, in many cases, have still to be learned.

In my personal experience the first of these arose through the building, under President Kwame Nkrumah's direction, of the Akosombo dam across the Volta River at Tema in Ghana, West Africa, in 1964. Though the dam was designed to create a great lake system which would provide the resource for the generation of hydro-electric power to advance Ghana's aluminium industry, it was also a threat to the livelihoods, the lands and the housing of many tribes and peoples in the hinterland of eastern Ghana. The greatest concentration of new housing was required in the Kete Krachi region and agriculturalists, sociologists, planners and architects were involved in effecting the transition from traditional village to planned settlement. Some 80,000 people were to be displaced and resettled, for whom four types of core houses were designed. With families ranging from five to twenty-five members, the houses had to have sufficient space for expansion, though the compound and settlement plans were designed to a regular quadrilateral geometry.

For my part, I had been charged with developing communication systems which would enable young Asante architects to converse with Gurunsi (Nabdam) tribespeople in the north of Ghana in the event that they, too, would have to be relocate, should the Volta waters rise still higher. The compounds of the Nabdam were complexes of cylindrical, single-cell units of moulded mud, linked with enclosing walls. Dwelling units were often flat-roofed, with low parapets and notched log ladders; granaries and stores were capped with cones of elephant-grass thatch (Prussin 1969). The land on which the houses were constructed belonged to the ancestors, to whom libations were offered by an intercessionary priest, the *tendaana,* who determined where new compounds should be built. I was deeply concerned that the compound forms and customs of the northern people would be overlooked in the urgency of resettlement. A subsequent book on the project confirmed my fears: a misleading photograph of 'a northern compound' shows rectilinear buildings with *brise soleils,* which were, in fact, one of the standard house types designed for the new settlements (Chambers 1970). Four house types were used, all employing lateritic soil–cement blocks, 4 in × 2 in timber purlins and aluminium sheet roofs. Generally, one room of 150 ft^2 was completed, a further roof provided for a 120-ft^2 room, and an L-plan floor slab permitted the building of a kitchen, stoop and porch. Soon, a settlement near Akosombo presented a 'problem of controlling a large number of unauthorised structures', mainly kitchens and 'bathrooms' made of used corrugated iron, bamboo and old packing cases (Danby, in Chambers 1970).

Entitled *The Volta Resettlement Experience,* the book gave accounts of the 'experience' of designers, agronomists and sociologists, but not of the experience of those who were resettled. E.A.K. Kalitsi, the Ghanaian in charge of the Volta Project, acknowledged nonetheless, that 'it is easier to evacuate people to the settlement towns than to keep them there'. Many of the evacuees soon drifted from the new sites: 'the spectre of the ghost town hangs over every settlement we have built', he wrote (Kalitsi in Chambers 1970). I did not remain in Ghana long enough to learn their eventual fate, but the problems of the ethics of intervention arose repeatedly, in contexts across the world. Some were in the name of 'improvement', others as 'advocacy planning' or 'aided self-help' in diverse contexts that generally involved 'emergency' methods.

Such was the case in Kutahya province, Turkey, where the towns of Gediz, Emet and Akçalaan had been destroyed, and over 300 villages demolished or severely damaged, in a major earthquake in 1970. The extended families of the peasant population lived in the upper floors of large, two-storeyed houses of timber frame and clay infill, their stores, crops and cattle being housed beneath them. As many as eighteen people might live in one house, with the parents occupying one room and each of their sons, with their wives and children, residing in others. A broad corridor space, the *sofa,* served as a communal gathering place for meals. Privacy, however, was strictly guarded and rooms could not be overlooked. When the earthquake struck, some 70,000 people were affected. Emergency housing was provided by the State, 50,000 homeless being accommodated in 15,000 newly constructed dwellings. More than a dozen years later I was engaged in a long-term evaluation of the new housing.

Designed by absentee architects in Ankara, the standard house took the form of a small, three-roomed, single-storey dwelling distantly related to the British wartime 'prefab'. This was suitable for the British 2.2 nuclear family, but the accommodation was quite unsuited to the extended peasant families. A markedly low level of occupancy of the houses which were provided under these policies reflected both this unsuitability and the designers' insensitivity to the need for privacy and other values related to the home (Aysan and Oliver 1987). The government plan house had large windows, which meant that occupants were on view; there was no *sofa,* and the living room opened on to the bedrooms; though the society was discrete about bodily functions, the access to the toilet was external and public. Consequently, for many families the house was totally unacceptable, and a dozen years after the earthquake entire villages of resettlement housing stood empty, never having been occupied. With no opportunity to express their needs and no consultation between the communities and housing authorities, many earthquake victims were obliged either to accept the housing or be denied any help at all. In the indigenous ethic of building, traditions of mutual assistance existed in the region, but these were ignored.

Planning was relentlessly linear, though sites were allocated by random selection so that opportunities for favoured locations were equal for all. This, however, resulted in the splitting up of families into nuclear units, often placed at considerable distances apart. Some villages, with larger land holdings, coped with these difficulties by adding on self-built extensions to act as a *sofa*, to screen the toilet and to provide necessary storage and animal shelter. As the emergency house was not designed to take extensions, this presented many problems that were crudely solved at the expense of safety. Eventually, peasant families were permitted to return to their ruinous homes and to slowly restore them to their original form, but it was clear that the imposition of standardised housing without consideration of the values of the afflicted communities resulted in their rejection or unskilled and vulnerable adaptation (Oliver 1988).

It was a story that was repeated scores of times in diverse cultural contexts, as I witnessed for myself in Central America, Eastern Europe, East Africa, the Indian sub-continent, China and elsewhere. Design decisions were taken on behalf of national and regional authorities in circumstances of resettlement or post-disaster housing, without regard for indigenous values and patterns of settlement. While the intentions were often with the interests of the subject communities in mind, the planning policies, building forms, spatial allocation and arrangement, and the use of 'modern materials' in construction were determined by professional planners and architects who, in the majority of cases, had not even visited the selected sites, much less discussed the proposed developments with those who were to live in them.

In some instances, there appear to have been ulterior motives for this, that bring the ethics of intervention further into question. Such was the case in Borneo, where indigenous peoples, such as the Dayaks, Dusun, Kenyah and others, live by traditional systems that they pursued long before Indonesia and Malaysia assumed power over their territories. One of the largest of the Dyak cultures are the Iban, who live in contiguous family units, or *bileks,* beneath common roofs that form 'long-houses'. In effect, the long-house is a village on piles, within the length of which runs a broad 'street', the *tempuan*, linking the individual family *bileks*. Communal work and social space, sleeping space for guests and often an outdoor platform, the *tanju*, also run in parallel along the long-house, which, in some cases, may be as much as 200 m or more in length. Animist in their beliefs, the Iban are 'swidden' farmers, whose movement, settlement, territorial claims and boundaries brought them into conflict with government regulations and administrations for most of the twentieth century (Freeman 1970).

Living on land which contained sought-after minerals and gravels, the Iban of northern Sarawak and Brunei were still under pressure when I visited some of their long-houses in the early 1990s. The long-houses ranged from a traditional structure built more than sixty years previously, to a large painted long-house, only three years old, with vinyl floor covering and strip-lighting in the *tempuan*, and glazed windows to the *bileks* that opened onto it. The residents of both were being induced to move to the outskirts of the city of Brunei. By the customary standards of resettlement housing, the houses on offer were superior in quality, with high concrete piles, tiled and pitched roofs, spacious accommodation and garden plots around each building. A house could be secured with a minimal payment which could be spread over several years. My Iban informants told me that the only other considerations were that the residents would give up swidden farming and move to the city, that they would no longer live in a long-house, and that they would adopt the Muslim faith. The cost of the new houses was the abandonment of their culture and the loss of their identity. At the time of viewing all but a couple of the new houses were standing empty.

If the price to pay for new housing was unacceptable to Iban in this region, related groups of Iban in other parts of Sarawak and Kalimantan have had their long-houses destroyed. They have been forced to move from their forest homelands, accused of causing destructive fires by the 'slash-and-burn' methods of swidden farming. Whether or not the conflagrations were deliberately fired to clear the undergrowth during the reckless plundering of the forest hardwoods for short-term profits is a matter of debate, but it is clear that ethically questionable interests, other than those of the Iban, are served by their removal and resettlement. Apart from dubious motivations, ethical problems arise when the housing is constrained by concepts of design that are not compatible with the life-ways, needs and values of the victim culture. Yet rehousing, as in post-disaster and refugee circumstances, is often initiated for altruistic reasons, and the results can be sympathetic.

Traditional building on the Greek island of Thira (or Santorini), in the Cyclades, has long been admired by architects. Subject to piracy and invasion in a long and troubled history, the islanders were prone to many influences. Yet they developed a way of building that was appropriate to the rough and undulating terrain, which was distinctive in its forms and construction. The volcanic explosion of Thira reputedly destroyed the Minoan civilisation in Crete, but the crater rim which constitutes the island has supported a small population that has farmed its volcanic soils for many centuries. Typically, the peasant houses were vaulted, though often extended with flat roofed terraces, built of black and red volcanic rock, and later with pumice, bonded with tephra (pozzalana), which 'is rich in silica and poor in lime, so that on mixing with a quantity of lime and water a solid homogeneous mass is produced, absolutely impervious to water'. The vault was 'laid on a framework of branches and weeds, tephra mortar joining long stones carefully placed in horizontal bands from springing to crown' (Radford and Clark 1974). The single cell was often internally divided into living and sleeping areas, while light and access were gained by two windows and a door in the gable end wall, and a skylight in the upper semi-circular gable. A plaster of pozzalana and water was laid over the wall surfaces, which were often colour-washed with ochre. Underground cisterns for the storage of rainwater were used in all houses.

To defend themselves against invaders and pirates, the wealthier families in the seventeenth century enclosed themselves in hilltop fortified settlements, or *kastelia*. Pyrgos, in the south centre of the island, was typical, the vaulted houses of the peasants being outside the *kasteli* on the lower slopes of the hill. This differentiated village structure continued until the island was hit by a disastrous earthquake in 1956. The earthquake caused extensive damage, such that only one church (or chapel) among more than two hundred on the island survived unscathed. In the town of Pyrgos the *kasteli* was totally destroyed and large areas of the rest of the town were demolished. Even so, partial vaults of severely damaged houses were still in evidence over forty years later. To avoid further landslides, much of the ruinous hilltop was capped with concrete when the reconstruction programme of the Greek Ministry of Public Works Housing Department commenced. The architectural team endeavoured to restore houses where possible, but approval for loans against rebuilding meant that many houses were replaced. However, literally hundreds of houses were constructed to accommodate the homeless. Following discussions with local people the vaulted roof of the vernacular buildings was 'chosen as a form in the new construction since it offered economy in cost, speed of construction and reflective qualities' (Noussia 1992). Most housing units consisted of parallel vaults, sometimes opening on to a loggia or a yard in which a cistern and wash-house could be built. The side walls of the house had a partially exposed ring beam so that a bearing ledge for subsequent extension was possible, a provision which acknowledged the local ethic that a family head should provide a dowry house or extension for his eldest daughter.

Over thirty-five years later, in the town of Pyrgos and similar villages where the earthquake victims had been extensively rehoused, the success of the building policy was evident. Large numbers of short rows of vaulted homes or free-standing single and double-vault units stood with little or no modification. Local builders had been instructed in the new methods, including reinforced concrete construction, and had been capable of extending other houses, setting further vaults at right angles, and even building above the vaults by spanning them with raised slabs. The over-riding impression was one of a continuing vernacular tradition, which did not hinder those who wished to enlarge their properties, but which established continuity between the past and the future while meeting, with safety and sensitivity, the physical, social and environmental needs of the culture. Regrettably, recent housing developments, hotels and the 'second homes' of Athenian vacationists have not recognised or responded positively to the example set by the reconstruction programme. However, this does not bring into question the achievement of its architects and builders, who did not intervene, but who worked with the community to produce a rare model of building appropriately within a vernacular context.

When these instances of intervention in housing are considered, certain fundamental lessons emerge. The ethics of one-off elite architecture may require that the designer meets the brief to the best of his creative abilities, but the ethics of housing for communities requires more. The architect may design responsibly, but the process fails when he ignores the values, mores, building skills, experience and wisdom of the cultures whose housing needs are to be met. Housing that involves the active participation of the community, which accommodates its values, relates to its vernacular traditions while meeting its aspirations and which remains substantially as the housing of and by the people is the most likely to succeed. If the housing of the billions in the twenty-first century is not to result in design debacles of unprecedented scale, these are lessons in the ethics of building that must be learned.

References and bibliography

Aysan, Yasemin and Oliver, Paul (1987) *Housing and Culture after Earthquakes*, Oxford: Oxford Polytehnic for the Overseas Development Administration.
Chakrabarti, Vibhuti (1997) 'Vastu Sastras', in Oliver (ed.) 552–3.

Chambers, Robert (ed.) (1970) *The Volta Resettlement Experience,* London: Pall Mall Press.

Danby, Miles (1970) 'House design', in R. Chambers (ed.) op. cit. 164–78.

Doumanis, Orestis and Oliver, Paul (eds) (1974) *Shelter in Greece,* Athens: Architecture in Greece Press.

Freeman, Derek (1970) *Report on the Iban,* London: The Athlone Press.

Griaule, Marcel and Dieterlen, Germaine (1954) 'The Dogon', in C. Darryl Forde (ed.) *African Worlds,* London: Oxford University Press.

Kalitsi, E.A.K. (1970) 'Present and future problems of administering resettlement towns', in R. Chambers (ed.) op. cit. 217–25.

Noussia, Antonia (1992) 'Revisiting the Tourist Landscape: The Dynamics of Change of the Traditional Environment in Santorini' in *Traditional Dwellings and Settlements Working Papers,* Vol. XXXV: 55–98.

Oliver, Paul (1988) *Dwellings: The House Across the World,* Oxford: Phaidon Press.

Oliver, Paul (ed.) (1997) *The Encyclopedia of Vernacular Architecture of the World,* 3 Vols. Cambridge: Cambridge University Press

Philippides, Dimitri (1983) 'Santorini', in D. Philippides (ed.) *Greek Traditional Architecture* 2 'Aegean: Cyclades', Athens: Melissa, 147–78.

Prussin, Labelle (1969) *Architecture in Northern Ghana. A Study in Forms and Functions,* Ghana, Berkeley: University of California Press.

Radford, A. and Clark, G. (1974) 'Cyclades: Studies of a building vernacular', in O. Doumanis, op. cit. 64–82.

Sulistayawati, A. (1997) 'Lontars (Bali)' , in Oliver (ed.), 560–1.

10

ETHICAL BUILDING IN THE EVERYDAY ENVIRONMENT

A multilayer approach to building and place design

Christopher Day

Ethics isn't something I normally think about at work. Building – and architecture – is; it's my job. But ethics are the underlying principles by which I unconsciously evaluate the myriad of decisions, large and small, that every day demands. Hence, an ethical stance unavoidably steers daily life, including work; including building. What does 'ethics' have to do with building?

First, some facts: 40 per cent (possibly 50 per cent) of all energy consumption, 50 per cent of materials taken from Nature, 50 per cent of waste,[1] and 50 per cent all CFC and HCFC use[2] is building related. These figures relate to what buildings are built of, and how we heat, cool, light and use them. If we add all the things we put into buildings, and use in and near buildings (which is nearly everything we buy) and the travel between buildings, the figures go up. Some of these things and some of this travel is unavoidable, but some is a result of *how buildings are designed.* There are rooms in which we *can't* live, without personalising and softening them with furnishings, ornaments and artwork. There are places we *can't* work in and places we *can't wait to get away from.*

In fact, buildings have major environmental costs. Once we become aware of the magnitude of the statistics, it becomes obvious that everything we build has major environmental repercussions. If we love the God-given beauty of Nature, we must surely feel we have *responsibilities* to live up to.

This is about answerability to 'Nature', but there is another aspect. In the modern world, we live 90 per cent of our lives amidst *built* environment – buildings, rooms, vehicles. If we feel any membership in a *human* community, we have responsibilities here too.

127

However, all of this brings up distinctly separate and apparently *conflicting* issues. Conservation and pollution reduction are *technical* issues – nothing to do with how we *feel*. Our responsibilities to the planet seem at variance with our need for surroundings that nourish us. Moreover, energy conservation and pollution reduction may seem to pull in opposite directions. The most efficient energy conservation practice uses cellular plastic insulation with minimal ventilation and few windows. Synthetic chemicals unavoidably cause industrial pollution. Their vapours, combined with minimal air exchange, are the cause of many 'sick buildings'.

The pursuit of *beauty* in our surroundings has (apparently) nothing to do with our ecological responsibilities. The concept of 'Nature' usually involves all but one level of creation, humanity. So we have *human* needs and *Nature's* needs and these are often in conflict.

Nature may be 'God-given', but the 'nature' around us is, in part, *man*-made. Townscape obviously is, as is agricultural landscape. In fact, there is little of the world – from Everest to Antarctica, the deep oceans, where oil spills lie, to the ozone-depleted stratosphere – that is not to some extent human influenced.

Are our concerns directed to what is good for *Nature* or what is good for *society*? If an undisturbed ecology is the best thing for 'Nature', how can this be compatible with what we need in modern life? Our needs, social and personal, material and cultural seem incompatible with those of Nature.

Faced with such a conflict of interest, it's all too easy just to say that the dilemma involves paradoxes that are totally irreconcilable, so let's just get on with daily life. But even if we decide that ecological responsibilities should override everything else, how does the rest of the world feel about it? How can we achieve it without (even benevolent) dictatorship?

This is the *either/or* world that we live in, and my view it is that *either/or-ism* which is at the heart of the problem:

- humanity *or* Nature
- utility *or* beauty
- ecology *or* society

Replace *or* with *and*, and we have a totally different perspective. This may be obvious, but it isn't *simple*. Take choosing a building material: thermal insulation, for instance. Heat flows through different substances at different rates. Dry air is a good insulator; it is the insulating component of materials of natural and mineral origin. But there are other chemicals, like polyisocyanate, urethane foam, that are better insulators than air. The more efficient ones, however, tend to be synthetic or at least, industrially processed, and leave a trail of industrial pollution in their manufacture. Moreover, their breakdown releases products which are hazardous to breathe, hazardous to the atmosphere or hazardous to handle. Plastic insulation materials are generally more convenient, and some are significantly more efficient than more common materials – but plastic manufacture typically involves some fifteen synthesis operations, each only 50 per cent efficient.[3] Of the original raw materials, only 0.02 per cent becomes end-product. And the rest? Walk past a chemical factory to see – and smell – the consequences.

But if we were to take more holistic criteria, we would ask for an insulation we could *live* with; a material that could *die* – be recycled back through the living kingdoms of Nature. If we set these conditions, it is obvious that the material would have *originated in life* – and probably would have had an insulating role when alive, perhaps wool, cork, wood and vegetable fibre products. Not surprisingly, these are non-toxic,[4] and require little manufacturing energy and pollution. They are also 'compostable', which means that they cycle back into the circle of life. This is about seeing beyond the physically present to the wider implications of the choices we make.

These holistic criteria bring up issues that apply to every material whatever the use. Where has it come from, and how? Where does it go, and how? There is a fundamental distinction between minimally processed, natural materials and highly industrially processed ones. Natural materials have come from living systems, and so are, by definition, life-compatible. A few are toxic or allergenic; most aren't. Most are but minimally processed, so are still close to source. Typically, they mature as they age, so they connect us to the experience of time, place and origins. Being 'borrowed' from living – and dying – Nature, they are stable as long as we maintain suitable environmental conditions. As soon as we stop, they re-enter the cycle of life and death, decay and growth. With human *care*, wooden buildings, for example Norwegian stave churches, have lasted nearly a thousand years. Without human care, many decay within a generation. *They need our care* and thus depend upon how we *feel* about them. In short, natural materials have come to us at minimal environmental cost; their present state demands our *caring* involvement; they connect us to a *living*, cyclic world; and their future state is, through composting, to re-enter these cycles.

Synthetic materials have been made at high energy and pollution cost. Many survive and deteriorate quite *independently of human care*. We have no opportunity to contribute and it makes very little difference how we feel about them. They connect us to a linear process, matter-bound and mono-dimensional; an industrial world, which is not about life – with its cycle of renewal – but about *non-reversible* chemical reactions. There is no *innate* reason why they should not be toxic. A few materials are stable, especially those which, like glass, are manufactured by heat processes. Most are, to some extent, harmful. If made from organic chemicals, there is a high likelihood they will react with our bodies as our chemical composition is closely related. At the end of their useful life, they do not readily re-enter living cycles in a healthy way.

Another conflict is between *social and ecological* priorities. Ecology is made up of cycles. In reality, cycles exist within cycles, pathways are multiple and patterns change from season to season and year to year, but this is too complex to actually build. So the cycles we design tend to be artificially simple, with limited pathways, limited patterns and stepped rather than with a fluidic response to external changes, like weather. We often have to put systems together with manufactured components, which can lead to a certain *mechanistic* feel.

However, once we think of systems as living organisms, rather than mechanical bits and pieces arranged together, we approach their design differently. Once we start to work with multiple pathways and patterns we also recognise that there can be multiple benefits. Inevitably this leads us to a broader involvement, engaging our feelings as well as our thinking, and inviting us to actually *enjoy* these cycles. Take, for example, the cycles of water; as rainwater, grey-water and sewage. The systems we devise to deal with this water – even sewage – can give delight at every stage:

- oxygenation by cascades, fountains, rills and 'Flowforms';
- pollutant processing by plants and associated micro-organisms – edge plants, floating and bottom rooted ones. And these need fish, molluscs and insects to stabilise their ecology. Soon we have birds and butterflies as well.

At the Rudolf Steiner Seminar in Järna, Sweden, sewage for 200–300 people is processed through seven plant-fringed lagoons, each with Flowform cascades to circulate, oxygenate and imprint rhythm into the water.[5] These sewage treatment ponds have developed into such rich and varied water-gardens that they have been featured on a TV gardening programme, without ever a mention of their sewage role. Deservedly they attract streams of visitors, for they are beautiful, tranquil – and aroma-free.

Grey-water can be cleansed through similar systems: reed-beds, duckweed-surfaced and plant-fringed pools. To minimise pollution risk, such a system is started with individual reed- and lily-beds outside each house or unit. Anyone pouring 'nasty chemicals' down the sink has to deal with the dead plants, not remotely distant in a communal system, but outside their own front door. After treatment, what was once sewage is now pure enough to discharge into rivers, recharge ground-water, irrigate plants or flush toilets. Rainwater and grey-water, being less polluted in the first place, are less demanding to treat and can be used more widely. In every case, the aims are always multiple: elimination of polluting waste outputs, benefiting from a resource, enhancing wildlife habitat and bringing tranquillity to eye and soul.

We have also used rainwater for cooling. In hot, dry climates, by saving all the rain that falls on roofs and hard surfaces, we can get the equivalent of up to five times the scant annual rainfall. This is to irrigate vegetation – for shade and cooling transpiration – which give about 4 °C cooling. The vegetation also cleans air and *absorbs* noise. The water is also for Flowforms, fountains and other water features. These also cool and clean air; and they *mask* noise. When such water features are placed in shade, opposite to sun-heated wall and roof surfaces, the two sides of a courtyard have a marked difference in temperature. This ancient technique (from Tadjikistan) is used to induce cooling breezes.

Beyond these technical functions, both leaf and water, dappled shade and dancing light can be orchestrated for delight. In more temperate, higher rainfall areas, we have used rills and pools alongside streets and pedestrian passages, for privacy distance, sunlight reflection and traffic calming, as well as air- and water-cleaning, temperature-extreme buffering – and, of course, amenity. Indoors, water features reoxygenate and rehumidify air as well as ionising and cleaning it and masking noise, all important in offices, hospitals, etc.

It was once assumed that people could *either* do things artistically *or* be socially or environmentally responsible. Hence the grotesquely brutal 'social' architecture of the 1960s and the 'energy-conservative' office blocks of the 1970s and 1980s. Although these were glass, they were effectively windowless for people working deep within them, and likewise dependent on air-conditioning as there was no access to fresh air. Nowadays, there are buildings so 'artistically' styled that they are not easy, nor pleasant, to use and are not at all ecological.

But we spend so much of our life in buildings! They can, and do, nourish or poison us. To nourish, they need to be artistic – not as dramatic, competing ego-statements, but in soul-feeding ways: gentle sensory stimulation, harmonious conflict resolution, spirit-uplifting. Aesthetics and ethics originate from the same source – the feelings.

In the quantifiable 1980s, the health and productivity effects of an approach that values the *feelings* could be shown to save money. In 1984, Roger Ulrich[6] found that hospital windows with tree views cut post-operative recovery time by 9 per cent compared with brick-wall views.[7] This works out at $500,000 per bed space over ten years, which certainly makes landscaping a profitable bargain.[8] When staff moved into the NMB bank headquarters created by Alberts and Van Huut, absenteeism declined and productivity increased by 15 per cent. Research on other projects that have prioritised occupant well-being has found similar improvement figures. What this means for commercial buildings, where 80 per cent of costs are staff salaries, is that a mere 6 per cent increased productivity would justify *quadrupling building costs*.[9]

Artistic work is vital to the *economics* of volunteer building projects. A lot of building work can seem to be just endless drudgery. People need some kind of compensating reward. Few volunteer projects can afford to make this reward monetary, but all can give reward in the form of artistic experience, the chance to create something from the heart. This doesn't cost any more, but without this fulfilment for volunteers, their numbers would decline.

It is widely held that economic and ecological priorities conflict. Jobs versus environment, ecology versus profitability, and so on. But ecological and economic priorities do not, in fact, have to conflict. Often it is the reverse. I am currently working on a sustainable, mixed-use, urban project in California, about 40 per cent of which is retail buildings. But, with urban-edge cut-price warehouses, what is the future of in-town shops? This is an even more acute question when cyber-shopping establishes itself. We took the view that urban retail can only compete if it offers something competing modes can't: delightful experience. This involves sensory interest, stimulating diversity, and other elements of *social* richness. It also depends on masking traffic noise with life-generated sounds, clean air and delightful scents – from flower blooms to baking. In a fiercely hot climate, leaf-dappled shade, natural cooling – by water features and naturally induced airflow – are also vital ingredients. In short, the *ecological* objectives of minimising energy and pollution, and maximising pollution absorption, copious and diverse vegetation and songbird habitat, and so on, are essential to the project's *social* success. Upon this, its *economic* viability depends.

The same concordance of ecological and economic priorities applies to the many parts of buildings. Air-conditioning, for instance, is expensive to run. At 35–45 per cent of the cost of a typical office building, its plant is expensive. It is also expensive to build space for and to maintain. Moreover, it needs major replacements every fifteen years.[10] Natural ventilation, by contrast, is free. It certainly makes demands on design, but rarely, if ever, any that cannot be overcome. In particular, it requires narrower buildings – but this means more daylight and views – which connect a person with place, time, weather and life outdoors – with the world, the cosmos, life beyond the desk. A gain, not a cost.

The same applies to centralised storm-water and sewage systems. Half the construction costs of cities are underground and renewed every thirty to fifty years. Localised supply and waste treatment are much cheaper.[11] Additionally, reed-beds are typically half as expensive as conventional sewage works to construct and one-tenth the cost to run.[12] In some apartment blocks in Sweden, urine is separated at source and sold to farmers for fertiliser.[13] Storm-water costs a great deal in sewer piping, flood control and, most particularly, flood damage. Hence, in Germany, which is 'downstream' in Europe, there are taxes on rainwater release. This has the result that many factories now have grass roofs. These spread the release of rainwater from a forty-minute thunderstorm evenly over twenty-four hours.

Built environment is often seen as being in conflict with Nature. But pre-industrial-revolution settlements typically fit so well into their surroundings that many are now popular tourist attractions. There are things buildings can do that Nature can't. Most notably, they can rapidly modify micro-climate. Trees can do this in a human generation, buildings, in a year. We have used buildings to screen traffic noise and use as windshields. This was especially important in an eco-village project in sub-arctic Sweden. Winds there are usually light, but at minus 30 °C, they seriously magnify the cold. We particularly focused on wind-protected sun-traps oriented to capture spring afternoon sunshine – when children returned home from school and the weather was warm enough (but still cold!) for outdoor play. We used the opposite principle in California: shaping buildings, in both plan and section, as wind-scoops for the predictable afternoon breezes. We also used building shape, colour and placing to maximise the temperature differential between tall sunny surfaces (dark-coloured to warm up) and shady areas, further cooled by evaporation from water features. This induces a cool breeze at person level.

There is an underlying conflict between man-made and natural that is so much a part of how we do things, that we rarely consider it:

- Nature is driven by the *past*.
- Humans are inspired by the *future*.
- All *places* are formed by the *past*. All *ideas* for building projects are in the *future*.

Unless we can marry *past* and *future*, everything we do will always be, at least in part, 'out-of-place'. This leads us to recognise that changes to place must be *process*-based. This process must listen to what already *is*, and grow from it.

I use a particular process in designing places and buildings, one which allows us to understand the essential being of a place, thing or situation. This builds upon a method developed by Dr Margaret Colquoun.[14] Central to this process is objectifying our (normally subjective) responses to a place. We study the place through its different *levels of being*:

- its physical substance
- its time- and life-related aspects – most notably its biography (which has brought it to the present) and how it will change in the future
- our emotional responses to its moods
- what the place would say of itself – its essence, genius loci, spirit of place.

We then allow the buildings themselves to find the forms appropriate to the place and situation by an incarnation process, which mirrors the study process:

- What should the project say – what is its essence?
- What activities will it engender – and *where* should these be located?
- What should their moods be? And what should be the character of their relationships to each other?
- The physical implications.

This is not just an environmental process, unavoidably it involves a social process. It depends upon involving users, and, in so doing, empowers and spurs inner growth in the individuals involved. Nowadays I try never to *design* places, but to let design *coalesce* out of the process. By its very nature, this technique must respond to both environment and community. So it is both ecologically *and* socially sensitive.

The following is an example of how this consensus-based design process works. At a Waldorf school in California, the process involved teachers and a development group, some twenty-four people, and had two aspects: what to do with their recently bought 'monstrosity' of a school; and how to develop the site with further buildings. For the existing building, we focused on the arrival journey – a first impression for visitors and a daily experience for the children. In this case, the time-life stage of observation was concerned with how our journey flowed as we walked this route: the abruptness, fluidity and rhythm of our movements, how space expanded and contracted, and the form and space gestures that met us. For future development, this stage focused on the biography of the site, how it had been violated and how it was continuing to change. When we looked at the moods of different parts, it showed up imbalances of elemental qualities: parts which were too sun-baked, hard or windy. This led to an understanding of how to remedy this damage. The development strategy was founded on *what feels right where*, but it also involved *what should be built when*. This is about *growth* processes – how places grow and from what generators ('growth-nodes') they start.

An important aspect of process-based design is that it *connects us to the continuum*. It also synthesises the needs of *people* with the needs of *place*. It is founded on the principle of respect, respect for all participants – there is no 'leader', all are equal. The techniques I use require us to set aside preconceived ideas. This allows us to see, listen to, and respect *what is there*, and so recognise *what wants to find form*. This four-level study allows us to be objective, not swayed by personal preference and pre-formed attitudes and ideas. It lets us listen, connect, *respect*. Respect is about *beauty;* lack of respect is about ugliness.

These levels of *place* are reflections of levels of being in *ourselves*:

- body
- life energy
- feeling soul
- individuality.

And these, themselves, are manifestations of the elemental principles of Nature:

- matter
- flow
- (communicable) mood
- warmth.

Or, more familiarly:

- earth
- water
- air
- fire.

This opens up the questions:

- What is 'Nature' in us?
- What are we in (and separate from) Nature? Aspects of how our environment and all its bits and pieces resonate with our inner beings.

This is about the design of places, but looking at the layers of the world, or ourselves, we can access deeper insights into the essence of things or situations. We can use related techniques to steer through other kinds of decision. So to return to simple, everyday things like our building material choice, we can use a similar approach:

- What is its substance?
- What is its connection to life?
- Is it pleasant to handle, live alongside?
- Can it be a contributor to a beautiful place?

As well as the material constituents of buildings, we can also assess their systems like waste, water, air and heating. For example, a ventilation system:

- What are the physical characteristics of the air we breathe?
- What life-connecting qualities do they bear?
- What sensory messages do they convey, and how do they influence our moods?
- What is the *essence* of the system?

Mechanically handled air is forced through ducts. Electromagnetic fields from fan motors, friction and ferrous (therefore magnetic) ductwork destroy ions, negative ions in particular. As well as conferring 'bracing' qualities, these clean micro-particles (including bacteria) from air also contribute to its cleanliness. Moreover, air is a vapour; it likes to flow in fluid spirals. Ducts, however, are mechanically formed, hence geometric. This mismatch of forms leads to stagnant eddies where mould and other micro-organisms can grow. These are the *physical* characteristics of mechanically handled air.

Natural air is oxygenated and invigorated by vegetation. The negative ion content of 1 cm^3 of clean rural air is 1,000; in mechanically ventilated offices, this drops to fifty. Although often polluted, particularly by traffic and industry, outdoor air is generally much cleaner than any indoor air it replaces. Hence, we talk of 'fresh air'.

The fans that push air through ducts are often audible, sometimes noisy or even reverberant; they are background contributors to stress. The air quality itself is lulling, sometimes soporific. Ventilation engineers do their best to provide an 'optimum environment'. As there is only one optimum, this effectively means constant conditions. Unchanging temperature, humidity and air-change rate is mechanically even. It does not stimulate our senses – which need constant subtle variations in stimulus to stay alert. We commonly refer to such air as 'dead'. Natural air, by contrast, changes from season to season, hour to hour, even minute to minute. It carries scents of season, weather, time of day and ongoing activities. It connects us, in other words, to life.

At the heart of mechanical ventilation is a system shaped by mechanical considerations. Although we try, of course, to deliver the best possible quality of air, these fundamental shaping considerations are quite independent from, and disinterested in, life. There is no innate reason why they should invigorate it. Natural ventilation, by contrast, is propelled by the forces of air itself – which we can boost by airflow induction, for instance with chimney effects or differential temperature. Air quality is renewed by living processes, photosynthesis in particular. It is driven by life and given quality by life. Indeed it is *all about life*.

Which do I prefer? Obvious as my choice may be, I don't need to base it on my personal, subjective preferences, but on objective appraisal of these four 'levels of being' of the competing systems: *matter, life-connection, mood-inductive character, fundamental essence*. We can also, as I have already mentioned, describe these as elemental levels, embodying the *principles* of *earth, water, air and fire*.

We can address elemental principles *materially* as conservation of resources, water and energy, and pollution minimisation (for air quality). But these principles are also *qualitative*. To nourish the human soul – *and* the ecological health of places – we need to balance and interweave earthiness, fluidity, airiness and thermal qualities. This is the *soul* side of micro-climatic design, building biology and ecological architecture. It is how *sustainable* design can *sustain* us. It isn't about numbers any more. It's not just that 50 per cent of energy, materials, waste, CFC and HCFC is a criminal price to pay for buildings. If buildings everywhere – not just those for 'greenies' – are for *human sustenance,* deeply and healingly, they must also be environmentally responsible. If they are *environmentally responsible* (fully and holistically) they must also sustain the human spirit.

Notes

1 Boonstra, D., Anink, C. and Mak, J. (1996) *Handbook of Sustainable Building*. European figures. London: James & James.

2 Edwards, Brian (1996) *Towards Sustainable Architecture*, Oxford: Butterworth Architecture.
3 Holger König (1989) *Wege zum Gesunden Bauen*, Freiburg: Ökobuch Verlag.
4 Except for those with uncommon allergies.
5 Designed by Arne Klingborg, Lars Friedlund and John Wilkes.
6 Of the University of Texas, San Antonio.
7 A total for 7.9 days for patients with tree view, 8.7 days for brick-wall view. Research by Roger Ulrich at Pennsylvania Hospital in 1984.
8 *Ensouling Healthcare Facilities* by Donald C. McKahan, Lennon Associates, Del Mar, CA, 1994.
9 *Building Values: Energy Guidelines for State Buildings*, prepared for the California Office of the State Architect 1976.
10 Brian Ford, Sustainable Urban Development through Design; RIBA CPD lecture at Cambridge University, 12 February 1998.
11 Margrit Kennedy, *Eco-settlements and Urban Renewal in Europe*, lecture at Eco-Villages Conference, Findhorn, Scotland, October 1995.
12 Jones, Julian (1995) 'Back to the Sewage Farm', *Resurgence* 169: March/April.
13 See the work of Nils Tiberg, professor of recycling at the University of Luleå, Sweden.
14 Of the Life Science Trust, Scotland.

11

CAN 'SPIRIT OF PLACE' BE A GUIDE TO ETHICAL BUILDING?

Isis Brook

Introduction

This chapter addresses some issues that arise from a nexus of ideas that is sometimes called *genius loci*, sometimes spirit of place and sometimes sense of place. This is a very old notion that has resurfaced and is undergoing a reformulation. The importance of this notion for the ethics of building rests in particular interpretations that see 'spirit of place' as something about a place that demands we respect it and work alongside it in terms of architectural design, building practice and appropriate daily use. However, this notion is ambiguous and variously expressed by writers in many fields of enquiry. This proliferation of interpretations and uses does nothing to help the development of a robust idea that could inform ethical building, though it may point to a necessary ambiguity.

The proliferation of definitions

Spirit of place and *sense of place* are used in humanistic geography, architecture, landscape design, planning, conservation, tourism, travel writing and other fields. Throughout this chapter I am going to use the term 'spirit of place' for the whole nexus of ideas associated with these terms, although this will slant the discussion strongly in the direction of the place itself, as opposed to meanings imposed on a setting. Sense of place is sometimes used in exactly the same way, but can also be used when the focus is shifted to human meanings and perhaps impositions. Sense of place is also used for what I would term 'sensing' place – to denote an effort to sensitively come to know the nature of a place.

The different ways in which the term 'spirit of place' is used and the lack of clear definitions given by writers suggests that the idea is ambiguous. The ambiguity does not seem to arise from the number of disciplines involved: it is not the case that architects mean one thing and geographers mean something else by the term. It is not even the case that, for example, one school of geographers means one thing and another school means something else. The term seems to shift its meaning even within one person's writing.

Rather than just stipulate a clear definition, I want to spend some time laying out the kind of interpretations that exist in the literature. These interpretations are used by people working in the areas outlined above; they have years of experience and may be presenting distinctive insights into this phenomenon. Alternatively, some interpretations may be inadequate and need to be cleared out of the way.

I will first clarify some major problems and then move on to what could be called the shades of meaning of 'spirit of place'. These are aspects of interpretation that any of the views may include. They could be seen as the conceptual collection from which writers on spirit of place seem to be drawing.

Major questions to ask of any definitions

One quite testing question that could be asked of a particular interpretation of spirit of place is whether it means that every place has one. Very often the literature picks out a particular city square, neighbourhood, woodland glade, etc., and proclaims it to have a spirit of place. This, it is claimed, is something not tangible in the way that the place's physical components are, but is nevertheless apparent to all but the most insensitive of observers. The implication would seem to be that only some places have this, and others are therefore deficient. The alternatives are, presumably, either that every place has a spirit of place, but in most places it is being ignored, hidden, driven underground, or that everywhere has a spirit, but in some places this quality is neutral or even bad.

A related question would be to enquire of the interpretation where the boundaries of the special place are. Is there a clear border, a thinning of the spirit of place's influence until it is too dilute to perceive? Or do the borders overlap and generate an intermingling of the spirits of place? How does the spirit of place of a city square or district relate to the spirit of place of the whole city? And are there regional spirits of place that influence the possible emergence of the smaller-scale spirits of place?

A crucial area of questioning is around the role of human beings in all of this. One way of getting at this would be to take the example of a place that has never been manipulated by humans and that seems to be widely recognised as having a spirit of place and ask, 'does it still have this quality without its human observers?' This would seem to get at one layer of distinction between whether a spirit of place is integral to the place and revealed to observers or whether it is a projection onto a place of human values. The question becomes more complex in the built environment where human patterns of use are seen as part of the spirit of place. However, populated places do not automatically fall into a different category of having to be interpreted from a human standpoint. Indeed, there is within the literature a strong strand of cutting through divisions between humans and environment. One thing that a spirit of place can be interpreted as doing is shaping the people who live in a place (Durrell 1988). So a place being populated does not automatically mean that a 'locicentric' view cannot be taken.

Shades of meaning

Just as the spirit of place seems to be something in or about a place that is not easily defined, so the conceptual collection below seems to be haunted by the meanings of this term rather than expressing it clearly. Each of these definitional components is presented as a synthesis of its appearance in the literature, but some of the names ascribed are my own shorthand. The purpose of setting these out is to lay bare the complexity of this nexus of ideas and to show the net of associations that its use can carry if its intended meaning is not clarified.

Abode of special beings

The reason that some places are felt to be special is that they are considered to be inhabited by gods/goddesses, spirits, fairies, etc., and that these are beings who live in this place and not elsewhere. In the West this meaning is connected to both Greek and Roman ideas and is seen most clearly in the idea of a sacred grove that is the home of a particular god or goddess. Perhaps this idea is universal as there seem to be similar beliefs in other cultures. Although the term 'spirit of place' might suggest such an interpretation, this is rarely used explicitly although it is used analogously and its antiquity makes it a strong underpinning theme.

Energy fields

On this view a place is not inhabited, but is a point of intense energy. Such places have a powerful effect on us due to the particular configuration of the land or due to their location within wider patterns of energy. These patterns may be determined by the land form or more abstract systems of interpretation. This is quite a difficult conceptual component to pin down; it tends to operate as a catch-all phrase to express something otherwise undefined or indefinable. The problem here is that, if it is saying anything, we should be able to press the idea and find out more. However, it seems to break down into one of two positions: either you 'get it' and see why nothing more could be said, or you need to understand and apply a complex system of meanings abstracted, often from another culture, and applied to this particular place. The former seems philosophically unrewarding and the latter is to move in exactly the wrong direction if you want to understand a particular place for the place it is.

Authenticity

Some places have come about through unconscious processes of habitation. They have grown in a place and have developed naturally to reflect that place. In general, authenticity applauds the undesigned and seemingly chance development of places. In one sense this is the idea of wilderness applied to built environments. The human inhabitants of, for example, the Tuscan hilltop village grew their environment as it grew them and thus their architecture has a fittingness because it is in accord with the spirit of the place. Living authentically 'in place' is said to be emotionally satisfying, but it is unclear if this state can be consciously regained. Can the 'designedly' undesigned be authentic? One would assume not, so any 'inauthentic' places are now beyond redemption. However, I am also unclear how we should interpret the notion of unconscious processes here. I am not sure that one can, or ever could, unconsciously build. Perhaps the Tuscan hilltop village dweller was engaged in as much conscious decision-making in choosing where and what to build as a 1960s modernist architect; it is just that today we applaud the Tuscan's decisions. We can applaud those decisions and see them as sensitive to and contributing to the spirit of place without de-humanising their designers.

Narrative

A place that tells its story, where the layers of past history are evident, and preferably not consciously preserved, is one that expresses a spirit of place. The present configuration of land, houses, ruins, and so on, is still working and connected to its past in a meaningful way. There is a diachronic integrity (Holland and O'Neill 1996) about the place: what is here now makes sense given what was here; it has a coherent narrative that connects its past to its present and could guide its future. Of course, just having a past would not count; everywhere has a past simply by virtue of being in space through time. If this notion is to elucidate spirit of place and consolidate its meaning, there must be significance placed on the coherence of the story and its working connection to the present. Themed street furniture displaying motifs of a town's now defunct cotton industry presumably do not count. But what about new office buildings whose windows repeat the staccato rhythm of the mill windows and the action of the machinery in the buildings they replace, the new industrial heart thus resonating with the old? Can the coherence of the narrative be dependent on the difference between the blatantly 'naff' and subtler design features? If even the latter is ruled out, then we seem to be back in the realms of unplanned authenticity. A final disquieting thought on narrative is that one could imagine a place that is characterised by disruption and arbitrary change, such that its spirit is that of exciting and pleasing discontinuity.

Local distinctiveness

A key feature of the idea of local distinctiveness is that of scale. Identifying with a specific place needs attention to detail, to what makes it distinctive: not in terms of important events or revered buildings, but the style of the ordinary in this specific place. This idea has informed much of the campaigning work of the pressure group Common Ground (Clifford and King 1993). Like narrative, this concept treads a fine, possibly unworkable, line between preserving the old and relishing the everyday, along with its inevitable change. Local distinctiveness is placed in opposition to national or international homogeneity. It is *for* local democracy and empowerment of ordinary people and *against* faceless government and multinational companies. The smallness of scale is crucial: thus local distinctiveness can affirm the family-run Indian restaurants in English towns as part of positive cultural change, but condemn the ubiquitous McDonalds.

Local distinctiveness does have the advantage of working with present circumstances, and it has something to say about every place, not just those that have missed unfashionable periods of development. This seems to escape some of the preciousness of ideas around authenticity and narrative. Also, local distinctiveness affirms the spirit of place notion that every place needs to be sensitively examined – or, better still, lived in – as an individual place in order to discover and work within its distinctiveness. This means that generalisations or standard planning solutions, beyond the injunction to work with what is there, cannot be applied.

When laying out these conceptual categories, and the ones that follow, it is clear that there are overlaps, parallel paths and sharp disjunctions. As a way of uncovering exactly what spirit of place could mean, this process, though bewildering, does have the virtue of being true to the richness and paradoxical nature of the idea. The next two (essence and character) are even closer together, but making distinctions between them does elucidate some crucial aspects.

Essence

I am grouping a number of things under essence and using it to get across the notion of interiority. The spirit of place, the 'something about this place', can be explained by it having an interior. Obviously, interior in this sense does not mean, for example, the interior of a mountain range that would be revealed by mining. It is attempting to get at something about that mountain range and using images of depth, indwelling, the soul, etc., to express it. Some uses of essence or entelechy or inscape may prompt a dualistic notion; there is rude matter and the soul that dwells within it. This could be viewed as moving back to the idea of the abode of special beings except that what is being expressed is more intimately connected with the material substance of the place even if it is of a different order. However, essence could also be a way of expressing something about the nature of the physical substance and the coming together of physical substances in characteristic ways. The problem of dualistic notions for spirit of place is that, whilst generating spiritual entities, they also reduce physical substance to dead matter. The predominance of dualism makes it hard to think outside those categories. Two interpretations of essence that step outside both dualism and its inherent diminishing of matter are Aristotle's idea of the form and Goethe's archetype. The Aristotelian essence, correctly understood (Pratt 1982: 207), creates the thing as the thing it is from within. The problem with this is that it could only account for the individual living things in a place, not for the spirit of a place. For this, one would need to extend the idea beyond the boundaries of organisms. Goethe's archetype is a more flexible idea (Pratt and Brook 1997) that could possibly be developed to understand place.

Character

Character is a notion that combines both depth and surface. Whereas essence can suggest an indwelling nature that is hinted at by the appearance of a place or one that is expressed in the appearance of the place, character tends to be used in a more forthright way. The character is not a persona. The term is not used to express a hidden nature behind an unpromising façade but the place as it both appears and is: as Norberg-Schultz says: 'A place is a space which has a distinct character' (1984: 5). Thus a place is not just a village green or a market square or an expanse of heath, but *this* one. They may or may not be typical of that type of place. For example, each of the places above may contain an eccentricity for their type that nevertheless does not detract from and may enhance their character. We can say that a particular thing – tree, building, signpost, etc. – is 'out of character', precisely because we can see that there is a character with which to be out. However, character is not used as another term for harmonious or balanced, it is not a marker of success in an aesthetic theory it is more like an emergent property of places which work (whatever 'work' might mean in their particular context).

Character does add dynamism to the idea of place. Just as a person's character is distinguished by traits, so a place is distinguished not as a static tableau but by what it is, through what it does. When we think of the meaning of the word character as the unique combination of traits that inform a person's actions and make what they do a coherent whole, we are perhaps close to what people mean when they say that a place has a distinctive character. Indeed, Casey describes the *genius loci* as 'the unique gestalt of traits that make a place this place'(1993: 303).

Whilst it might seem that the term 'character' is well placed as a central concept for spirit of place there are, I believe, two dangers to be avoided: overuse and anthropomorphism. Examples of overuse of the term are when it no longer expresses a unique configuration of traits, but merely something quaint. Alternatively, it is used so broadly that it can even describe the now discredited idea of zones so that, for example, housing and industry are separated because the housing zone has a residential character. However, when we restrict the use to one more closely aligned with human character we are in danger of thinking of places as people. The problem with anthropomorphising places is that it short-circuits the moral argument that it may be possible to respect places. It tends in the direction of saying that places are like people and since people have moral standing, places should also have moral standing. It only requires the observation that places are not like people, that this is a metaphor, to undermine the attribution of moral standing or respect for a place.

Moreover, anthropomorphism also prevents us from seeing a place as the thing it is. We can see similar confusion at play when we anthropomorphise animals. Consider a similar example. When my brother was a small child he killed a spider and my mother, hoping to instil in him some compassion and a dislike of needless killing, said 'now what will his wife and children do?' My brother promptly burst into tears and was thenceforth always kind to animals. As a way of getting a small child to think about the effect of his actions it was a good response. Being moved to think about things from the spider's perspective might even prompt an interest in finding out exactly what that perspective really is. However, stopping at the anthropomorphised sympathy does not allow us to treat spiders in the way most appropriate to their welfare. By thinking of the spider as a quasi human we actually fail to think of it as the thing it is. Indeed in this example, from the 1960s, we can even see outdated cultural norms: if it is a spider out in the world, in danger of encountering a small child, it must be male. Rather than trap the being in a misinformed, albeit friendly, conceptual category we need to find out more about it including its otherness, its difference from us.

There is no doubt that thinking of places as 'like people' can have pedagogical uses, as it can be a way of getting us thinking about places as other than a resource or a grid reference or an example of habitat type X or townscape type Y. However, we need to be alert to its metaphorical nature; it is a technique to help us along the way to experiencing place, not a description of the reality of any particular place.

With this tendency to error highlighted we can perhaps just revisit the potential strengths of the notion of place having a character. These are the dynamism of traits, the sense of a place as unique and the coherence of the inner dynamic with its outer appearance. Character does seem a useful conceptual component of spirit of place and, clearly defined, could be a complete replacement. It does seem to express the way a place can be experienced as more than the sum of its parts, that the place has an overarching character that we can identify and describe. However, do we need this extra thing? Perhaps the parts of a place could be understood as doing all the work because of the way they form a whole.

Ecosystem

On this view a thorough understanding of the place means its parts (e.g. geology, flora, fauna, weather, human patterns of use) and, significantly, the way they work together. Things fit together in an ecosystem such that the dynamics of the system is seen as the cohering force. Whether we view the ecosystem as a quasi-organism or a future directed system, this gives us a something beyond its parts that could be used to argue for its moral standing and to explain the experience of meeting something other than a mere collection of rocks and plants. One strength of the ecosystem conceptual component would seem to rest on its apparent scientific respectability. However, ecology has moved on and has abandoned the 'organismic' view of ecosystems (Worster 1985: 332–3). To maintain scientific respectability, we need to view ecosystems as made up of individually goal-directed organisms with no interest in even the stability of the system. The now outdated organism or holistic process view of an ecosystem may have been trying to identify the same entity as spirit of place has always attempted to express. That is, the unique holding together in a characteristic way that we experience in some places.

Pantheism

Various positions and interpretations on the nature of the relationship between God and the world could be examined as playing into ideas about spirit of place. The abode of the special beings section (see p. 141) dealt with understandings about local deities or metaphysical beings. Under pantheism I wish to signal another range of ideas that see the world, particularly the natural world, as infused with a single deity. Thus, on this view, the world houses, is part of or is the same thing as God. The world might be seen as a 'holy manifestation' (Wood 1985: 157) or the body of God. This could be seen as a stronger claim for care and respect than the theist's view that the Earth is God's creation. To a culture used to revering God and excelling in buildings to honour God, it seems reasonable to suppose that the wonder of the natural world, when noticed, is tied up with these beliefs. Whether viewed as God's creation or God's body, we read into this an injunction to respect the Earth, but it seems that a similar short circuit could be happening here. God has respect, the world is an expression of God's nature, therefore the world has respect. It might be that the awe and wonder that we feel about the world, often triggered by special places could prompt the appropriate respect without a mediating belief structure.

Pantheism can add to ideas of spirit of place an impressive heritage and links with nature mysticism. For many it is possible to see some places as clear expressions of God and thereby enhance the feeling of their sacredness. However, the placeless hinterlands that spirit of place ideas are used to criticise have to be seen as desecrated (they, rather than rugged wilderness, are now seen as 'fallen') though still, paradoxically, part of God.

Panpsychism

Panpsychism is the doctrine that all things, including inanimate things, have their own form of consciousness or alternatively that all things share in a world or infinite consciousness. Again this is an ancient idea that has seen occasional resurgences, most recently in environmental ethics. Here, mind-like qualities are attributed as a means to extend the kind of things that can have moral standing. (For a critique, see Andrews 1998). As with ecosystems, one problem to get around, if this is to be applied to place, is the relationship between the mind-like qualities of the individual rocks, streams, plants, and so on, and attributing a mind-like quality to their amalgamation in a specific place. If the world consciousness view is taken, the problem becomes one of making distinctions, as with pantheism, between places one wants to claim have a spirit of place and the experience of some spaces as placeless. One possibility is that every entity, be it a tree or a paving slab, has its own mind- like qualities and in some places these qualities create something together, a kind of place-mind, and in other places this does not happen; they just do not gel in the same way. Perhaps we can experience the difference in a way analogous to the way that groups of students sometimes build a new group entity and others remain separate individuals. There is a tangible difference, but it is one that is hard to predict or explain.

The role of the architect would then include identifying the place-mind and thinking through the implications of, for example, adding a particular structure. Presumably this would involve knowing the particular mind-like qualities of the different building materials as well as their adaptation when in particular spatial configurations, then thinking through how that will gel with and modify the place-mind in the proposed place. Moreover, the extraction of materials would also have implications for their place of origin or current location and this would also need to be taken into account. As a way of prompting responsibility and thoughtfulness, panpsychism seems a useful component to spirit of place, but there could be problems over and above creating a fear of any action at all.

The inclusive nature of the doctrine is driven by the rejection of an anthropocentric hierarchy of valuing and yet it seems to fall directly into this by attributing mind-like qualities (something we have no doubt about humans having) to entities where the possession of mind-like qualities is speculative. Playing with such ideas might open up possibilities of changing unhelpful worldviews, but it is not clear that it will help us to understand the real nature of mountains or streams or cobbled paving. As with the potential anthropomorphism in the notion of character, it seems to misapply an attribute to things in order that we should respect them. This could be at the expense of giving us a better understanding of the things as the things they are. The way forward for architects and builders is surely, as it always has been, to develop a sensitive respect for the materials as they occur and when they have been well used and combined in a fitting context.

And many more

Spirit of place is sometimes used as a way of expressing the health of a place – the feel we get from the flourishing of a healthy ecosystem, or the vibrancy of good community feeling in a place. Perhaps health here is operating as a metaphor for the emergent property, discussed under 'character', that we experience about places that work.

Occasionally the role of spirit of place seems to be to express something that is not quantifiable in scientific terms. This 'scientifically intangible something' is not investigated further as the point seems to be to critique science rather than to understand the phenomenon itself.

The term also gets used when claiming that it is possible to create a spirit of place: if you just use the correct design principles or natural materials or have the right attitude to daily use. This, of course, contradicts aspects of authenticity and narrative and undermines the role of spirit of place as claiming irreplaceability. If we can create such places on a blank canvas, then the idea fails to provide sound reasons for nurturing and respect of particular places. However, it does hold out hope for the seemingly irredeemable placeless locations.

Possible ways forward

The shades of meaning above reflect a complex, multifaceted nexus of ideas, but does spirit of place have a sound foundation or is it just a hopeless confusion? I want to propose three possible ways forward.

One response to the confusion that the notion of spirit of place seems capable of generating is to say that there is no such thing. The confusion and contradictions involved are a sure sign of a missing referent (Rapaport 1993). If any such things exist there would be a greater clarity already about what they are.

The second possible way through the confusion is to take an instrumental strategy. We could ask what we want the idea for – what purposes is it meant to serve? Then keep the best definitions and perhaps find a better term for those purposes. Spirit of place is used to protect places from development or to create sensitive changes. It can inform architectural style and prevent homogenisation (Relph 1976). It is used to explain and to promote successful community life. However, to be persuasive, to explain why building A is preferable to building B or the route of road A is preferable to route B, it needs more clarity. Especially if building A and route A are more expensive or (especially contentious in the current context) less energy efficient.

The third way forward, and one which I believe will eventually provide the robustness we need on much firmer ground than instrumental strategies can supply, is to say that the spirit of place describes reality. When we try to describe some places it becomes necessary to include something that is not an inventory of their contents or a description of our feelings about them. To discover exactly what it is and to find the best ways of speaking about it means that we need to become sensitive investigators of places. Places that it is claimed have a strong spirit of place and those that seem the very antithesis of the idea. How we do that is a complex issue; we might try to step outside of our cultural presuppositions, our personal likes and dislikes or current design training in order to meet places (Brook 1998). Only then can we discover if this nexus of ideas has any purchase on a place itself.

Discovering a spirit of place does not mean we cannot then build or change a place. We could combine these observations with the best of current environmental understanding and, where appropriate, aesthetic sensitivity, political theory, historical insight, and so on, to lend to the spirit of place the best of our cultural discernment.

Acknowledgements

Work on this chapter was supported by the Arts and Humanities Research Board. I am also indebted to the participants at the Ethics of Building conference and the staff and postgraduates in the Philosophy Department at Lancaster University who raised many helpful points when I presented a germinal version of this chapter.

References

Andrews, J. (1998) 'Weak Panpsychism and Environmental Ethics', *Environmental Values* 7: 381–96.

Brook, I. (1998) 'Goethean Science as a Way to Read Landscape', *Landscape Research* 23(1): 51–69.

Casey, E. S. (1993) *Getting Back into Place,* Indianapolis: Indiana University Press.

Clifford, S. and King, A. (1993) *Local Distinctiveness,* London: Common Ground.

Durrell, L. (1988) *Spirit of Place,* London: Faber and Faber.

Holland, A. and O'Neill, J. (1996) 'The Integrity of Nature Over Time: Some Problems', *The Thingmount Working Paper Series on the Philosophy of Conservation,* Lancaster University: Philosophy Department.

Norberg-Schulz, Christian (1984) *Genius Loci: Towards a Phenomenology of Architecture*, New York: Rizzoli.

Pratt, V. (1982) 'Aristotle and the Essence of Natural History', *History and Philosophy of the Life Sciences* 4(2): 203–33.

Pratt, V. and Brook, I. (1997) 'Goethe's Archetype and the Romantic Self' *Studies in History and Philosophy of Science*, 26: 351–65.

Rapaport, Amos (1993) 'A Critical Look at the Concept "Place"', in Rana P. B. Singh (ed.) *The Spirit and Power of Place: Human Environment and Sacrality* Varanasi: National Geographical Society of India.

Relph, E. (1976) *Place and Placelessness*, London: Pion.

Wood, H. W. Jr (1985) 'Modern Pantheism as an Approach to Environmental Ethics', *Environmental Ethics* 7: 151–63.

Worster D. (1985) *Nature's Economy: A History of Ecological Ideas*, Cambridge: Cambridge University Press.

Part III

STEPS TOWARDS A THEORY OF THE ETHICS OF THE BUILT ENVIRONMENT

12

THE CONCEPTUAL BASIS OF BUILDING ETHICS

Mustafa Pultar

The nature of building(s) and people's attitudes towards them are determined by two types of factors: *environmental* and *cultural*. Among the latter, ethical predicates are probably the most influential; not only because they determine how buildings are evaluated by people, but also because they form the basic precepts through which professionals act in designing and constructing them, and through which resources are allocated in competition with other socio-economic needs.

Ethical precepts that dictate action have their origin in the values that people hold. Despite this importance of values in the formation of ethical precepts, there appears to be no well-established, coherent and systematic framework for a discussion of value-related issues in the analysis of building(s). The problem of value has received much attention in philosophy and in the behavioural sciences, where

> [N]umerous books have been written on the subject, but [even there] often the reader comes away more confused than enlightened because the author has not defined his terms and has used the concept so loosely and broadly that his meaning cannot even be inferred.
>
> (Kilby 1993: 31)

The problem is addressed here by examining concepts that may be used in a discussion of values and interrelating them to form a framework. It is based on the place and importance of value-related concepts in the life-cycle of building. Prost has supported the same approach:

> Rather than speak of architecture in a very general sense from the point of view of aesthetics and technology...the focus [should] be on architectural production... Ethical inquiry in architecture cannot

involve individual responsibility only but must consider all social actors and lead to social awareness and responsibility.

(Prost 1994: 152)

The model presented here may appear to be founded on the conception of a professional, industrialised building process, but some reflection will reveal how it can be applied to many different instances of building.

A process model of building

The life-cycle of building is similar to that of a majority of human activities, in that it consists of a four-stage process: *problem formulation*, *problem solution*, *implementation* and *use*. In formalised, professional building, these four stages correspond, respectively, to planning and programming, design, construction and use. The process is cyclic; most building reaches the end of its useful life for a variety of reasons, and leads, thereby, to a repetition of the cycle in the form of renovation, refurbishing, readaptation of use or completely new building. A graphical model of this process is shown in Figure 12.1, which illustrates one representative cycle.

At the outset, a misfit is recognised between the present state of building and some ideal conditions that are deemed to be desirable for that environment. The former is described in terms of building descriptors, the latter conditions express what kind or level of the pertinent building descriptors are acceptable or ideal. These conditions are obviously bound to people's conceptions of what is good and ought to be preferred. The misfit may result, on the one hand, from an observed deterioration over time of the state defined by the building descriptors. Alternatively, people's conception of the desirable conditions may change over time as would happen, for example, with changes in fashion or the socio-economic status of the occupants. The misfit may be felt intuitively or, as in today's formalised construction, made explicit in the form of an architectural brief; in either instance there results a building problem.

During design, decisions are made about how a projected state of building should be so that the misfit between the state descriptors and the desirable conditions shall be resolved. The product of design reflects the designers' interpretation of the problem, as well as their own convictions about the desirable conditions that they deem are preferable in a particular situation. These latter may be, and often are, quite different to those of the owner.

Construction involves a major transformation of materials, energy, finance and manpower into the building product. Characterised by an

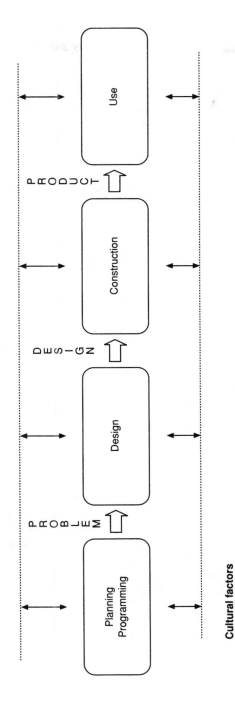

Figure 12.1 Process model of building.

intense concentration of economic resources, construction necessarily reflects the interests of all the parties concerned. What are considered to be good and desirable during construction are likely to be quite different for owner and designer.

Use is that stage of the building life-cycle where the building's impact extends not only to the users but also to the social and built environment at large; and this for long periods of time. Very often the immediate users of and the people indirectly involved in building(s) have very little say in its formation until this stage. It may even be the case that they remain unknown until much later.

Building activity exists in interdependence with numerous environmental and cultural factors, with technology, knowledge and value systems forming the basic components of the latter. Neither environmental factors nor knowledge and technology, however, determine on their own or together, to any fundamental extent, the nature of a building design or the quality observed by the users. What does determine them are the beliefs that owners, users, building professionals and others hold as to what *ought* to be desired and preferred. In essence, these are ethical beliefs, and, in this sense, people's ethical beliefs are the ultimate determinants of how buildings are appraised.

Values in ethics

If ethical considerations in building are to be of any operational consequence at all, we need to view them differently than do the traditional speculative discussions in philosophy, and approach building ethics with a scientific understanding which allows it to be studied empirically. One such approach, which will form the basis of the discussion in this chapter, views ethics as the science of 'oughtness'. Bahm, a proponent of this approach, claims that '[T]he most basic problem facing ethics as a pure science is understanding the nature of oughtness' (Bahm 1994: 3). He goes on to state that the nature of rightness and wrongness, obligation and duty, codes, standards, norms, mores and laws are all related to oughtness, further indicating that these are mere synonyms for it. He regards values as the fundamental notion in a study of ethics: 'Fully adequate understanding of oughtness and rightness involves understanding values' (Bahm 1994: 28).

Bahm proposes:

> ...as essential to ethics, some principles for choosing...[which] will seem self-evident. All of them can be tested by rigorous examination.

All of them presuppose that persons have values...and that at least some of these values can be known and considered in making right and wrong choices.

(Bahm 1994: 27–28)

The said principles consist of the choice of a 'good' over a 'bad', of a 'greater good' over a 'lesser good', and of a 'lesser bad' over a 'greater bad'. By reference to a spectrum of goodnesses, these principles can be consolidated into a single one, namely the choice of a greater good over a lesser good.

Values and value judgement

The question of value has been treated to great extents from philosophical, psychological and economic perspectives. Among these, the approach taken by the behavioural sciences seems, at first, to lend itself to the study of value in building. A widely quoted definition of this understanding of value, given by the anthropologist Kluckhohn, sees a value as a 'conception, explicit or implicit, distinctive of an individual or characteristic of a group, of the desirable which influences the selection from available modes, means and ends of action' (Kluckhohn 1951: 395). This definition stems mainly from work that involves people's personal, social and moral values in affecting their behaviour, and subsequent studies have continued in that vein (Rokeach 1973; Schwartz and Bilsky 1987). Kilby (1993: 31), working from the same perspective, states explicitly that he ignores all of the technical meanings of value except the one in behavioural science – a common trait of such studies. Furthermore, what is characteristic of values understood in this sense is that the thing valued, the precept used in judging it as good, and the act of valuing it, are all fused into the same notion.

Studies of ethics in building, on the other hand, need an alternate conception of value since building is closely connected with technical, socio-economic and perceptual phenomena and since different parties involved in the life-cycle of building do not conceive the question of value in the same manner. There is, therefore, a need to approach the question of value from a wider perspective. The conception utilised in axiology, the science of value in general, allows us to do this.

Citing the work of Hartman (1967), who conceived of ethics as the knowledge of goodness, Forrest defines goodness as 'degree of concept meaning fulfilment' (Forrest 1994: 2). This definition implies fit to some ideal or perfect state. Goodness is understood to be variable; there can be different degrees of fit to an ideal. The definition also incorporates the notion of badness and exhibits a gradation from good to bad (Bahm 1993).

The construct which expresses this variability of goodness is defined by Forrest as value: 'Value is goodness gradation specificity' (Forrest 1994: 23). Analogous to 'number' being a construct for resolving questions of abundance (quantity) gradation, value is a construct, which pertains to questions of goodness gradation. Thus, for any concrete or abstract object which displays a particular goodness gradation, including the binary gradation of good and not good, to define a value which describes that gradation should be possible.

In many instances, values have a hierarchical nature in that some values constitute generic classes; these generic classes may be thought of as incorporating different values that have a common character: a feature of similarity. For example, the value of reliability incorporates the values of functionality and durability, which, in turn, are special instances of reliability. Even these may be thought of as generic classes of other more narrowly defined values. Such hierarchy relations may extend through different types of values and may not be unique.

Traditionally, values have been differentiated as to whether they are intrinsic or operational (Bahm 1993: 40–42). Korsgaard (1983) has argued that these are, in fact, two dualities: intrinsic versus extrinsic and operational (means) versus non-operational (ends). Green (1996) has given a discussion of this argument regarding environmental values.

Intrinsic value pertains only to the attributes of the object itself, independent of its circumstances. Many building values such as strength, durability, safety and executional mastery are intrinsic in character. Extrinsic value, on the other hand, resides in the relation of the object to its circumstances (Green 1996: 32). Typical examples of extrinsic values in building can be found in the contextuality of a building in consequence of its site and its historical importance, or in its uniqueness as the sole remaining instance of a particular style in a particular city.

An object has operational value if it is good for achieving an end. To a housing developer, a building has value as a means to profitability; to a designer, computer aids have operational value for achieving consistency. The end value of a building, however, does not appear to be very distinct and seems to coincide with its extrinsic value, as magnanimity is for a corporation.

Values are constructs that associate potential goodness attributes with objects. They do not indicate, however, what form the goodness gradation associated with that value is to take. Value association involves not only denoting the value but also describing its nature and the conditions of its desirability or acceptability. In other words, it also requires establishing its goodness gradation. Rewording Kluckhohn's definition to read 'beliefs, distinctive of a group of professionals or users, of the desirable conditions which influences their decisions and perceptions' provides an explanation of this kind of association. Such beliefs are called *value judgements*, and because they express what ought to be considered good, they are ethical dictates. In building, specifying the structural requirements of strength may be given as an example of explicit value judgement. A social value such as conformity with a particular style illustrates implicitly held value judgements.

These examples highlight a characteristic of value judgements. Even though strength is a value, its goodness gradation can only be established in reference to the load-carrying capacity of a structural system in a building. Similarly, thermal comfort can be established, primarily, in reference to the internal temperature. Thus, value judgements necessitate the association of some building descriptor with the corresponding value. As a naïve example, Figure 12.2 shows the value judgement for thermal comfort in the form of a goodness gradation (level of comfort) associated with a descriptor (internal temperature). This example is a singularly well-defined case because it associates a continuously measurable descriptor with a continuous goodness gradation. Most value judgements, however, simply associate a binary goodness gradation with a value, as is the case for strength: the load-carrying capacity is either above a predetermined threshold (acceptable) or below it (not acceptable). Others may be associated with categorical or ordinal goodness gradations.

Many of the descriptors related to values in the engineering and economic aspects of building are defined explicitly. Usually this is the outcome of an involved cognitional process and often the product of

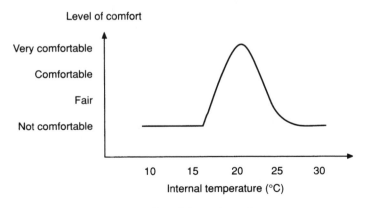

Figure 12.2 Goodness gradation of thermal comfort.

cultural aggregation in the profession. Major problems seem to occur, however, in the association of descriptors with social values and in the measurement of these descriptors. Even though some scales exist, such as the Rokeach (1973) scale of values, few well-established procedures of measurement have been developed for a majority of the behavioural and perceptual values involved in building(s).

Values and value judgements in building

A convenient basis for identifying and differentiating values is to consider the kind of human needs that they are related to. From this viewpoint, values that affect the nature and outcome of human activities may be classified under three general categories: *technical, socio-cultural* and *percepto-cognitional* values.

Technical values are related to the satisfaction of biological and bio-social human needs, as well as non-human requirements. Three generic values in this context are *reliability, efficiency* and *compatibility*. Reliability is concerned with the probability that a problem solution will perform its function satisfactorily. In the building context, one instance of reliability may be interpreted, for example, to mean the probability that a building will provide the requisite meso-environmental conditions. Efficiency concerns the ratio of the utility obtained to the amount of the resources supplied. In building, examples of descriptors associated with efficiency are such quantities as amount of useful space or quality obtained per unit of investment, or the thermal efficiency of the heating system. Compatibility is a value related to the inverse of the degree of conflict that the solution implemented will create with the people, and the physical and socio-cultural context, as well as other entities in the environment. A foremost example of technical compatibility is safety. Figure 12.3 shows a preliminary classification of technical values in building. The various lines seen therein are intended to indicate the hierarchy relations among the values as discussed above.

Compatibility also pertains to the general class of socio-cultural values. As shown in Figure 12.4, social compatibility comprises values of past and future continuity, suitability to the social and cultural context, and conformity to good professional practice.

Also affecting the formation and perception of the built environment are percepto-cognitional values, among which may be mentioned the generic values of evocativeness, mastery and 'dishabituality' (see Figure 12.5). Evocativeness is a value related to the extent to which the senses, emotions and intellect of observers and users are evoked. For example, such evocation may consist in giving an impression of magnanimity or

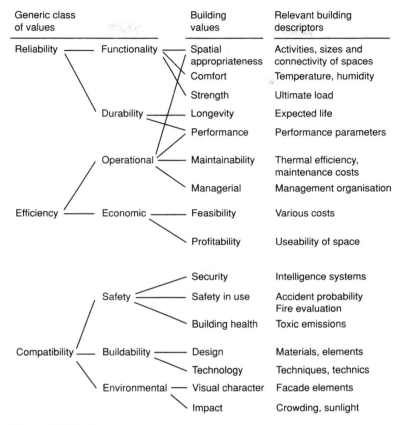

Figure 12.3 Technical values.

historical continuity, or evoking feelings of homely cosiness or community. Dishabituality is a measure of the novelty and the unfamiliarity of the solution. In building this might correspond to the provision of novel spaces, vistas that people are unaccustomed to and novel uses of materials and other architectural elements. Mastery comprises qualities that are conveyed by formal aesthetic characteristics such as the unity of the design, the refinement in details and the degree of perfection attained in design and construction.

In building, there are many values ranging from those associated with structural parameters to those associated with acoustic variables, from material costs to formal aesthetic measures. Several different values fall under the same generic value: for example, the safety of the building against collapse during earthquakes, safety from household accidents or

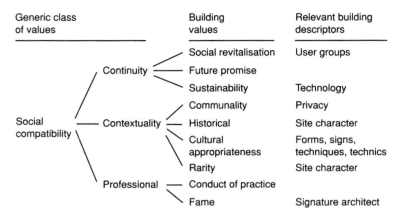

Figure 12.4 Socio-cultural values.

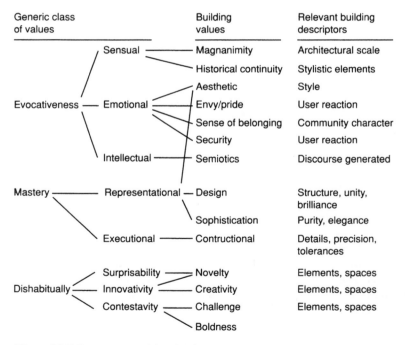

Figure 12.5 Percepto-cognitional values.

toxic emissions from the building materials and the availability of sunlight in light of adjacent buildings are all instances of compatibility existing simultaneously in building. This diversity in the range of values is a major problem in studies of building values.

Another problem relates to the fact that it is not only building, the product, but the whole process of building, as illustrated in Figure 12.1, that constitutes the subject area of building values. It is not possible to enumerate all building values here, but the short list below may serve to illustrate their diverse nature:

1 compatibility of the building with the physiological and psychological health of the occupants (Day 1990);
2 advantages of the social organisation through which the planning has been achieved, such as a participatory process;
3 extent of the discourse that the building has generated in architectural circles;
4 compatibility with the topography and climate of the environment;
5 innovativity of the techniques used in the construction;
6 appropriateness of the spatial solution *vis-à-vis* the cultural value systems of the occupants;
7 honesty of the building professionals (Manheim 1983).

Value judgements in building are formed mainly through the accretion of successful examples and the practice of criticism. They are disseminated throughout the building professions through education, professional guidance and control, and through society by 'enculturation'. Parallel to all cultural phenomena, value judgements vary through time and in space. Whereas judgements related to technical values have a tendency to remain fairly constant, other value judgements change more often and are more variable from group to group, from society to society.

Explicitly stated value judgements are encountered in the clauses of professional standards, building codes and other codes of practice. Ordinarily, such clauses are not considered as value judgements; and they rarely create much disagreement. Much more controversial, however, are socio-cultural and percepto-cognitional value judgements which are not expressed explicitly but are carried implicitly by professionals in their individual style of practice or in the cultural accumulation of the profession. In addition to not having clearly defined descriptors, such values have implicit value judgements associated with them and they incorporate their goodness gradation also implicitly, often in binary form. Values commonly used in architectural criticism such as creativity, sensitivity, perceptivity, boldnes and brilliance are examples of such values.

Value systems

The value-related features that characterise particular people, groups and societies are not their value judgements, but rather their value systems. A value system is the abstract collection of value judgements held by a person or a group regarding the various values involved in a phenomenon. Within a value system, value judgements do not exist independently of each other; they are related through various interactions and conflicts. As shown by Schwartz and Bilsky (1987), the conflicts that exist between quality judgements and economic interests are very noticeable examples.

Two main questions appear in the formulation of value systems: how to compromise different value judgements and how to aggregate them. Regarding the former, the value system must contain additional rules that prioritise value judgements and dictate when and how precedence may take place. In the case of conflicting judgements, the value system must have means of resolving this conflict. These rules and means will involve preferences among various goodnesses, and are, therefore, in the nature of ethical dictates. Because they express what ought to be done concerning particular phenomena, the study of value systems is essentially a problem in ethics rather than an axiological one.

Regarding the problem of aggregation, it is often helpful to find a common value in terms of which different values may be expressed. Cost is one example of such a convenient value. When such a common value cannot be formulated, various value judgements may be aggregated by weighting them and forming a composite. Somerville, for example, discusses the aggregation of benefit and harm: 'Value judgements are involved here as to what counts as benefit and harm, and as to what weight should be given to each' (Somerville 1994: 77). Stern *et al.* (1993: 328) have used a similar approach to model the motivation to act on the environment.

Value systems are more variable in time, and between groups and societies, than are value judgements. It is not difficult to imagine, simply by looking at the types of building values shown in Figures 12.3 to 12.5, that although clients, architects, builders, contractors and local administrators might tend to judge individual values similarly, they will tend to differ significantly in the priorities they give to some of these values over others.

Valuation and worth

The discussion above has been general in character in that no reference was made to particular instances of building. To bring the study of values to an operational level, we need to consider the evaluation of instances.

Establishing the goodness level of a particular instance (i.e. building) on the goodness gradation of a value is a process that may be called valuation. The level established in this manner is the worth of that instance for that value. For example, the structural analysis (i.e. the valuation) of some particular load-carrying system (instance) establishes that its strength (value) is strong (worth). Thus, a building descriptor, mediated through valuation, results in a worth for that building. This example also illustrates some salient features of valuation:

1 Valuation may consist of a procedure varying from a simple one, as can be done by a layperson, to a detailed professional study.
2 It may be done at different stages of the building process and for different purposes: predictively, as during design; selectively, as in an architectural competition; or *post facto*, as in building assessment.
3 Because the valuation of an actual building will involve many co-existing value judgements, in order to determine composite worth, some procedure of composite valuation needs to be formulated using the premises of value systems.

Overall quality in a building is a typical example of composite worth, incorporating the worth of all values pertaining to a building. Because it is mediated by value systems, it is continuous and variable throughout the life-cycle of the building and also with respect to the groups that are doing the valuation, thus emphasising the essential subjectivity of building appraisals.

Some value-related issues in building

Many of the problems that generate debate on building may be reformulated in the light of value systems. One such issue concerns the conflict that is observed between different groups. For example, there appears to be constant conflict in the valuations and approaches of professionals versus users, in the attitudes of architects versus engineers, in the interests of contractors versus clients. Although it may not necessarily help in resolving these differences, a reanalysis of these problems in value-related terms will certainly be instrumental in understanding them.

Another occasion becomes apparent in building design competitions. Competition documents expressing a problem are prepared by a planning/ programming group that also sets performance criteria and acceptable standards. The actual choice of the solution to be implemented, however, is mediated by the value system of the jury. It is very easy to foresee different winners emerging if different juries are to judge the same entries. The perennial complaints by designers that documents are not clear, or too restrictive, or have not been taken into consideration by the juries are likely to find clarity when viewed in a value-related perspective. A major portion of the energy that is devoted to education in building goes to forming the value systems of the students. This effort would be better guided by a consciousness of value systems through a study of the values involved and their formation, examining past and present value systems held by different groups. Similarly, value-related analysis may also be used in the studies of designer attitudes and behaviour.

The fundamental value concepts discussed above provide a basis for discussing building ethics. Further progress in ethical issues in building may be attained through the following studies:

1 identifying values in building, and developing operational procedures for value judgement;
2 examining and documenting value systems of different groups involved in building, taking account of variations in cultural backgrounds;
3 observing and documenting changes over time in the value systems of different groups involved in building and the manner in which these changes take place;
4 studies of the formation, dissemination and diffusion of value systems;
5 studies of user groups to document their preferences in choosing buildings and in their attitudes towards them.

References

Bahm, A.J. (1993) *Axiology: The Science of Values*, Amsterdam: Rodopi.
Bahm, A.J. (1994) *Ethics: The Science of Oughtness*, Amsterdam: Rodopi.
Day, C. (1990) *Places of the Soul: Architecture and Environmental Design as a Healing Art*, Wellingford: Aquarian Press.
Forrest, F.G. (1994) *Valuemetrics: The Science of Personal and Professional Ethics*, Amsterdam: Rodopi.
Green, K. (1996) 'Two Distinctions in Environmental Goodness', *Environmental Values*, 5: 31–46.
Hartman, R.J. (1967) *The Structure of Value: Foundations of Scientific Axiology*, Carbondale, IL: Southern Illinois University Press.
Kilby, R.W. (1993) *The Study of Human Values*, Lanham, MD: University Press of America.

Kluckhohn, C. (1951) 'Values and value-orientations in the theory of action: An exploration in definition and classification', in T. Parsons and E. A. Shils (eds) *Toward A General Theory of Action*, Cambridge, MA: Harvard University Press.

Korsgaard, C.M. (1983) 'Two distinctions in goodness', *The Philosophical Review* 95: 169–95.

Manheim, M.L. (1983) 'Values and Professional Practice', in J. H. Schaub and K. Pavlovic (eds) *Engineering Professionalism and Ethics*, Malabar, FL: Robert E. Krieger Publishing.

Prost, R. (1994) 'L'architecture considérée sous l'angle du processus', in L. Pelletier and A. Pérez-Goméz (eds) *Architecture, Ethics and Technology*, Montreal: McGill-Queen's University Press.

Rokeach, M. (1973) *The Nature of Human Values*, New York: Free Press.

Schwartz, S.H. and Bilsky, W. (1987) 'Toward a Theory of the Universal Content and Structure of Values: Extensions and Cross Cultural Replications', *Journal of Personality and Social Psychology* 58(5): 878–91.

Somerville, M.A. (1994) 'Ethics and architects: Spaces, voids and travelling-in-hope', in L. Pelletier and A. Pérez-Goméz (eds) *Architecture, Ethics and Technology*, Montreal: McGill-Queen's University Press.

Stern, C., Dietz, K. and Kalof, L. (1993) 'Value Orientations, Gender and Environmental Concern', *Environment and Behavior* 25(3): 322–48.

13

HOW TO THINK ABOUT THE ETHICS OF ARCHITECTURE

Saul Fisher

Philosophical ethicists have not yet fully explored, or even mapped out, the problems posed by architectural practice. While some have attempted such explorations, their accounts suffer assorted philosophical deficits, and generally miss the aim of reasoned moral analysis. I believe that the most fruitful attempts to think about such issues in philosophical terms, in lieu of an analytical architectural ethics, are found in the body of architectural law. There we may glimpse some promising philosophical considerations pertaining to such matters as intellectual property, the judgement of others' actions and responsibilities to others.

Why does architecture require a dedicated ethical analysis?

I begin by considering why architecture merits its own branch of applied ethics. In brief, architecture has special moral issues as a consequence of its proper, idiosyncratic features, which distinguish it among the arts, the professions and social practices.

To capture the interest of philosophical ethicists, we need to think of architecture as a particular series of choices among actions. Architecture is a practice as well as a product, and being a practice of any sort entails behaviours that fall into kinds. Philosophical ethicists typically categorise kinds of behaviours as right or wrong, and as having good or bad consequences or as brought about by good or bad intentions. The *practice* of architecture, then, entails behaviours our choices of which may be illuminated by ethical analysis. What, then, is special to architecture that makes for distinctive sorts of behavioural choices, and so warrants a dedicated ethical analysis? Some special ethical problems architecture faces result from its blend of the concrete with the ideational; this blend yields a clash of physical and intellectual property rights. Other problems result from architecture's mix of the utilitarian with the artistic, which leads to the promotion of competing preferences and interests – those of self versus those of the greater whole. In addition, architectural practice compounds individual effort with social needs and desires, and so requires architects to balance obligations to their work as art *and* as token of a building type, where value is judged by functional success.

One consequence of such blends and oppositions of interests is that we cannot expect to directly import ethical solutions for architectural practice from the applied ethics canon that addresses other, distinct disciplines. These problems are hybrids, reflective of preferences and meta-preferences distinctive to architecture and so requiring specially designed solutions for architecture. One might think that a natural model for professional moral guidance is business ethics, but there is no profession or business that is quite like architecture, which alone generates products of great utility *and* artistic value. In business ethics, one does not quite get at these issues because of the focus on traditional financial relationships, without the additional factors of aesthetic value, intellectual property, or the status of shelter as a human need. This last factor in particular suggests social issues special to architecture that are, to date, little discussed in the existing canon of applied ethics. Thus, on a practical level, architects and others must learn how to decide between claims as to what constitutes better housing and under what conditions. However, this also raises the theoretical, ethical issue as to what makes housing an obligation, and in what ways that such an obligation accrues to architects. Such considerations arise from the peculiar nature of architecture as a profession committed to the creation of a socially beneficial and functional art. There is no other discipline with just this mix of commitments, or consequently, problematic ethical choices. Addressing *how* one makes such choices, then, is unlike that which ethicists have done before; at least for ethicists in the analytic philosophical tradition.

Current models of addressing ethical problems in architecture

There have been, of course, other efforts to address something called 'architectural ethics'. It is not clear, though, that the subject tackled in these efforts corresponds to moral thinking as analytic philosophers understand it, or that such efforts suitably speak to the proper issues at hand. I am particularly concerned to show the failings of three such efforts: *professional codes of ethics*, the Continental philosophical perspective of Karsten Harries (1997) and *architectural-theoretic views,* such as critical regionalism. Each approach, I argue, suffers its own special flaws. The first approach (employed in architectural codes of ethics) impresses us with the need for high-minded principles and particular rules of conduct, yet presents such thinking in canned documents that promote organisational authority at the expense of individual responsibility for moral choice. The Continental approach pursued by Harries focuses on architecture's role as product, not practice, and so results in an obscure notion of buildings and their environments as judged to be right or wrong, or good or bad. Finally, Critical Regionalism, a movement that promotes cultural bounds as a resolution of architecture's ethical dilemmas, fails to identify any deep ethical difficulties, much less resolve them. Furthermore, Critical Regionalism introduces an insupportable cultural relativism, which proscribes meaningful, intersubjective ethical analysis.

Professional codes of ethics

In recent years, many professional organisations have formulated codes of ethics or conduct, and in architecture some very careful work has been undertaken by the Royal Institute of British Architects (RIBA) in the UK, and the American Institute of Architects (AIA) and the National Council of Architectural Registrations Boards (NCARB) in the US. As is common with such codes, for architects, the goal has been to formulate general guiding moral principles and particular rules of conduct to express the considered opinion of the profession on ethical matters in order to protect the profession and guard against liability problems. To enforce this opinion, organisations bring the weight of their promotional and disciplinary powers to bear on adherence to the code. All of this is built upon careful thinking about ethics, yet the finished product cannot qualify as ethical reasoning *per se*. Though these codes are perfectly suitable as professional statements, they are *codes* after all; hence ethics by stipulation. Further, they do not address ethical issues of architecture that arise out of the design function, as opposed to business, fiduciary, insurance or liability functions.

Those codes of ethics typically include sets of general principles or rules, and subsidiary guidelines governing specific behaviours. They may also feature sets of global claims intended to characterise the organisation's *ethos*: the theoretical grounds for having chosen the general principles. This reflects the standard way of organising normative, principled moral thinking, and makes for easy analysis of different sorts of moral frameworks. Kantian, utilitarian and even virtue ethics can be easily assessed along similar lines. What is striking about professional codes of ethics, as compared with philosophical or even theological ethics, is that the moral thinking so structured is inappropriately rigid. Whatever moral claims were deemed worthy by the professional association at a particular stage have been pronounced as codified, with allowance for change by decision of the organisation. This is hardly the stuff of moral philosophy that focuses on flexible, individual ethical choice. Further, such codes present the content of moral claims without the benefit of the supporting reasoning. It is a mistake, then, to take this fixed moral pronouncement as completing one's duties towards thinking about right and wrong. Surely such thinking needs to be an *ongoing* professional activity, and the best evidence of this need lies in the serious failings of such codes as they currently stand.

Ethics codes adopted by professional organisations have some characteristic deficiencies. First, the motivation for obedience is driven by compulsion: agreement is required for membership, and violation is punishable by reprimand, suspension or expulsion. This is a classic case of 'doing right for the wrong reason'. Second, the focus and motivation for the principles derives from an assessment of the professional's role and behaviour: in this case, the architect. Other stakeholders in architectural practice, such as owners, contractors and end-users, naturally figure less prominently. Hence the codes tend to prescribe what is morally correct for architects alone, to the neglect of others' proper roles; this cannot yield a well-rounded moral picture of architectural practice. Finally, professional codes are written from the perspective of the professional organisation, and so do not necessarily honour the preferences, meta-preference or global moral concerns of other parties, whether individual practitioners or non-architect stakeholders in architectural practice.

Another sort of problem is that the codes do not always hold up to close logical inspection. For example, the RIBA Code contains a principle that requires members to mind the interests of those using their product *and* remain loyal to the client *and* employer. Yet this represents three plausibly distinct interests, with no suggestion as to how one should balance or prioritise them. Further, to uphold this principle, members are advised to retain impartial judgements when acting between parties. Yet if we assume that there *is* some way of prioritising among the three previously mentioned interests, then by the same measure members should exercise partiality accordingly. If all such problems were resolved, we should have consistent codes. But, consistency itself does not guarantee that compliant behaviour is ethical by rational standards beyond the codes.

The common thread through these problems is that they reflect the unchanging nature of the codes and their grounding in the professional needs of architects. Whatever the benefits to the profession, the professional codes approach does not satisfy the obligations of architects to think through the moral issues of their practice with constant and deep probing. *That* would not be practical, some may complain. Indeed, it would be theoretical, and we have, occasionally, obligations to theoretical pursuits.

The Continental 'ethics' of Karsten Harries

A different approach to architectural ethics is quite satisfactory in its degree of theoretical bent; this is the Continental perspective of Karsten Harries. While his perspective is reassuringly grounded in *some* philosophical tradition, I suggest that Harries offers a flawed view of an architectural ethics, based on inadequate theories of what counts as ethics or, for that matter, architecture. His view is that architecture has a lost ethical role which can be attained if we restore some of its older, lost features. He argues as follows:

1 Architecture lacks certain features that would make it 'authentic'.
2 With authenticity comes *ethos*: the values of living in a community.

Thus

3 If we restore those features, then architecture will reflect the prized values of community life.

This piece of reasoning ought not to work at all because it trades on the Greek root of 'ethics', insisting that architecture's ethical role *should* commit the art form to communal, sacral values Harries believes to be enshrined in '*ethos*'. Such is argument by philology, otherwise known as guilt by association. Let us accept, however, the possibility that architecture should reflect values as a function of its being a social practice, and while that is a bit more minimal than Harries's second premise, it might be enough to get his argument going.

It won't get us far, though, given the burdens of the rest of his argument. One principal question is what Harries intends by architecture's 'authenticity' and what features would be needed to restore this lost lustre. His fall-from-grace tale is as follows. Before the advent of technology, buildings reflected the natural, communal and sacral state of man's grasp of, and values towards, the world around him and his existence in it (this is a primordial state referred to by Heidegger as 'being-in-the-world'). Technology and the modern 'aesthetic' perspective have introduced a gross distortion by emphasising architecture's decorative and 'constructive' natures, and the architect's role as an individual creator with a voice distinctive from that of the community. What special restorative features does this story entail?

The suggestion is that architecture can become authentic again if technology does not drive design, and if architects submerge their individualistic desires to design buildings that betray a personal aesthetic. Architects are likely to find these prescriptions backwards and stifling but of greater interest is the lack of guarantee that following this path would lead to a more 'authentic' or 'ethical' architecture of the sort Harries envisions. Architecture is a human artefact and no matter the aesthetic or performative constraints we impose, it inevitably reflects our mediated conception of our relation to the world. Architecture designed around perceptions of communal needs, preferences and behaviours is nonetheless architecture designed around the architect's idiosyncratic perceptions.

In sum, attaining Harries's authenticity would not give us his *ethos*, because we cannot ensure community values in architecture by aesthetic fiat, or by reducing the significance of the architect as an individual creator. Given *these* failings, we need not assess the unargued claim that we *should* promote community values, nor need we consider which community or which values. One other failing *is* worth mention, however, because it undercuts Harries's views from the start. He treats architecture primarily as a product, not a practice, which results in an ethical perspective that attaches moral values and their realisation to buildings, not to the people who build them. This is a form of mysticism. A building might be inhumane in that it is bleak or uninhabitable. It does not follow, nor is it intelligible to suggest, that the building itself has inhumane values. It is on the basis of this misassignment of values that Harries offers us the impossible vision of artefacts reflecting values without the moral input of the individual (moral) agents who create those artefacts. Naturally, some other Continental approach to architectural ethics might be more satisfactory. *Whatever* approach to guiding moral choices of architects is workable, it needs to recognise the significance of the architect's moral agency.

Architectural-theoretic approaches: the critical regionalist perspective

Architectural theorists, for their part, are acutely attuned to moral problems of the practice of architecture. While there are prominent perspectives on such problems among architectural theorists, it is not clear that their adherents conceive of them as 'ethical theories' *per se*. I focus on one popular perspective, and I propose that the form of argumentation among such views is commonly flawed.

Several movements or schools of contemporary architectural thought suggest that there is an ethical crisis that architecture should be meeting and is not, and that following in the path of said school of thought should better the state of affairs. One such school is Critical Regionalism (CR), which proposes that architecture faces a crisis of loss in values because (1) modernism has been co-opted by corporate architectural sensibilities and (2) post-modernism is morally bankrupt for glorifying past, wrong ideals and contemporary possessive individualism (Frampton 1983). Resolution of this crisis, according to the CR proponent, requires an emphasis on the revelation of architectural form within a design framework sensitive to local context. Let us briefly examine the argument for CR:

1 It is ethically unjustifiable for architects to pursue 'corporate' modernist or post-modernist design; doing so neglects the social charge of architecture.
2 Advancing this social charge requires eschewing 'homogenised' mass culture. Hence a design aesthetic is ethical if it is context-driven and restores architecture's social focus in a locally sensitive fashion. Thus
3 one ethically viable design aesthetic preserves modernist formalism but retreats from modernist commitments to a universal aesthetic. CR is such an aesthetic, and its adherents practice ethically by rejecting mass culture while retaining a modernist commitment to structure that reveals form – in designs that reflect local culture.

I conceive of three problems here. The first premise suggests that modernist or post-modernist design as adapted in 'late capitalism' are morally indefensible. Anyone who has worked in a post-war office building may sympathise with this claim. Yet these are awful work environments because the engineering was 'bad' with respect to workspace, i.e. a straightforward design or engineering problem that has little to do with capitalism or any other economic model. And if one has difficulties with capitalism, such as objections to possessive individualism, then the last place to seek change should be architecture. This is so, not because architects will defend individualism to the end, but because they are generally out of the loop when it comes to development. In this sense, the CR proponent has a quibble with developers and planners, not architects, who (after all) ostensibly have some obligation to their clients.

Premise two is not much better: given an ethical problem with the present, glib mass culture, it does not follow that the solution is a context or locality-driven culture. Further, this unsupported proposal entails a retreat to an onerous moral relativism. We do not rectify a problematic universal culture by celebrating many distinctive cultures if each is as problematic as the first. We are likely to be better off with a single alternative culture, amenable to all yet a bit less glib and entertainment-driven. That is probably difficult to achieve, and numerous critics have interpreted accordingly the career of architectural modernism as a failure to have this sort of agenda widely adopted. The level of difficulty, however, signals to me a reason to press that agenda further, not abandon it altogether.

Finally, the form of this argument fails to support any such global candidate for addressing the full range of architecture's ethical problems. Consider the CR argument in outline form: architecture faces some particular ethical crisis x because of reliance on design aesthetic y; crisis x can be averted by adopting design aesthetic without features f; design aesthetic z does not have features f and so presents a satisfactory solution to x. Now, this may be good and well for x but tells us nothing about how z would fare in resolving other sorts of ethical crises or difficulties and, as I have suggested, there are many such difficulties, none of which are addressed by CR. The problem is that z should really satisfy a range of conditions and all we have been told is that given one such condition the proposed solution z should work for the lack of features f. One challenge to such architectural-theoretic approaches is to formulate solutions to ethical difficulties without employing arguments of this form.

My cursory review highlights various flaws of these perspectives on assessing moral problems and potential solutions. Broadly, what plagues professional codes, Harries's view and critical regionalism alike is some manner of misconstruing the problems of architectural ethics: what truly constitutes moral dilemmas for architects. None of this should be taken remotely as endorsing an ethical cynicism or nihilism. Following my earlier suggestion, there *are* moral dilemmas special to architecture; there is an architectural ethics *en soi* concerned with rational resolution of such dilemmas. Hence we need a means of carefully identifying those dilemmas and suggesting how they can be addressed with scholarly rigour. Our task is to identify the right tools for doing so.

An analytic ethics of architecture

I propose that our best tool kit for architectural ethics consists in the argument-oriented framework and ground rules of analytic philosophy. By following the broader analytic ethics tradition, we place architectural *practice*, and thus the architect as moral agent, at the focus of moral thought. There is little in the philosophical literature to guide us directly in this task. Yet the resources of an analytic approach extend beyond the history of philosophy to the wealth of argument in architectural law, which ranges over such issues as property, liability and honesty. This new approach can help us identify responsibilities among parties to architectural practice, define who or what in architectural interactions has moral agency (hence rights) and describe morally defensible distribution in architecture, as judged by utility, equality or other measures.

The analytic approach to philosophy can be broadly defined as the assessment of competing philosophical positions strictly by the arguments that are adduced in their behalf. Analytic philosophical ethics is the application to moral thought of this logical weighing of claims and supporting reasons. The analytic approach *as a philosophical method* is generally indifferent to definitions of the scope of ethics. Yet by tradition, analytic moral philosophers pay closest attention to a running contest among prominent candidates for universal moral guidelines, including Kantian, utilitarian and virtue ethics. Along the way, analytic ethics has yielded potential accounts of foundational moral concepts (what is responsibility? what is equality?), offered views on meta-ethical matters (can ethics be universal? is ethical thinking biologically determined?), and developed various areas of application, generally to the professions. I suggested earlier that applied ethics is the general class of which architectural ethics is most appropriately a member discipline, and that the distinctive nature of architecture requires a distinctive subject matter. At the foundation of all applied studies, however, are broader issues of the basic discipline. Some questions of architectural ethics that an analytic approach, following traditional *non-applied* ethical concerns, might usefully address include:

- *Responsibilities.* What are the obligations of architects to other persons? What are broad ethical standards on which such obligations may be based? How could we ensure that such standards are reasonable and might be met? What other sorts of obligations do architects have, for example, to historic preservation or environmental protection?
- *Rights.* Who or what has rights, why, and whose trump whose: environments, communities, developers, builders, engineers, architects...buildings?
- *Utility.* What determines the usefulness of architectural goods such as buildings, restorations, reconstructions or plans? Their

social character? Individual preferences of the creator, owner, end-users or public-at-large? Is there a fair way to sum over such preferences?

If the general run of professional ethics is any guide, the greatest interest architectural ethics may generate will not be in such deeply theoretical matters but in those issues pertaining to moral considerations that impact the quotidian and business-oriented practice of architecture. In addition to the practical issues I cited previously, here are several others: Which property rights, intellectual, domestic or commercial, should trump the others, and on what basis? Should degrees of liability for one's designs be directly proportional to the innovative structural character of a design? When does inventive marketing of innovative designs become outright misrepresentation? Is it ethically acceptable at any point until then?

These general moral issues are not difficult to identify, perhaps they are even obvious, given the road map of the existing applied and pure ethics literature. It is harder to spell out the relevant competing claims and supporting arguments with proper attention to architectural concerns, because there is no literature in analytic ethics that addresses issues in architecture. One other, related, starting point for plotting out the competitive landscape of claims and arguments is the existing body of *architectural law*. Legal regulations, judgements and considerations constitute a preliminary resource for grasping some possible lines of reasoning about ethical issues regarding architecture. There are numerous areas one might explore here, and I offer only a small sample: three ways one can mine the law to understand some stakes and strategies of architectural ethics, ranging over intellectual property, the architect's role as arbitrator and one's responsibilities to others.

Intellectual property

Is architecture a service or product? The legal position that it is strictly a service means that architects would not have a stake on copyright, because they would then be creators-by-contract, and here legal tradition has it that rights to the expression of ideas so created accrue to the contracting party. The legal position that it is a product supports the architect's claim to copyright, given that the expression is the architect's creation, whatever services are performed in the course of production (Greenstreet 1998; and Cushman and Hedemann 1995: ch. 11). Such intellectual property questions have been well debated by philosophers but the significance of these debates for architects, and a way of deciding between the status of service and product, have not yet been realised.

The role of architect as judge in disputes between owner and contractor

The architect has a dual role as designer and administrator of an architectural project, and according to American and British law (and the architectural profession's recommendations for contracts) this dual role justifies the architect adjudicating between the owner and contractor in matters of dispute and questions of performance. The legal philosophical questions here are significant: why should one party x paid by another party y be a suitable candidate to judge in disputes between y and a third party z? (Sweet 1994: 639–40) Is utility a sufficient justification? The professional code suggests that all participants should be judged fairly, but what is the proper standard of fairness? Beyond these general legal and philosophical questions lie ethical questions particular to architecture: when are specifications sufficiently poorly satisfied to warrant a judgement with punishing consequences? How is fealty to the owner's interests preserved alongside fairness to the contractor? How could fairness be preserved at all when judging the satisfactory realisation of one's own design? What moral characteristics are necessary and sufficient to the role of judge in design-related disputes, and what facets of being an architect constrain or promote those characteristics?

Responsibility to others' design

Architecture is frequently an accretive enterprise, and adding to or altering another architect's design often entails a responsibility to sensitivity concerning original intent and execution. But what warrants this responsibility, and under what conditions is it in effect? The law weighs in on such questions in the form of historic preservation and landmarking laws. The underlying thinking is that some aesthetic concerns are matters in the public interest and may trump private interests. This might constitute requisite conditions for preservation regulation but does not tell us the source of individual architects' responsibilities to existing structures. These sources may well go beyond public interest, for example extending to one's personal commitment as a design professional to the integrity of work by one's fellow professionals.

This sample of architectural legal issues is a promising starting point for launching a philosophical approach to architectural ethics. In the law we find a tradition of addressing moral issues of architectural practice towards the ends of regulation and dispute resolution, and through consideration of competing doctrines and reasoned argument. As is typical in relations between the law and philosophical ethics, the former may serve as a resource for the latter, given the shared accent on argumentation. Of course the ground rules are a bit more flexible in philosophical ethics and there is distinctly less emphasis on received doctrine as a pre-legitimised source of authority. The principal philosophical contribution in the end, though, lies not in the form but the content of architectural law, in its setting out pertinent questions for moral philosophy to ponder, and some contending responses. Happily, much good work by professional architectural organisations and counsel has gone into thinking about these issues from a legal perspective, out of practical necessity, given liability considerations, the need for dispute resolution and the minimal security of the profession.

Moral philosophy presents a different, more maximalist challenge to professional architects, however. Some may think it a proactive approach: questions of liability, dispute resolution and the profession's very security or reputation should not even arise if all parties adhere to moral standards that go beyond the actual law. That at least is one popular conception of the law, as less stringent than proper ethical reasoning should dictate. Popular conceptions aside, philosophical ethics is more maximalist than law, in architecture and elsewhere, rather in the sense that it is a critical enterprise that takes no foundational beliefs for granted. This is the perspective from which persons typically wonder whether, though some act *x* is legal or warranted by professional code, it is right (and the other way around). In the consideration of moral grounds for architectural practice, then, the law and professionally promoted legal documents provide necessary road maps to the better structured extant moral thinking. Yet this body of thought should be taken by the philosophically inclined as largely built on pre-critical assumptions, constrained by particular legal and professional concerns. Further, while the range of issues addressed is a rich source for philosophical analysis, there are detectable gaps. The law tells us what we *must do* or *cannot do*. These are legal obligations and proscriptions. It says nothing of what we *should* or *should not do* beyond what is required of us. These are supererogatory and permissible yet blameworthy acts, which we look to moral philosophy (among other sources) to help define.

Let us end with an example of the last sort of case. If Smith can legally create a work that reflects numerous central aspects of design thinking clearly found in the work of Jones, without violating copyright, is Smith's resulting work morally blameworthy? There are two intuitive and popular answers: yes, just in case Smith has knowingly borrowed from Jones without proper attribution and permission; and no, because architectural history *just is* a history of borrowing and copying, usually without attribution or permission. Whichever side one argues for, the issue is not to be settled by reference to copyright law, and probably not even by reference to the jurisprudence underlying and around that law. For this is to beg the question concerning the moral viability of such legal tradition (interesting, of course, in its own right). Rather, the answer is likely to be settled (for our moral sensibility, anyway) by reference to the relevant sorts of ethical analysis and not a little reflection on the nature of architecture and its practice. Is architectural history truly one long pattern of aesthetic theft? If it is, would that warrant recidivism? What features of architecture would lend itself to such borrowing, and might those features lead us to justify it? What are the relevant obligations in this context of one architect to another, to the profession and to architectural history? We are quickly led far afield from purely legal considerations, into uncharted territory we can recognise as belonging to philosophical ethics and even metaphysics. Let us venture forth, philosophers, architects, and other interested parties, surveying and positional instruments in hand. It is not the sturdy moral compass of the true believer that will guide us here, but the enhanced vision and polished lenses of rigorous analysis and argumentation.

References

American Institute of Architects. 'Code of Ethics and Professional Conduct'. Online. http://www.e-architect.com/institute/codeethics.asp

Cushman, R.F., Hedemann, G.C. (eds) (1995) *Architect and Engineer Liability: Claims against Design Professionals (Construction Law Library)*, 2nd edn. New York: Wiley Law.

Frampton, K. (1983) 'Towards a Critical Regionalism: Six Points for an Architecture of Resistance', in H. Foster (ed.) *The Anti-Aesthetic*, Port Townsend,WA: Bay Press.

Greenstreet, R. (1989) 'Law: Architectural Ethics', *Progressive Architecture* 70(7): 43, 46, 48.

Greenstreet, R. (1998) 'The Case for Copyright', *AIArchitect*, March. Online. http://www.e-architect.com/news/aiarchitect/mar98/copyright.asp

Harries, K. (1997) *The Ethical Functions of Architecture*, Cambridge, MA: MIT Press.

National Council of Architectural Registration Boards. 'Rules of Conduct'. Online. http://www.ncarb.org

Royal Institute of British Architects. 'Code of Professional Conduct'. Online. http://www.riba.org/riba/copc01.htm

Sweet, J. (1994) *Legal Aspects of Architecture, Engineering and the Construction Process*, 5th edn, St. Paul, MN: West Pub. Co.

14

THE TAJ MAHAL AND THE SPIDER'S WEB

Keekok Lee

Introduction

The Guardian recently carried (spring 1999) an article about the highlights of twentieth-century architecture. First, it drew attention to a North American list of such items, criticising those who compiled it for celebrating the 'big and the spectacular', gigantic constructions, such as the Hoover Dam, being prominent. By way of contrast, the writer of the article drew up an alternative list (more British or perhaps 'European' in character) in which Lubetkin's penguin pool in London Zoo and Frank Lloyd Wright's *Fallingwater* featured. However, what is germane to the preoccupation of this chapter is the surprising inclusion of the spider's web. Journalistic tricks of attention-grabbing apart, its mention surely stands out like a sore thumb and is distinctly the 'odd item out.' Why it is odd, in philosophical terms, is precisely what this chapter sets out to explore and clarify.

The artefactual and the natural

One red herring must first be got out of the way. This chapter does not deny that the spider's web is a construction in the same way as the Taj Mahal or *Fallingwater* is a construction. The former is built by the spider, the latter by humans. If the term 'artefact' is to be used to refer to constructions, then there is a legitimate sense in which both the web and The Taj Mahal are 'artefacts'– their difference would then be marked by calling the one 'spider artefact' and the other 'human artefact.' However, philosophical issues and problems are not, and should not hang upon, purely verbal matters. To concede that both may be called 'artefacts' is not to concede that there are no deep philosophical differences between them. There is one crucial difference; and to mark it, the word 'artefact' will be defined in this chapter in such a way as to refer only to the category identified just now as 'human artefacts', and to exclude the category 'spider artefacts.' In the terminology proposed here, the former category is called 'the artefactual' and the latter category which stands duty for all 'non-human artefacts' (in the sense first alluded to) will now be part of what is termed 'the natural.'[1]

It will be obvious as the chapter proceeds why this terminology is proposed, and why the proposal may not be dismissed as being arbitrary. But for the moment, let us observe that there is a legitimate distinction to be made between the built environment on the one hand and the 'non-built' or 'natural' environment on the other. The built environment refers to that which is constituted by human artefacts, of which architecture (that is, buildings) is a prime exemplar. However, other obvious artefacts include works of fine art such as the *Mona Lisa* or more mundane objects such as tables, chairs, items of clothing, and machines like cars and computers. But it can also be used even more widely, as we shall see, to include any object fabricated by humans, not necessarily one which is fashioned out of inert or dead matter, such as a field of so-called high-yield wheat, which may be said to belong to the domain of the artefactual.

The strategy of this chapter lies in defining 'the natural' as the foil of 'the artefactual.' In giving a philosophical account of the notion of artefact and (thereby of the artefactual), it would also then have succeeded in giving an account (albeit not the fullest) of the notion of the natural.[2]

Defining 'artefact'

The most succinct definition of 'artefact' which one can give is to say that an artefact is the material embodiment of human intentionality. In other words, not all expressions of human intentionality necessarily involve the production of artefacts. For instance, while numbers and the rules of adding and subtracting are deliberately drawn up by humans for the purpose of calculation and computation, they are themselves not artefacts, although they may lead to the production of artefacts such as the abacus or the electronic calculator. A good many intentionally executed activities like singing and dancing involve no artefacts. In other words, techniques themselves are to be distinguished from the things which materially embody them; some, though not all, techniques lead to artefacts. Singing requires only the techniques of using voice, lungs and control of other related parts of the body; a recorded performance of a song, on the other hand, either as a vinyl record, a tape or a CD disc, is an artefact whose production in turn involves further artefacts like microphone and other machines.

On this definition, an artefact is a sub-class of human intentionality.[3] Its emphasis on the characteristic of material embodiment means that in almost all, if not all instances, artefacts are technological products. In the dim historical past, the technology involved would be very minimal and primitive, so to speak – an adze would require some chipping and shaping, whereas a stealth-bomber would embody the latest in scientific technology. In the past, indeed up to the mid-nineteenth century, the technology generally used in manufacturing artefacts is craft-based rather than science-induced. However, since then, the technology which is employed, and considered to be the most sophisticated, advanced and the most powerful, is generated by fundamental theoretical discoveries in science; witness the difference between the steam engine and the space ship, or that between the land races and genetically modified crops.

Aristotle's four causes

Another way of giving a philosophical account of the notion of artefact is to lean on Aristotle's four causes. In Aristotle's philosophy, the four causes provide an explanatory schema not only to cover all phenomena, but are also meant to be a complete explanation of a phenomenon or event. However, this chapter is not meant to be an application of Aristotelian philosophy as such; much more modestly, it is merely an attempt to borrow the four causes in a very limited fashion to cast light on the notion of artefact as understood in this context.

The four causes are: *material*, *efficient*, *formal* and *final*. Put simplistically, the material refers to the matter out of which the artefact is made, the efficient to the agent which makes or causes the artefact to be made, the formal to the plan or blueprint (either expressed on writing material or carried in the head) of what is intended to be constructed, the final to the reason which accounts for why the artefact is built.

In the case of an artefact (as Aristotle himself noted), the four causes can be separated out, not merely intellectually, but also physically and, in principle, can be assigned to four separately identified agencies or sources. The Taj Mahal was (is) made of marble. Builders or artisans were, either directly or indirectly, employed by Shah Jahan to construct the building. Its commissioned architect(s) drew up plans (ultimately endorsed by Shah Jahan, presumably). Shah Jahan had a very special reason for wanting such a monument to be erected; it was to commemorate his beloved wife. In other words, in trying to understand the artefact, the Taj Mahal, once one has gone through its four causes, one would have understood all that could ever be understood about it. The most complete explanation would have been given of it; in theory, one would have come to know all there was (is) to be known about it.

Note that in this example of the Taj Mahal, out of the four causes, three of them involved human agencies and their intentionalities. However, its material cause, namely, marble, appears to have nothing to do with human agency: marble is a 'natural kind', the product of geological processes in Earth's long historical past before the evolution of humans. Of course, in order to build the Taj Mahal, workmen had to quarry the marble, cut and shape the blocks. But the marble's existence itself, with the kind of material structure it possesses, has nothing to do with human agency and its intentionality. Does it follow then that the matter, through which humans express and in which they embed their intentionality, is itself necessarily beyond human manipulation and fabrication?

To answer this question, one needs to go back to an earlier section (p. 185), which very briefly refers to the history of technology. There we observed that technology is dynamic and changes in the light of many factors, a very important one since the mid-nineteenth century being the role played by basic theoretical scientific discoveries in technological innovations. This means that for more than 150 years, the matter out of which artefacts could be made did not need to belong to natural kinds, for example marble or wood. We can, for instance, also make them out of plastic, a substance not found in Nature, though manufactured from oil which is itself a natural kind. This we can do, thanks to the understanding given to us by basic sciences like that of organic chemistry. We have long ceased to build out of stone or wood only; bricks, and later concrete, have become 'normal' building material. As the twenty-first century dawns, other artefactual material will come into use, not only for construction of buildings but also in nearly all, if not all, areas of manufacture.[4]

This shows that it is a matter of contingency, not of necessity, that the material cause of artefacts should be 'natural kinds'. It follows then that, in increasingly numerous instances, all the four causes today in practice, and not merely in principle, can be assigned to human agency and its intentionality. On this account, it also follows that any object, whose four or at least three causes (the latter covers those instances where the material cause belongs to a natural kind) can be thus traced, would qualify to be an artefact. According to this definition, the artefactual can be abiotic (marble or plutonium), exbiotic (wood or skin) or biotic (traditionally bred plants and animals or genetically modified ones).

The built environment in the narrowest understanding of that term, which primarily includes constructions, whether houses or dams, relies on the abiotic or exbiotic. In its slightly broader meaning the built environment, which includes tables, shoes and machine-artefacts like computers and bicycles, relies also on the abiotic and the exbiotic. But in its broadest meaning, it includes the pets we keep, the domesticated animals we rear, the domesticated crops we grow, of which the latest model is the so-called genetically engineered or modified organisms, not excluding those we cultivate in vats. In this widest sense, the built environment coincides with the domain of the artefactual.

Ontological difference between the built environment and the natural environment

In the light of the above account, we can now further clarify the ontological difference between the artefactual and the natural. The artefactual is that domain of entities which has come into existence, continues to exist and will eventually go out of existence as the result of deliberate human design and intention. Its ontological foil is the domain of the natural, consisting of those entities and their processes which have come into existence, continue to exist and will eventually go out of existence entirely independently of deliberate human design and intention.

A world without humans and their intentions and purposes is a world without the artefactual. Without humans, there would be no Taj Mahal, no Hoover Dam, no *Fallingwater*, but there would be spider webs and plover nests. In a world before humankind evolved, spiders existed and spun their webs. In a world to come, when perhaps we humans have become extinct, it is conceivable that spiders would continue to exist and would continue to spin their webs. This then explains why the spider's web is the 'odd item out' in the list of constructions mentioned right at the beginning of this chapter. The spider's web and architectural artefacts are two different types of being; they belong to two different and distinct ontological categories.

To prevent misunderstanding, let me clarify one point. When it is held that artefacts come into existence, continue to exist and will eventually go out of existence at human behest and intervention, this should not be interpreted to deny two things: (1) that artefacts eventually decay and crumble away into dust, and (2) that they may alter in the purpose with which they are regarded. In addressing the first point, one must acknowledge that ultimately all objects, whether natural or artefactual in origin, would disintegrate, becoming in the end mere atoms of carbon, hydrogen, and so on. No matter how much care and attention we humans lavish upon a particular artefact, we can only slow down the processes of disintegration, not transcend them. However, the point to emphasise in the light of this is that, unless we intervene to retard the processes of decay and disintegration, those processes will inexorably occur. The Taj Mahal today is threatened by pollutants in the air, and unless we come up with a technological device to protect its fabric, the monument will, sooner rather than later, disintegrate. We may not be able to intervene to save it as, in reality, no effective technological fix may be found, or that even if such device exists, it would be too expensive to use it.

Second, the original purpose (final cause) of the artefact may have long gone, but contemporary humans can reinvest it with a new purpose. Shah Jahan died and so have any of his and his wife's descendants (assuming this to be correct). However, we (not only Indians) cherish the monument and sustain it, for a very different reason, as a part of world (not merely Indian) heritage, as an expression of human artistic and artisan creativity. The artefact continues to enrich our lives in spite of the demise of the purpose for which it was originally constructed.

Applying the last person argument

The ontological difference between the built environment and the natural environment may be further brought out by a thought experiment, the so-called last person argument. Imagine that you are the last person on Earth, and after your death, no other being with the equivalent of human consciousness would ever appear. The technology is available for a device to go off, when you have breathed your last, which would destroy Earth and all the natural items on it. Are you morally permitted to press that destructive button? If the answer is no, then it is because the natural domain has a value which is based on its distinctive ontological status, namely that its history and its future are independent of human history and its future. Before the first human ever appeared and after the last human has gone, Nature existed and would continue to exist. Natural entities and their processes have their own trajectories; some entities had come and gone long ago, with others taking their place. However, they did so at their own pace and their successors would continue to do so after *Homo sapiens* became extinct. That is why we have no moral right to take them all with us when we go.

Now ask the same question but with regard to artefacts: should you programme that button to destroy them all after your own demise? Are you morally permitted to do so? The answer to both questions would be 'yes,' even though the items might include the Taj Mahal, Chartres Cathedral, the *Mona Lisa* and so much more of great artistic beauty.[5] This is because artefacts have come into existence entirely to serve human ends and purposes; in a world without humans, the ends they have been designed to serve would *ipso facto* have also disappeared. In a world minus humans, the Taj Mahal is but a pile of inert matter. The trees which would eventually take root in its fabric and the animals, large and small, which would find niches in it could and would have no grasp of its meaning and significance. To destroy it would not then amount to an act of vandalism, as its value is only intelligible within a human context. Humans alone, while creating their handiwork, endow it with meaning. In the absence of humans, the preservation of artefacts would be empirically impossible as well as philosophically unintelligible. Whether one destroys them in one fell swoop or simply lets natural decay take over is of no moral or philosophical relevance.

Appreciating the Taj Mahal and appreciating the spider's web

The *Mona Lisa* or the *Piéta* might be exquisitely beautiful as works of art, but they are artefacts in the same way that mundane, purely functional and utilitarian objects like a chipboard table and a ballpoint pen are artefacts. While no one is passionate about preserving chipboard tables and ballpoint pens (a single item preserved in a museum of cultural objects would suffice), many are passionate about preserving the works of outstanding artists like Leonardo da Vinci and Michelangelo. And they would be right to do so. If their works express beauty (or at least one canon of beauty), they ought to be preserved, as they embody quintessentially a particular form of human creativity. Without going into the philosophy of aesthetics, one could say that on a world heritage list of objects to be preserved, one could find exemplars of exceptional aesthetic quality in every human culture, even though they belong to very different artistic traditions.

Preservation of artistic artefacts entails maintaining them as near as it is (technologically, economically and culturally) possible in the state and condition deemed to manifest their aesthetic perfection.[6] Any change from such a state is deemed to be a change for the worse and must, therefore, be arrested. Cherishing them means precisely this.

Imagine for a moment, transposing such an ideal from culture to Nature. Natural landscapes are often likened to works of art: there is beauty, after all, to be found in both art and Nature. However, appreciating Nature, like appreciating art, comes in different cultural packages at different periods of history. At one period, a particular type of landscape might be regarded as frightening, as was the landscape of the Lake District and the Peak District in the seventeenth century. The drivers of coaches passing through such areas used to pull down the blinds so that their passengers would not be frightened by the scenery outside the windows.

But after the Romantic Movement, such landscapes have come to be regarded even as picturesque, and many derive pleasure from driving through them, while fewer in number get satisfaction walking in them. They are now part of English heritage.

Although it is true that such landscapes are heavily humanised in many ways, it does not, however, undermine the fact that humans have not been responsible for their general geological structures and forms (barring the flooding of a valley or two, turning them into reservoirs). These are not the work of humans but of natural forces in Earth's geological past. Today, we happen to find some of these forms beautiful and emotionally gratifying. This could then make some people assume an analogy between beauty found in Nature and beauty found in works of art. As a result of this unthinking assumption, those who own (in part or in whole) or manage such landscapes are tempted also uncritically to assume that there is a similar duty to preserve such beauty in Nature for the enjoyment of posterity in the same way that museums of fine art and custodians of other art works have a duty to preserve the objects under their care for the appreciation of generations to come. One must cherish both.

But we have already seen what cherishing artistic artefacts entails. It means arresting change or deviation from the state of their perfection, whatever that state might be deemed to be. Were the roof of Chartres Cathedral to leak, we must repair it with the same sort of material as the damaged parts and using the same techniques (or as nearly the same as is possible). Analogously if Yew Tree Tarn (a tarn in the Lake District) were to start leaking, then too one must repair the leak, to prevent it from drying out altogether, that is to say, to arrest or at least retard the processes which would stop it eventually being a tarn.[7] Part of the charm of the Lake District is precisely to stumble across tarns while rambling on the fells. The enjoyment and the satisfaction would be diminished if one were to stumble upon a hole in the ground with some stones at the bottom of it, or a bog.

However, according to the perspective pursued by this chapter, tempting though this strategy might be, it would be philosophically wrong to follow it. Nature is not static but dynamic. Its forces and processes are continuously at work transforming whatever is to become something else. In terms of human time, a mountain is permanent, but in terms of geological time, it is not. Of all the geological forms, lakes (and tarns) are said to be the most ephemeral. Lakes, the moment they come into existence, start changing in the direction of being, perhaps, first a marsh, then a meadow and eventually even a forest. Coastlines, too, in geological terms, do not endure very long. The Cornish coastline is not only spectacularly beautiful in parts, but also richly endowed in terms of romance. Yet it is undoubtedly eroding away before our very eyes. If we had the technology to do so, should we shore it up to arrest its erosion? If coastlines are our artefacts, 'yes', but 'no' if they are not. Nature and artefacts do not belong to the same ontological category, although it is obviously the case that there is plenty we find beautiful in both. Natural items (and their processes) have come into existence, continue to exist and will go out of existence independently of us. Artefacts, however, are entities which we have consciously and deliberately chosen to bring into existence and which we choose in some cases to maintain, in order to retard the processes of change leading to decay.[8] The Taj Mahal is indeed beautiful and fragile in this sense, and hence requires protection; the spider's web is beautiful, too, but the transience of its beauty is part of what is meant by saying that it belongs to the domain of the natural, not that of the artefactual.

Notes

1 This usage is ultimately dependent on retaining the distinction between 'Nature', on the one hand, and 'human' on the other. However, I do not intend the distinction to be a dualistic one; it is meant, instead, as 'ontological dyadism'; see Lee (1999).

2 For a full account of both categories – the artefactual and the natural – see Lee (1999).

3 For an account which equates 'artefact' with all expressions of human intentionality, including beliefs, see below:

By an 'artifact' I mean here an object which has been intentionally made or produced for a certain purpose. According to this characterisation, an artifact necessarily has a maker or an author, or several authors, who are responsible for its existence... Artifacts are products of <u>intentional making</u>. Human activities produce innumerable new objects which are entirely unintentional (or unintended); such objects and materials are not artifacts in the strict sense of the word. When a person intends to make an object, the content of the intention is not the object itself, but rather some description of an object; the agent intends to make an object of a certain kind or type. Thus what I want to suggest is that artifacts in the strict sense can be distinguished from other products of human activity in the same way as acts are distinguished from other movements of the body; a movement is an action only if it is intentional under some description (Davidson 1980: 43–61), and I take an object to be an artifact in the strict sense of the word only if it is intentionally produced by an agent under some description of the object. The intention 'ties' to the object a number of concepts or predicates which define its intended properties. These properties constitute the <u>intended character</u> of the object. I shall denote the intended character of an object <u>o</u> by '<u>IC(o)</u>'. Thus an object <u>o</u> is a proper artifact only if it satisfies the following

Dependence Condition: ... The existence and some of the properties of <u>o</u> depend on an agent's (or author's) intention to make an object of kind <u>IC(o)</u>.

(Hilpinen 1995: 138–39)

My account of the notion is, therefore, not as wide as Hilpinen's as I have defined it in terms of the material embodiment of human intentionality, the operative word being 'material.'

4 See Ball (1998); also Manzini (1989).

5 Strictly speaking, this applies only to the built environment in the first two narrower senses of the term. In the largest sense, which includes biotic artefacts such as domesticated plants and animals, one could make a case for saving them from such destruction. This is because these organisms, though the products of human design, nevertheless, possess mechanisms which will permit them to survive when humans are gone. Of course, many would die, in any case, without human maintenance; but of those which survive, they could then live lives which in the long run render them no longer the bearers of human intentionality, even if their origin might have been anthropogenically designed and caused.

6 The word 'deemed' here is critical as there are very different conceptions of what that state or condition of artistic perfection is – in art restoration, some scholars argue that the original vibrancy of the colours of a mural be respected, others that the quieter tones of faded colours, with which contemporary viewers are familiar and have long grown to love, have greater priority in the appreciation of its aesthetic perfection.

7 Yew Tree Tarn is in that part of the Lake District owned by the National Trust, which did repair it a few years ago. For a more detailed discussion of this case and the philosophical issues raised by it, see Lee (1995: 213–25).

8 Of course, we have also chosen, in recent times, to design death-dates into most of our artefacts – built-in obsolence and 'death' is a critical strategy in an economic system which holds exponential rate of growth as axiomatic to its success.

References

Ball, P. (1998) *Made to Measure: New Materials for the 21st Century*, Princeton: Princeton University Press.

Hilpinen, R. (1995) 'Belief Systems as Artifacts', *Monist* 28.

Lee, K. (1995) 'Beauty For Ever?' *Environmental Values* 4: 213–25.

Lee, K. (1999) *The Natural and the Artefactual: The Implications of Deep Science and Deep Technology for Environmental Philosophy*, Lanham: Lexington Books.

Manzini, E. (1989) *The Materials of Invention*, Cambridge, MA: The MIT Press.

15

ETHICAL ARGUMENTS ABOUT THE AESTHETICS OF ARCHITECTURE

Nigel Taylor

...there is not a building that I know of, lately raised, wherein it is not sufficiently evident that neither the architect nor builder has done his best. It is the especial character of modern work...Ours has as constantly the look of money's worth, of a stopping short wherever and whenever we can, of a lazy compliance with low conditions ...

(John Ruskin 1849: 37)

...in the last resort, great art will be distinguished from that which is merely aesthetically clever by a nobility that, in the final analysis, is moral; or, rather, the nobility in life which we call 'moral' is itself aesthetic... There is, in fact, a true, not a false, analogy between ethical and aesthetic values: the correspondence between them may even amount to an identity. The 'dignity' of architecture is the same as the dignity we recognise in character. Thus, when once we have discerned it aesthetically in architecture, there may arise in the mind its moral echo.

(Geoffrey Scott 1914: 161–2)

Introduction: ethics, aesthetics and architectural criticism

Are there any ethical grounds for praising, or criticising, the aesthetic content of buildings? This is the question examined in this chapter. I emphasise that I am concerned here only with ethical arguments about the *aesthetics* of architecture. There are of course ethical arguments about other, non-aesthetic aspects of building, such as the economic and social processes of producing buildings, what kinds of buildings get built and who for, the ecological impact of buildings (e.g. in terms of their use of materials, their heating and energy consumption), and so on. However, although the answers given to these ethical questions may affect the form, and hence the aesthetic content of buildings, in this chapter I am concerned only with whether the aesthetic content of buildings *in itself* can be a legitimate matter of moral praise or criticism.[1]

At first blush, the answer to my question might seem obviously 'yes', at least with respect to some buildings. Consider, for example, Auschwitz. As Jan van Pelt and Dwork (1996) remind us, some people designed the buildings of Auschwitz concentration camp. Surely, then, *these* buildings were ethically wrong.

Yet this extreme and apparently 'obvious' case highlights the difficulty of directing ethical criticisms at the *aesthetic form* of buildings. There are two problems. First, are we to blame the *buildings* of Auschwitz for the awful things that went on in and around them? Surely such criticism misses its proper target; the moral criticism should rather be directed at the people who organised and carried out the mass slaughter at Auschwitz. In other words, *moral* criticism presupposes moral agency, and so is only appropriately applied to *people* and their *actions*, not to inanimate objects, such as buildings. To be sure, ethical criticism of the relevant people might include those involved in designing the buildings of Auschwitz, but note again, the criticism is levelled at *those people*, not the buildings as such. As for the inanimate objects which buildings are, their moral innocence is shown by the fact that a building constructed for an evil purpose, such as a dungeon, might later be used for a good purpose, such as an exhibition space or a chapel, and vice versa. As Thomas Markus (1993: 25) wrote of Auschwitz: 'For all the world this looked like a pavilion hospital'. And indeed, it *could* have been: those self-same buildings could have been designed, or used, to treat the sick.

Second, even if we were morally to object to the very existence of a certain type of building because of its *purpose or function*, such as a slaughter-house, we might yet find such a building aesthetically pleasing in its *physical form*, just as we might acknowledge that an executioner's axe or a samurai warrior's sword can be beautiful objects. Correspondingly, there can be buildings which house activities we morally approve of (e.g. a hospital or a school) but whose form we find aesthetically objectionable. So even in cases where we feel justified in morally criticising a *building*, we need to distinguish criticism of the building because of its *use* from criticism because of its aesthetic content or *form*.

To be sure, if we know that a building whose form we enjoy has been used for an ethically objectionable use, then this is bound to colour the way we see that building. Nevertheless, the distinction just made can still hold; even though we feel sombre when looking at a building constructed or used for morally objectionable purposes, we *may* still acknowledge that the form of such a building is aesthetically pleasing. Consider, for example, the Parthenon in Athens. Without knowing anything of its history we may find this building beautiful. Now imagine that sometime later we learn that this temple was built for ritual slaughter. Would we now suddenly say, *of its aesthetic appearance*, that it is morally bad, or that its *style* is morally wrong? Surely not. Whilst disapproving of its original purpose we would more likely, and quite reasonably, continue to regard the building as a beautiful object.[2]

Is there, then, no place for moral criticism of *built form*, as distinct from the *purposes* of some buildings?

From Pugin and Ruskin in the nineteenth century, through the whole period of architectural modernism in the twentieth century, there has been a recurrent theme of ethical criticism in architecture. Certain built forms have therefore been praised, or criticised, according to whether or not they have embodied certain favoured moral principles. In this chapter (see pp. 195–201), I shall re-examine some of these ethical arguments about the aesthetic content of built form. I shall distinguish and assess three important ethical arguments, which have been widely deployed over the past 150 years, and I shall argue that none of them provides compelling reasons for favouring, or criticising, particular aesthetic forms or styles of building.

Even if this analysis of 'modern' ethical criticism in architecture is accepted, there may of course be other, more persuasive arguments that would enable us to appraise the aesthetic content of buildings from an ethical point of view. And in fact, after disposing of the three arguments just mentioned, I shall outline another (see pp. 201–205), fourth kind of ethical criticism of architectural aesthetics which, I claim, is justified. This argument concerns the degree to which a building has been designed with due aesthetic attentiveness or 'care', both as a whole (including its relation to its environmental context) and in detail. Something like this was, I think, what Ruskin was getting at in the first quotation at the head of this chapter, and so although I shall reject most aspects of Ruskin's ethical criticism of architecture, I shall at least defend this aspect of his criticism.

Three ethical criticisms of the aesthetics of architecture

First, I will discuss, and criticise, three kinds of ethical criticism of built form which have been deployed by some architectural theorists over the past 150 years. The three arguments I examine are, first, those which support or criticise architectural forms in terms of their structural *'honesty'*; second, those which deploy ethical reasons for favouring (or criticising) a particular aesthetic *style*; and, third, arguments which evaluate buildings in terms of whether they conform to certain allegedly desirable or 'progressive' tendencies in a given culture or period (so-called *'spirit of the age'* arguments). I shall claim that none of these arguments succeeds, and so, like Scott (1914), I shall term each an ethical *fallacy*.

Ethical fallacy I: honesty and deceit in building

Pugin (1841) and Ruskin (1849) were key figures in initiating ethical criticism in relation to architecture, and central to their criticism was the question of whether the form of buildings was 'true' or 'honest'. As Ruskin put it:

> We may not be able to command good, or beautiful, or inventive, architecture; but we can command an honest architecture: the meagreness of poverty may be pardoned, the sternness of utility respected; but what is there but scorn for the meanness of deception?
> (Ruskin 1849: 61)

Ruskin distinguished three kinds of architectural deceits: first, 'structural deceits', where there is in the design of the building 'a mode of support other than the true one' (ibid.: 63); second, 'surface deceits' where the treatment of a surface is such that it induces 'the supposition of some form of material which does not actually exist; as commonly in the painting of wood to represent marble, or in the painting of ornaments in deceptive relief, etc.' (ibid.: 80); and third, 'operative deceits', by which Ruskin meant 'the substitution of cast or machine work for that of the hand' (ibid.: 94).

Interestingly, Ruskin acknowledges the difficulty of deploying each of these criticisms, so that his treatment of each is correspondingly complex and subtle (critics might say laboured and unconvincing). As he candidly admitted with regard to all of his 'deceits':

> there are certain degrees of them, which, owing to their frequent usage, or to other causes, have so far lost the nature of deceit as to be admissible... So that there arise, in the application of the strict rules of right, many exceptions and niceties of conscience.
> (Ruskin 1849: 62)

Thus in discussing structural deceits, although Ruskin held 'that building will generally be the noblest, which to an intelligent eye reveals the great secrets of its structure...' he allows that the 'architect is not *bound* to exhibit structure; nor are we to complain of him for concealing it, any more than we should regret that the outer surfaces of the human frame conceal much of its anatomy'(ibid.: 63). It turns out, then, that the 'rules of right' are not *'strict'* after all. And this becomes a problem for the kind of argument which Ruskin wants to sustain. For however sensitive his own observations on the rightness of buildings may be, and however much we may agree with his judgements, without some clear rules or criteria for distinguishing right from wrong concealments of structure or surface, Ruskin's judgements become, from some other people's point of view, arbitrary, causing his ethical criticism of architectural deceits to disintegrate.

Geoffrey Scott was clear about this. He undercut Ruskin's moral argument by drawing attention to the fact that some architectural deceits are deliberately devised in order to achieve some satisfactory aesthetic effect, and that such devices can be to the positive good of the overall design. He gives the following example:

> I am probably *not* persuaded into believing that the false window of a Renaissance front is a real one, and the more familiar I am with Renaissance architecture, the less likely am I to believe it; but neither do I wish to believe it, nor does it matter to me if, by chance, I am persuaded. I want the window for the sake of the balance which it can give to the design.
>
> (Scott 1914: 152–3).

The example is a significant one because, as Scott goes on to point out, even if we accept that it is a morally good principle to avoid deceiving the observer, sometimes (as the above example shows) there can be a conflict between this moral value and an aesthetic value, and in such circumstances why should this moral value take precedence? As Scott observes of the Renaissance architects who occasionally put in false windows: '...these architects placed aesthetic values in the scale of their importance, and where economic and other barriers stood in their way, preferred at least, and foremost, to indicate *design'* (ibid.: 153–4).

One of the favourite targets of critics such as Ruskin was baroque architecture, because of its ostentatious forms and ornaments. But Scott presses home his argument by pointing out that all art, including the art of architecture, involves the creation of deliberate aesthetic effects which are 'deceitful', so that, on this basis, all styles, not just the baroque, would come under Ruskin's moral axe:

An impartial spectator who found so much contrived – and so ingenuously – for his delight would, on taking thought, no more complain of all these substitutions – these false perspectives and painted shadows – than grow indignant because, in the Greek cornice, he is shown false eggs and darts. For this is no mere flippancy. Imitation runs through all art; and Plato was more logical who rejected art, on this account, altogether, than those critics who draw a line at the baroque.

(Scott 1914: 154)

Ethical fallacy II: the moral superiority of a particular style

Aside from questions of 'honesty' in building, Pugin and Ruskin also argued that certain kinds of architectural *styles* were morally superior. In particular, both argued that the gothic style was morally supreme. For Pugin, this moral accolade was granted because he was an ardent (Catholic) Christian, and he held (with peculiar logic) that gothic architecture was the most 'Christian' architecture. Ruskin favoured the gothic style because its forms mirrored the organic forms of Nature. Here is Ruskin using this argument to praise the gothic, whilst criticising Doric classicism:

...all beautiful lines are adaptations of those which are commonest in external creation; ...man cannot advance in the invention of beauty, without directly imitating natural form. Thus, in the Doric temple the triglyph and cornice are unimitative;... No one would call these members beautiful... The cylindrical pillar is always beautiful, for God has so moulded the stem of every tree that is pleasant to the eyes. The pointed arch is beautiful; it is the termination of every leaf... It will evidently follow, upon our application of this test of natural resemblance, that we shall at once conclude that all perfectly beautiful forms must be composed of curves; since there is hardly any common natural form in which it is possible to discover a straight line...forms which are *not* taken from natural objects *must* be ugly.

(Ruskin 1849: 188–9, 195, 190)

As Scott observed, the nineteenth-century preference for natural forms, and hence for the gothic, was partly inspired by literary (and especially poetic) romanticism. But he also emphasises how, in Ruskin, this preference for natural form was also moral:

To be 'natural' was no longer a point merely of poetic charm – it was a point of sanctity. With Ruskin…the argument from Nature is always final… On the one side was Nature: the curves of the waves, the line of the unfolding leaf, the pattern of the crystal… On the other stood the principles of Palladio, and all the pedantry of rule and measure, made barren by conscious intellect. The choice between them was a moral choice…

(Scott 1914: 76, 78)

The problem with Ruskin's argument is simple; it is that his assertions that 'man cannot advance in the invention of beauty, without directly imitating natural form', so that 'we shall at once conclude that all perfectly beautiful forms must be composed of curves' are simply disputed by those who find beauty in (say) the formal geometry of classical architecture (see Tzonis and Lefaivre 1986: Part 1). In short, the idea that a particular aesthetic style (be it gothic, classical or any other) is *morally* superior to other styles is unsustainable. By all means we may engage in arguments about the relative aesthetic merits of different styles. But these arguments are precisely that: they are solely *aesthetic* arguments, not moral ones. Accordingly, what persuades us in these instances is not some higher moral imperative, but simply (though importantly) a particular aesthetic viewpoint and sensibility.

Ethical fallacy III: historicist 'Spirit of the Age' arguments

Both the foregoing moral arguments about architecture seek to find some moral justification for particular architectural forms based on arguments about architectural form: its revealed structure in the case of the first argument, and its style in the case of the second. However, a third kind of moral argument about architectural form derives from considerations separate from matters of architectural form itself, such as some more general moral or political argument.

An example of this kind of argument is a 'historicist' argument which holds that buildings should be designed out of certain materials, or have a certain form, because this reflects the emergent technology of a particular period in a society's history. This argument was much used by propagandists of the modern movement in architecture in the first half of the twentieth century, who claimed that the architecture of 'the modern age' should be constructed from contemporary industrial materials, such as iron and steel, plate glass and reinforced concrete, rather than traditional building materials, such as stone and brick. In the same vein, certain building forms were justified because they reflected contemporary construction technology and/or production methods, e.g. the skyscraper, forms constructed from prefabricated units, etc. In either case, buildings so designed and constructed were praised because they were 'progressive' in reflecting and expressing the culture or technology of the age in which they were built.[3]

Watkin (1977) calls this kind of justification for certain architectural forms a 'spirit of the age' argument. It suggests that, whether or not we find the resultant buildings aesthetically pleasing, we should endorse them because they reflect the contemporary age; as Watkin puts it, such buildings 'have an authority and an inevitability which it would be improper to question' (ibid., p. 6). If we unpick the logical structure of this argument, we can state the argument as follows:

1 *Premise.* There is, in any given period of history (such as our own time), a distinctive technology and culture.
2 *Inference.* Therefore, buildings should be designed and built in a way and in materials which use and express this technology and culture.

Thus stated, we can see clearly the pitfalls of this argument. For a start, the premise itself is open to dispute. For, with the exception of some highly stable, pre-modern cultures, it is both conceptually and empirically difficult (and therefore controversial) to identify what is most characteristic of a particular age or culture. This is especially so in relation to Europe and North America over the last 150 years, where the pace of technological and social change has been such as to make it especially difficult, at any one time, to pin down what is the distinctive or dominant 'spirit of the age' (unless of course one identifies it with change itself, as some writers have done,[4] in which case no one style would be sanctioned anyway). Claims about what constitutes the 'spirit' of a given age or culture are therefore contestable, from which it follows that any conclusions about what architectural forms are appropriate to a certain age are correspondingly contestable.

But even if we could, for a certain period or culture, identify what is distinctive and dominant about it, the inference that we should make buildings which reflect this period or culture is itself contestable. Suppose, for example, that the dominant spirit of the age were a Nazi one. Most people would say we should resist this spirit and so design buildings which *challenge*, rather than conform to it. In short, we still require an independent argument for accepting that we should, morally, behave (and build) in accordance with the spirit of a given age or culture.

A variant on the spirit of the age argument is that which Watkin

(1977: 8) calls a 'rationalist' argument, which claims that certain building forms or styles are more rational than others, and so, on the assumption that we wish not to be irrational, we ought to adopt these building forms. Again, such an argument was much used by early modernist architectural theorists. Thus a 'purely functional' architecture (with its bare, undecorated forms) was sometimes said to be more 'rational' than architectural forms which contained 'unnecessary' stylisation or ornamentation. As Adolf Loos wrote, combining this argument with the historicist 'spirit of the age' argument discussed above: 'The evolution of culture is synonymous with the removal of ornament from utilitarian objects... We have outgrown ornament' (Loos 1908: 20). But this argument is no more convincing than the plain 'spirit of the age' argument considered above. For it presumes that only certain architectural forms are rational, without giving us any reasons why this is so (and giving reasons is the mark of rationality). It abstracts from Vitruvius' three conditions of good architecture of 'commodity, firmness and delight' only the condition of 'commodity' (i.e. function), and then privileges this with the accolade of rationality. But why the other two conditions, and notably the condition of 'delight', are not also 'rational', we are not told, nor is any argument supplied to persuade us.

Aesthetic attention to the whole of a building, and its details, as an ethic for architectural design

If the arguments in the previous section are accepted, then they close three avenues of ethical arguments about the aesthetic form of buildings, namely ethical arguments about the 'honesty' of built-form; ethical arguments which seek to privilege only a particular aesthetic style; and ethical arguments based on claims about the spirit of the age. Are there, then, *any* persuasive ethical grounds for criticising, or praising, the aesthetic content of a building? I think there can be, and in this concluding section I set out what I claim is a more tenable basis for the ethical criticism of the aesthetics of architecture.

My argument can be simply put by an imaginary case. Imagine a building, which we find aesthetically displeasing, and where this displeasure arises in large part because all kinds of features and details in the building appear to have been thrown together carelessly, without any thought or sensitivity. Imagine, too, that part of our displeasure arises because the building as a whole appears as if it has just been 'plonked' down on its site without any apparent consideration of how it fits on the site or relates to its surroundings. Such a building might literally offend us. It would offend us aesthetically, but, more than that, part of our offence might be ethical. Thus we might reasonably be angered or outraged, not just by the look of the thing, but also by the visible evidence that the person who designed it didn't show sufficient *care* about the aesthetic impact of his building. And this moral objection would be supported by the fact that buildings, unlike (say) paintings or books, are things we are compelled to look at, for architecture (unlike painting and literature) is necessarily a *public* art. Consequently, any lack of care given to the design of a building is also, in effect, a lack of care shown to the public who have to live with it. In these circumstances, therefore, our aesthetic criticism is not solely aesthetic, but also, at the same time, moral; it is an ethical criticism of the aesthetic content of the building.

It is important to be clear about what this argument is not claiming. Thus, I might happen not to like a particular kind of architectural style, and so experience aesthetic displeasure in seeing a building in that style. However, that *by itself* would offer no purchase to the above argument. For my ethical argument can only be sustained if it is evident from a building that it has not been designed with due care. And if, in spite of my dislike of a building's style, I cannot level this charge of carelessness against the building and its designer, then my argument has no foothold. This important point makes clear that it is no part of my argument to claim that a particular *aesthetic style* can be ethically good or bad. That was Ruskin's mistake, as we saw earlier. I may not like a particular style, but that is *solely* an aesthetic judgement, not a moral one.

To cite an actual example, I may not like Daniel Libeskind's angular 'deconstructionist' design for the extension of the Victoria and Albert museum in London; I may have preferred to see a design which deferred to the old 'V and A' in much the same way that Venturi's extension to the National Gallery defers to Wilkins's nineteenth-century building. Furthermore, I may feel strongly, and so get 'worked up' about this, campaigning vigorously to halt the Libeskind design in favour of one to my taste. Aesthetic feelings, after all, are *feelings*, and so potentially matters of passion, not just 'refined taste'. Nevertheless, however passionately held, the dispute at this level remains solely an aesthetic one, and it would be unreasonable of me to direct a *moral* criticism at the Libeskind design just because I object to its *style*. Thus, although my ethical argument concerns the aesthetic content of buildings, in this case my argument would only gain purchase if I could demonstrate that, in his design, Libeskind had simply not bothered. Of course, I might seek ethically to criticise Libeskind's extension because its jagged, jutting forms are not restful to my eye, or do not harmonise with the adjacent buildings, and I might say that this shows a lack of 'care' for the context of the extension. But this would be to use the notion of 'care' (and 'carelessness') in a different way from that endorsed by my argument. For the Libeskind extension does not exhibit a lack of care in the sense of its designer not having taken care in his design. On the contrary, it seems clear that Libeskind's slanting, jagged forms are deliberate and that this is something that Libeskind thought (and in *this* sense 'cared') about, and consciously designed. Whatever else it is, Libeskind's extension is not mere oversight or carelessness. Still, of course, my aesthetic objection may remain, and remain passionately, but not as a moral objection to its aesthetic form.

The moral argument advanced here, then, can only be directed at buildings, or parts of buildings, where there has clearly been a lack of careful aesthetic attention to the design. And there are two initial ways in which we might 'test' a building in relation to this argument. First, one can rigorously examine the parts and the details of a building, to see whether they have received careful attention, both in themselves and in relation to the building as a whole. Second, one can examine the building as a whole, including its appearance as a detail in the landscape or townscape (which any individual building is), in order to see whether there has been an equal attention to the design of the building in relation to its context.

Something like the argument put here has been advanced by Roger Scruton (1979). Acknowledging that our aesthetic experience of architecture is intellectual or cognitive, as well as sensory,[5] Scruton argues that there is a moral component to aesthetic experience and judgement, and that this reveals itself in judgements about what is 'appropriate' in building. As he puts it: 'central to aesthetic judgement [is] the notion of the appropriate... To build well is to find appropriate form' (ibid.: 225, 240). And further:

> the concept of the "appropriate" compels us to follow...the path from aesthetic taste to practical reason, from the sense of how things should look to the judgement of how they should be. The sense of the appropriate exists as an embodiment of moral thought...
>
> (Scruton 1979: 230)

Scruton explores this notion of moral appropriateness particularly in relation to the detailing of buildings, arguing that the possession of a 'sense of detail' is central to understanding what is appropriate in building design. He cites, as a vivid illustration of this, a 'simple' long brick wall by a railway in London (see Figure 15.1).

Though apparently a 'simple' structure (one of the most simple structures there are), Scruton shows that it is obvious that the wall has

Figure 15.1 Westbourne Park Villas, London, railway wall (reprinted with permission from Roger Scruton (1979) *The Aesthethics of Architecture*, London: Methuen & Co., p. 231).

been most carefully designed. Thus it swells out gently from its top to its base. The base rests on a projecting plinth, the top bricks of which are rounded to echo the swell of the wall. At the top, the wall is capped by a projecting cornice, and along the length of the wall are regularly spaced buttresses which stand out from the swelling surface of the wall like pilasters. Scruton goes on:

> The buttresses have strong quoins of hard-baked blue brick, matching the base, while the interstices are soft, matt, pink brick, scuffed and pitted with use. The wall follows the street, but in its own rhythm…attractively counterpointing the scarcely visible curvature of the pavement. The buttresses answer each other, each leading the eye onward between points of rest. The backward curve of the upper wall gives an effective emphasis to the "cornice" and enhances the apparent weight of the whole. The pleasure that is felt in passing such a wall is not simply the recognition of sound construction or workmanship. It is a sense of the natural fittingness of part to part, of an achieved articulation… The properly detailed wall has an accumulation of moral character…
>
> (Scruton 1979: 231–2)

Scruton shows here that this wall exhibits an attentiveness to detail, to the relationship of detail to the whole and to the wall's relationship with its immediate environment. In other words, Scruton shows that the anonymous designers of this wall *cared* about the wall they designed, in all its aspects. And 'caring' is a moral concept. To care like this for how something looks, and thereby for the people who will look at it, is to exhibit not just an aesthetic but also a moral concern. Or rather, it is to exhibit an aesthetic attentiveness which is itself moral.

Notes

1 Given this focus, I should clarify what I take the 'aesthetic' content of buildings to include for the purposes of this chapter. I assume here that the aesthetic content of a building is, primarily, its sensory content. Accordingly, our aesthetic experience of a building is, primarily, a sensory experience. Although this experience can include all the senses (we smell, touch and hear buildings), I shall be mostly concerned here with the visual appearance of buildings. I say that our aesthetic experience of buildings is only 'primarily' sensory because it is important to acknowledge that a *purely* sensory conception of aesthetic experience is too simple and crude. For as thinking creatures, we do not just innocently 'look' at buildings; we also judge and interpret them, and such judgement is essentially a cognitive activity. That is why buildings have 'meaning' for us, as well as sensory content. Indeed, I shall argue in the final section of this chapter that our cognitive experience of buildings provides one of the grounds for a legitimate kind of ethical evaluation of the aesthetic content of buildings.
2 The example here is not just hypothetical (Hersey 1988).
3 This argument was sometimes combined with the argument about 'honesty' considered earlier, so that modern buildings which revealed, rather than concealed, their steel-frame structure, or their concrete walling, would be praised because of this 'truthfulness to materials'.
4 Thus, Berman (1982: 15) writes: 'Modern environments and experiences cut across all boundaries of geography and ethnicity, of class and nationality, of religion and ideology: in this sense, modernity can be said to unite all mankind. But it is a paradoxical unity, a unity of disunity: it pours us into a maelstrom of perpetual disintegration and renewal, of struggle and contradiction, of ambiguity and anguish. To be modern is to be part of a universe in which, as Marx said, "all that is solid melts into air"'.
5 As Scruton says, understanding aesthetic experience is part of the philosophy of mind (see also note 1 above).

References

Berman, M. (1982) *All That is Solid Melts into Air: The Experience of Modernity*, London: Verso.

Hersey, G. (1988) *The Lost Meaning of Classical Architecture*, Cambridge, MA: MIT Press.

Jan van Pelt, R. and Dwork, D. (1996) *Auschwitz: 1270 to the Present*, New Haven and London: Yale University Press.

Loos, A. (1975; first pub.1908) 'Ornament and Crime', in U. Conrads (ed.) *Programs and Manifestoes on 20th Century Architecture*, Cambridge, MA: MIT Press.

Markus, T.A. (1993) *Buildings and Power: Freedom and Control in the Origin of Modern Building Types*, London: Routledge.

Pugin, A.W. (1973; first pub.1841) *The True Principles of Pointed or Christian Architecture*, London: Academy Editions.

Ruskin, J. (1904; first pub.1849) *The Seven Lamps of Architecture*, London: George Allen.

Scott, G. (1980; first pub. 1914) *The Architecture of Humanism: A Study in the History of Taste*, London: The Architectural Press.

Scruton, R. (1979) *The Aesthetics of Architecture*, London: Methuen.

Tzonis, A. and Lefaivre, L. (1986) *Classical Architecture: The Poetics of Order*, Cambridge, MA: MIT Press.

Watkin, D. (1977) *Morality and Architecture*, Oxford: Clarendon Press.

16

TOWARDS AN ETHICS (OR AT LEAST A VALUE THEORY) OF THE BUILT ENVIRONMENT

Warwick Fox

The question of the ethics of the built environment

I want to address the question of the ethics of the built environment in what I take to be its most fundamental form. This might seem only appropriate in a book on this subject. Even so, I think that to the extent that most people might think about this question at all, they would probably find it extremely difficult to focus fairly and squarely on the question of the ethics of the built environment in the sense in which I want to here. The issue can be put this way. I think that most people, and certainly most philosophers, would not consider the built environment to be an appropriate focus of moral concern *in its own right*. Instead, I think that most people, including philosophers, would consider that questions regarding built environments should only enter into *moral* discussion in so far as these environments are considered to matter to, impact upon, or in some way affect, those kinds of beings or entities in respect of which we think we have *direct* moral obligations. This directly morally relevant class of beings or entities has typically been restricted to other people (sometimes not all other people). (I have elsewhere described this traditional focus of ethics as 'the closed moral universe of the Old Ethics'; see Fox, forthcoming, for a full discussion.) More controversially, the morally relevant class might be taken to include sentient creatures in general, life forms in general (i.e. whether sentient or non-sentient) or even widely distributed systems that maintain some sort of holistic integrity over time, like ecosystems and the ecosphere. But whatever the case, the *non*-rational, *non*-sentient, *non*-living, *non*-self-organising, *non*-self-renewing *built* environment is not generally thought of as being of moral consequence in its own right. The value and relevance of the built environment to ethical discussion is generally considered to be purely of a secondary, derivative, or indirect kind.

This response immediately raises the following challenge: Do we even need an ethics of the built environment *per se*? If the built environment is only of moral consequence to the extent that it is useful or in some sense valuable *to* other kinds of entities then surely all we need is an ethics that applies to those kinds of entities. It will then follow as a logical consequence that in respecting those entities we will have to take into account those things that are useful or in some sense valuable to them, including, where relevant, the built environment. Since the built environment *per se* is only of moral consequence in this indirect way, the very idea of an ethics of the built environment *per se* is unnecessary, surplus to moral requirements.

However, if that is really all there is to be said about the ethics of the built environment *per se* then we are left argumentatively/rationally helpless to respond to the following sort of situation. Consider two examples of the built environment: houses, office buildings, roads – take your pick. Suppose that they are of similar *overall* usefulness or value to people, to sentient creatures, and even to life forms in general (for the sake of the argument, we'll set aside the philosophical questions regarding whether or not something can really be said to be useful or valuable to an entity that is non-sentient). Suppose that these two examples of the built environment even have the same overall impact on the self-renewing properties of their surrounding ecosystem and the ecosphere in general. *By definition*, then, there is no *indirect* morally based reason to favour one of these built environments over the other, since they are just as useful or valuable as each other to all the main candidates for membership of the moral class.

Now suppose that one of these examples of the built environment – let's assume it's a building – is simply imposed upon its natural and built environments in a very arbitrary way, a way that bears no particular relationship to these environments in terms of its design (even though, as we have said, its measurable physical/environmental impact upon the world is no worse than that of the other building). And suppose that, in contrast, the other building is designed in such a way that it clearly relates to, or *coheres* with, its natural and built environments. Now, to you, being the design-sensitive person you are(!), the former building might be such a distressing sight to behold that your gut reaction might be that 'there ought to be a law against it'. Indeed, I think this is a very common experience in today's world – and, of course, there *are* laws and regulations that would forbid such building in *some* areas and places. Yet, as we've already said, in this hypothetical instance, your view (and those of any others who happen to share it) is cancelled out, or at least swamped, by the preferences of other people who:

1 may not like the design of the building either but whose preferences for its *overall* usefulness to them are significantly stronger than yours;
2 may simply not care very much one way or the other – or not even really know how they feel about its design (also a common experience I think); or
3 may in fact actually like the design of the building or have grown to like it (e.g. they might only care about how exciting the design of the building itself is and not care or even notice whether the building fits in with its larger natural and built environmental contexts).

If space allowed we could flesh out the above abstract comparison with all sorts of particular, real-world (or least potentially real-world) examples. But, in each case, what would be at stake with respect to the *buildings themselves* in these comparisons would be 'simply' a matter of the extent to which their designs suit, fit in or cohere with their context. I have guaranteed this in the abstract comparison above by making it clear that the *overall* usefulness or value of the buildings under discussion is the same with respect to all the most likely candidates for inclusion in the moral class. But so what? What's so important about such a comparison? Isn't it the case that emphasising the contextual 'fit' of a building's design might be seen as a concern that lies a long way down any 'ethics of the built environment' priority list? Surely there are many nitty-gritty issues that are ultimately both more urgent and more important than finessing the design details of a building in the direction of greater contextual 'fit' (whatever that might mean). A quick list of some of these (allegedly) more urgent and important issues might include (1) matters relating to employment; (2) social equity (e.g. Who pays for the building or subsidises it? Who gets to use it? Where will any profits from this usage go?); (3) accessibility of the site by foot, public transport and private vehicle; (4) accessibility to the building itself for the elderly, infirm and disabled; (5) public participation in the design process; and (6) impact upon the natural environment in terms of both the building's construction and ongoing operation (the building's ecological footprint). In the face of all these important issues, it is easy to imagine a hard-headed politician or businessman lampooning a concern for a building that fits its context as expressive of, say, 'the aesthetic preferences of the cappuccino crowd'. And why should 'the aesthetic preferences of the cappuccino crowd' be allowed to stand in the way of the 'most reasonable cost option' for a building that is as good as any other (perhaps even better) on most other grounds?

However, the reason I have highlighted the contrasting *designs* example, which can lead to challenges of the above kind, is precisely because it serves to present the question of the ethics of the built environment in its sharpest and most fundamental form. This follows from the fact that *all* the issues mentioned above in regard to the ethics of the built environment – employment, social equity, accessibility of the site by various means, accessibility to the building, public participation in its design and ecological sustainability – can potentially be reduced to the question of what is best *for* or most useful *to* some class of entities that are thought of as being of moral consequence in their own right. But if all these questions can be reduced in this way then we are back to the questions I asked at the outset: Do we even need an ethics of the built environment *per se*? If ethical questions concerning the built environment are reducible in this way then isn't the very idea of an ethics of the built environment *per se* surplus to moral requirements?

On the other hand, if it could be shown that the 'mere' *design* of one building should be preferred to another *in principle* (i.e. regardless of whether or not the two buildings are of the same overall usefulness or value to whatever moral class one wishes to specify), then we have established the ground for an ethics of the built environment *as such*. Moreover, like other general evaluative principles, any principle that served to underpin, legitimate and even require this differential evaluation of the two designs would presumably have to be one of considerable depth or generality. And if this were the case then it would be reasonable to expect that this principle would necessarily flow into a great many *other* aspects of our judgements with respect to the construction of buildings, *including the list of 'nitty-gritty' concerns given above* (i.e. this principle would apply to these concerns regardless of the extent to which these concerns might *also* be analysable in terms of issues of usefulness or value to some morally relevant class). Under these circumstances, it would seem that one could then speak of 'the ethics of building' or 'the ethics of the built environment' as a wide ranging *bona fide* area of enquiry in its own right.

Responsive cohesion as the foundation of value theory in general and, hence, ethics in particular

I want to propose that there is in fact a *foundational* principle at work in value theory in general and *ipso facto* ethics in particular ('*ipso facto* ethics in particular' because ethics is centrally an evaluative enterprise and, hence, necessarily a part of value theory). Moreover, I want to claim that when this foundational principle is applied to the built environment, it does indeed require that we judge some forms of the built environment as better than others, even when considered 'merely' at the level of the extent to which their designs suit, fit in or cohere with their context. I refer to this foundational principle as the principle of *responsive cohesion* and will argue for it below. The usual caveat is required in a contribution of this length as to the necessary brevity of the argument that follows for such a strong claim, but I nevertheless trust that what follows will be more than simply suggestive in its overall thrust.

Beginning with ethics in particular, we can observe that, whatever our particular preferences in ethical theory at the fine-grained level (some version of virtue ethics? duty/principle based ethics? consequentialist ethics?), the ethical theories that reflective judges consider to be best are those that exemplify the principle of responsive cohesion in terms of both their method and their content. I will consider these in turn.

In terms of method, a good ethical theory is one that is open to continual feedback and mutual accommodation between the theory and the personal evaluations of moral agents. For example, suppose that someone claims that the best ethical approach is one in which moral agents should strive for the greatest happiness of the greatest number of people (a version of consequentialist ethics, specifically utilitarianism, which might, on the face of it, sound like a fairly sensible and appealing position). It would seem that a straightforward consequence of this view, as written, is that it would be morally permissible to sacrifice the life of an innocent person (or perhaps a presumed-innocent-until-proven-guilty person as in, for example, the handing over of a *pre*-trial prisoner to a lynch mob) if that seemed to be the best way to secure the greatest happiness of the greatest number of people. (This is a common form of objection against utilitarianism.) However, this course of action is likely to rub against the personal evaluations of good and bad actions, or right and wrong actions, of a great many reflective people. They are then confronted with a choice. On the one hand, they can consider the merits of the theory more closely and perhaps come to the view that, on balance, the arguments in its favour are so compelling that they ought to modify their *personal evaluations* in the face of them, and so come to accept this (originally) unpalatable course of action as justifiable. On the other hand, they can consider the reasons for their objections to this course of action more closely, and perhaps come to the view that, on balance, these reasons are so compelling that the *theory* ought to be modified in order to accommodate these objections – or perhaps even be abandoned in favour of a better theory. Either way, this process then continues as the revised personal evaluations or theory are repeatedly tested against each other with respect to new problems.

This procedure of moving to and fro between personal evaluations and an ethical theory in order to reach a point of mutual accommodation represents the basic method in rationally based ethical discussion. The influential American philosopher John Rawls (1972) has famously described this method in ethics as 'the method of reflective equilibrium'. Indeed, Rawls's descriptive label for this method is so famous that some people now seem to associate the *method itself* with Rawls. However, Rawls hardly *invented* this method; rather, he simply helped to highlight this way of proceeding in ethics by giving it a name and explicitly drawing attention to it *as* a method (i.e. as opposed simply to employing this method in an implicit way, as is typically done). Rawls himself was aware both of this and of the fact that 'the process of mutual adjustment of principles and considered judgements is not peculiar to moral philosophy' (Rawls 1972: 20).

I would be more inclined to refer to the basic method of rationally based ethical discussion outlined here as 'the method of responsive cohesion'. (Owing to space limitations, I cannot outline my reasons for this preference in relation to Rawls's terminology here, but I do so elsewhere: see Fox, forthcoming.) The term *cohere* literally means to cling, hold, stick or adhere together (from Latin *cohaerere*, from *co* together and *haerere* to cling, adhere). The adjectival term *responsive* (from Latin *respondsum,* answer) suggests that the way in which we should strive to reach a state in which theory and personal evaluations cohere or 'cling together' is through a process in which each side is responsive to, or answers to, the challenges thrown up by the other side. This responsiveness can take the accommodating form of accepting the challenge that has been made, and thus modifying the side against which the challenge was made, or the oppositional form of a critical counter-challenge to the other side. The upshot of this process is that cohesion between the two sides is ultimately brought about, assuming this goal *is* reached, through a process of mutual accommodation, adjustment, adaptation or reconciliation between theory and evaluations.

In contrast to the method of responsive cohesion (or Rawls's reflective equilibrium), bad procedure in ethical theorising consists in the extremes that lie on either side. One extreme is that of coming up with a rigidly fixed code that is completely impervious to criticism based on considered personal evaluations, for example a code that is claimed to be 'God given', or sanctioned by an inflexible tradition, or sanctioned by a King (or equivalent power) who has a 'divine right' to rule. The general message is this: the code is right, any contrary personal evaluations you have are in error; ergo, the correct 'method' of reconciliation is this: you must modify your personal evaluations whenever they conflict with the code.

The other extreme to that of having a completely rigid code or 'theory' is that of eschewing the organising function of theory altogether. On this scenario, one's personal evaluations are always right, whatever they are, and don't need to be justified or modified in the light of any thoughtful arguments to the contrary. In other words, anything one thinks is OK goes: relativism and nihilism rule, OK? It's hard to know which of these extremes is worse: the unchallengeable static, rigid order of the former or the equally unchallengeable all-over-the-place chaos of the latter. In contrast, ensuring that ethical theories and personal evaluations are *responsive* to each other, and so working towards a *cohesion* (or 'clinging together') between theories and evaluations on that basis, would seem to be infinitely preferable.

Having briefly considered the question of the best method of ethics, let us now turn to the question of the *content* of ethics. With respect to this area too, I want to argue that, whatever our particular preferences in ethical theory at a fine-grained level, the ethical theories that reflective judges generally consider to be best are those that exhibit the principle of responsive cohesion in terms of their content. Expressed simply, thoughtful reflection generally suggests that, whatever their specific details, the best approaches to ethics are those in which we are permitted the freedom to be responsive to our own goals and desires, but not to the extent of trampling on the interests of others in doing so. Why not? The answer is that at the same time as we are permitted the freedom to be responsive to our own goals and desires, we are also required to be responsive to others who are also permitted the freedom to be responsive to *their* own goals and desires. The upshot is a considerable degree of freedom within which to pursue our own goals and desires, but not so much freedom that we are morally permitted to ride roughshod over the interests of others in doing so. There are arguments about the extent of the infringements that each of us ought to be able to make upon the interests of others, about exactly what classes or kinds of 'others' are deemed to have moral claims upon us, and so on, but this remains the broad outline of the content of those ethical theories that we consider to be worth taking seriously. It is a shared commitment to this general kind of understanding that defines a responsive – and hence adaptive – *moral community* (where 'community' refers to a form of social arrangement that coheres or 'clings together' because of its own internal social dynamics). In a moral community of this kind, individuals are viewed as being loosely (hence, fluidly) coupled to each other rather than tightly coupled (in which case individual freedom is diminished) or not connected at all (in which case the sense, and the fact, of living in a community disappears).

This solution to the moral problem – the solution of significant individual freedom within a loosely coupled moral community – exemplifies the general principle of responsive cohesion between moral agents. This is because this form of cohesion is brought about through the process of moral agents being responsive to both their own goals and desires and the needs of others to be responsive to *their* own goals and desires. This, again, represents a middle way between the extremes on either side. On the one hand, there is the extreme of what we could call 'moral slavery', where the freedom to pursue one's own goals and desires is largely or even completely curtailed by the extent of our moral obligations to others and/or in respect of some overarching authority. This represents a 'tightly coupled' and/or rigidly organised moral community in which one is not permitted the freedom – or sufficient freedom – to be responsive to one's *own* goals and desires. On the other hand, there is the possibility that Thomas Hobbes famously associated with the raw 'state of nature' in which there is a 'war of every man against every man' – in other words, social disorganisation, anarchy, chaos. This represents the complete lack of a moral community in which one is *only* responsive to one's own goals and desires and not at all responsive to the goals and desires of others (unless it happens to be one's pleasure to be so). In contrast to these extremes, it is those ethical theories that exemplify the principle of responsive cohesion in their content that reflective judges generally consider to be the main candidates for being taken seriously when it comes to guiding the actual ways in which we ought to live, which, after all, is the main point of ethics.

To this point, then, I have tried to show that, whatever their specific details, good ethical theories are those that exemplify the foundational principle of responsive cohesion at the level of both method and content. The next point to make is that ethics is just one area among others, albeit a very significant one, in which we make evaluative judgements, that is, judgements of good and bad, better and worse. Although philosophers tend to think of value theory (or *axiology*, from Greek *axios,* worthy) as consisting primarily of ethics and aesthetics, it is clear that we in fact make judgements of better and worse in a great many other areas of life too. For example, we make judgements of better and worse in regard to issues concerning epistemology in general and science in particular, the personal psychologies or mental states of others, politics, skills (including sports), the quality of the natural environment and the quality of the built environment. Perhaps the philosophical tendency to confine the realm of value theory (axiology) to ethics and aesthetics reflects little more than the fact that philosophy still largely retains these disciplines as its own. But however that may be, it is clear that *all* the major areas of life that I have just listed are grist for the mill of value theory, broadly conceived.

The way in which the argument I am presenting develops in these 'extra-ethical' value theory contexts can only be indicated here rather than developed at any length, but the general point is this: I want to claim that, whether they realise it or not, informed observers make judgements of better and worse in each of these contexts on the basis of a general principle that could reasonably be described as one of responsive cohesion. Many other more fine-grained sorts of considerations will enter into judgements in each area that are specific to that area of course, but the principle of responsive cohesion is always at work at the very foundation of these judgements. Let us consider some examples, albeit with appalling brevity.

With respect to epistemology and science

Reflective judges generally consider that the best ways of coming to know 'the way the world is' involve a responsive cohesion between theory and observations: on the one hand, theory is answerable to relevant observations and, on the other, what counts as a relevant observation is answerable to (a function of) the theory that one is testing. (This is similar, but not identical, to the situation in ethical methodology, where, as we have seen, ethical theory informs personal evaluations and personal evaluations inform ethical theory.) This approach to knowing the world stands in contrast to the extremes on either side. On the one hand, there is the extreme of rigid adherence to a theory in spite of substantial contrary evidence (theoretical rigidity/stasis). On the other hand, there is the extreme of rejecting the organising role of rigorously tested theory altogether, in which case one either lives in 'a wilderness of single instances' (observational chaos) or extrapolates from experience left, right and centre ('wild speculation', theoretical chaos).

With respect to personal psychologies

Reflective judges generally consider that a person is in the best psychological state when there is a responsive cohesion between their various internal psychological forces (in which case their thoughts, emotions and desires – or cognition, affect and volition – are judged as being well integrated) and between the person as a whole and their external surroundings (in which case their responses are judged as being appropriate to, in keeping with or coherent with their surroundings). This stands in contrast to the extremes on either side. On the one hand, there is the contrast of rigidity in a person's inner psychological organisation and ways of dealing with the world (psychological and behavioural rigidity/inflexibility). In this case, we might colloquially describe the person as 'stuck in a rut', 'acting like a zombie', and so on. On the other hand, there is the contrast of a lack of cohesion in a person's internal psychological organisation and ways of dealing with the world (psychological chaos and/or causing havoc through their behaviour). In this case, we might colloquially describe the person as 'falling apart', 'all over the place', 'a mess', 'not together', and so on.

With respect to politics

Reflective judges generally consider that the best forms of politics are those in which there are mechanisms in place to ensure mutual feedback and accommodation (thus, responsive cohesion) between government and people (a situation that is loosely analogous to the relationship that obtains between theory and observations in science or theory and personal evaluations in ethics). In this situation, people are answerable to the laws passed by government and government is answerable to the people through the institutions of free elections, a free press, freedom of expression generally, an independent judiciary, and so on. This responsive cohesion approach to politics stands in contrast to the extremes on either side. On the one hand, there is the contrast of rigid, totalitarian forms of 'government' in which the people must be responsive to the 'government', but in which there are no mechanisms to ensure that the 'government' must be responsive to the people. This typically results in a rigidly imposed form of political cohesion rather than a responsive form of political cohesion, and its grip is often only broken through a rebellion that flips the society (at least temporarily) from a situation of rigidly imposed control to one of social anarchy and chaos. This situation represents the extreme that lies on the other side of a responsive cohesion approach to politics, namely the extreme in which the legitimacy and organising function of government is rejected altogether.

With respect to skills and the arts

Reflective judges generally consider that the best examples of skills and arts (whether we are talking about chess, furniture making, high diving, music, drama, novels or painting) exhibit an internal responsive cohesion in that they are judged to 'hang together' well (or be cohesive) through the various ways in which each aspect of the whole is seen to answer to (or be responsive to) the other aspects. As ever, this responsive cohesion approach to the topic under consideration stands in contrast to the extremes on either side. In this case, there is, on the one hand, the contrast of a skill or art that coheres in a way that is judged to be rigid, forced, imposed or 'wooden' (i.e. where the elements of the skill or art are judged as being unresponsive to each other, all of which bespeaks a rigidity of imaginative or technical capacity). On the other hand, there is the contrast of a skill or art that lacks cohesion and so is judged as being 'all over the place', as 'not hanging together' or, like a high dive or a bad move in chess, as coming 'unstuck'.

Skills and arts can also be judged in terms of their responsiveness to the tradition (or cultural context) within which they are located. In contrast to the above emphasis on the degree of *internal* responsive cohesion of a skill or art, this can be thought of as referring to the *external* (or *contextual*) responsive cohesion of a skill or art. Again, reflective judges generally consider that the best examples of skills and arts are those that not only make sense within, and so *cohere* with, a recognisable tradition but also *respond to* that tradition and so add to its development. This, again, stands in contrast to the extremes on either side. On the one hand, if an example of a skill or art blindly repeats a tradition, then it is cohesive with that tradition in a rigid (or unresponsive) way, even if the resulting product displays considerable *internal* responsive cohesion. It then pays the price of being judged as 'cliched', 'stereotypical', 'hackneyed', 'formulaic', 'plodding', 'unimaginative', and so on, in its design or execution. On the other hand, if an example of a skill or art bears no obvious connection with the tradition in which it claims to partake (i.e. if it doesn't answer to that tradition in any recognisable way) then it doesn't make any sense in terms of that tradition and is judged as a bad example of its kind. It is dismissed as 'novelty for novelty's sake,' 'pretentious', having 'more style (if it has that) than substance', and much worse!

With respect to the quality of the natural environment

Reflective judges generally consider that the best examples of natural environments – those natural environments that we openly refer to as being *well* preserved – are those that exemplify long-standing mutual accommodation (i.e. responsive cohesion) between the forms of life that inhabit them and their environment. In well-preserved natural environments, the forms of life that inhabit the environment have been interacting with each other and their environment for considerable periods of time in evolutionary terms. They have not recently been significantly disrupted by such things as an asteroid impact, the arrival of large numbers of highly invasive plants and animals or anthropogenic destruction of habitat. The upshot is that well-preserved natural environments possess an unmistakably cohesive or systemic quality, but one which is, of course, fluid and dynamic, since they are continually subject to all manner of internally generated fluctuations borne of the multifarious ways in which the forms of life that inhabit them respond to each other and their environment in seeking to survive and reproduce. This ecological form of responsive cohesion stands in contrast to the extremes on either side. On the one hand, there is the contrast of a natural environment being 'managed' by being 'deep frozen.' On the other hand, there is the contrast of an 'open-slather,' 'anything goes' policy (ecological chaos). Deep freezing an ecology rigidly maintains the existing cohesion of natural processes but robs them of their dynamic or responsive nature whereas the 'anything goes' approach maintains the dynamic or responsive nature of these processes but robs them of their long-standing cohesion.

The foregoing analysis represents an abbreviated version of the case for the claim that the quality or property of responsive cohesion is a foundational principle not only in informed judgements about the method and content of ethics but also in other major areas of life in which we make judgements of better and worse. That said, where we draw the line as to exactly where ethics ends and the *rest* of value theory begins is a moot point. For example, we clearly think that the way in which we treat other people belongs to the realm of ethics, whereas we don't generally think of one's evaluation of, say, scientific theories as an *ethical* issue. But these waters can be muddied very quickly. For example, where there *are* very sound evidentially backed reasons for judging one theory as better than another (e.g. the theory of evolution by means of natural selection as opposed to the views of 'creation science') then it is no longer clear that this judgement is purely a matter of value theory that lacks an ethical dimension. All we would need to do to turn this issue into an overtly ethical one would be to invoke the sort of principle advanced by the British philosopher W. K. Clifford (1845–79) in a famous paper significantly entitled 'The Ethics of Belief' (1877) in which he claimed that 'It is wrong always, everywhere, and for anyone [i.e. it is *categorically* wrong, or wrong *in principle*], to believe anything on insufficient evidence' (a view that saw Clifford himself move from Catholicism to agnosticism). If one agrees that insisting on a preference for one theory when there are far stronger grounds for preferring another is not simply perverse but rather wrong in principle, then the realm of

218

epistemology becomes intertwined with the realm of ethics and it becomes possible to speak of *epistemological ethics*, or what Clifford called the *ethics* of belief.

Given this lack of clarity or widespread agreement as to exactly where what we call ethics ends and where the rest of the general study of value and evaluation begins, I am (as indicated by my title) happy to speak in this context about the development of either an *ethics* of the built environment or, more generally, a *value theory* of the built environment. But whatever the terminology, my central claim here has been to establish and uphold the claim that the principle of responsive cohesion lies at the very foundation of our best and most informed judgements of better and worse.

Responsive cohesion and the built environment

I have argued that the principle of responsive cohesion represents the *foundational* principle that is at work in our best evaluations with respect to a wide range of evaluative domains. Indeed, given the breadth of the evaluative domains I have considered, the clear implication of my argument is that this principle lies at the foundation of whatever evaluative domain one cares to nominate. Even the *method* by which we arrive at our best judgements of better and worse – namely, the approach of making evaluative theories and personal evaluations answer (respond) to each other in order to work towards a cohesiveness between them – exemplifies this foundational principle. What happens, then, when the principle of responsive cohesion is applied to the built environment? Let us go back to the comparison I offered at the outset between two buildings that are of the same overall usefulness or value to whatever class of entities is deemed to be deserving of moral consideration (including even the natural environment itself if required), but that differ only in their design such that one blends in with its natural and built environments whereas the other sticks out like the proverbial sore thumb. If we accept the foundational nature of the principle of responsive cohesion in making judgements of better and worse then we clearly possess a strong basis for objecting to the latter building *in principle* (i.e. irrespective of the overall usefulness or value of the building *to* any morally relevant class of entities). This is because this example makes it quite explicit that the latter building fails to exemplify the principle of responsive cohesion with respect to its natural and built environments.

But the principle of responsive cohesion also allows us to say rather more than that about the construction of the built environment. For example, the principle of responsive cohesion also has built into it the idea that we should construct buildings (or built environments) that represent a creative adaptation to their ecological, social and built contexts *in that overall order of preference*. Why that overall order of preference? The answer turns on the fact that the ecological context generated and continues to support humans and, hence, the human social context, and the human social context generated and continues to support the built environment context. The principle of responsive cohesion clearly suggests that while a newly introduced feature can, will and ought to be able to alter its generative and supportive context (as, say, any organism modifies its environment), it is the new feature that ought, overall, to be made to defer to its generative and supportive context for this simple reason: for a new *feature* to *radically* alter its generative and supportive *context* is to undo a lot of already existing responsive cohesion. We would also say, colloquially but rightly, that it is 'crazy': a good example would be adding some new notes to a beautiful, responsively cohesive symphony (i.e. a symphony that 'hangs together' well, precisely because of the way in which its various elements 'answer' to each other), finding that the new notes don't 'work'/fit/cohere, and then proceeding to tear apart the already existing responsive cohesion of the symphony in order to recreate the work around the ill-fitting notes. Responsive cohesion is best preserved overall where the generative and supportive context (whether it be a symphony or the natural environment) has the lion's share of the influence with respect to the new feature (whether that new feature be a musical theme, human society or an aspect of the built environment). The architect Christopher Day captures the general thrust of this point quite simply when he says that 'To be harmonious, the new needs to be an organic development of what is already there, not an imposed alien' (Day 1990: 18).

As ever, the principle of responsive cohesion stands in contrast to the extremes on either side. With respect to the built environment this means the following. On the one hand, there is the contrast of the kind of rigid forms (often massive in scale), rigidly imposed upon the landscape that characterise so much of contemporary building. On the other hand, there is the contrast of the kind of 'anything goes,' 'all-over-the-place' architectural 'free-for-all' that can arise as an allegedly 'liberating' reaction to the former. These are exactly the extremes that the architectural theorist Christian Norberg-Schulz identifies as 'general monotony' on the one hand and 'arbitrary fancies' on the other hand, when he says: 'The modern environment in fact offers very little of the surprises and discoveries which make the experience of old towns so fascinating. When attempts to break the general monotony are made, they mostly appear as arbitrary fancies' (Norberg-Schulz 1980: 190). In contrast, 'responsive cohesion' seems to be a very good way of describing (in formal language) what it is that makes 'the experience of [some] old towns so fascinating'; of describing what it is that can lend to the built environment the sense that it exemplifies a 'timeless way of building,' to borrow Christopher Alexander's (1979) evocative term.

We've tried the spiritually deadening, rigidly imposed dormitory-suburbs-drive-to-the-shopping-mall approach to the built environment. A number of architectural leaders have recently been experimenting with the allegedly-ironically-'playful'-but-to-others-somewhat-imaginatively-desperate historical pastiche approach of post-modernist architecture (much of which will surely end up looking like anything *but* a 'timeless way of building'). And we've tried much in between that hasn't worked well either, ecologically or for the human spirit. The approach I have advocated here, based on the foundational principle of responsive cohesion, suggests that we now need to turn (and, to some extent, *re*turn, albeit in a modern context) to the preservation and creation of built environments that exemplify a responsive cohesion both internally and with respect to their ecological, social and built contexts (*in that overall order of preference*). Eschewing rigidly imposed, monotonous order on the one hand and novelty for its own sake ('arbitrary fancies') on the other hand, the principle of responsive cohesion points the way to a built environment that both coheres with living systems and is enlivening to the human spirit.

References

Alexander, C.A. (1979) *The Timeless Way of Building*, New York: Oxford University Press.

Clifford, W.K. (1877) 'The Ethics of Belief', *Contemporary Review*. Reprinted in *Lectures and Essays*, London: Macmillan, 1879.

Day, C. (1990) *Places of the Soul: Architecture and Environmental Design as a Healing Art*, London: Thorsons (HarperCollins).

Fox, W. *The New Ethics* (in preparation).

Norberg-Schulz, C. (1980) *Genius Loci: Towards a Phenomenology of Architecture*, New York: Rizzoli International Publications.

Rawls, J. (1972) *A Theory of Justice*, Oxford: Oxford University Press.

17

CONCLUSION

Towards an agenda for the ethics of the built environment

Warwick Fox

As stated in Chapter 1, the aim of this volume has been to contribute towards the accumulation of a critical mass of ideas and questions that will enable the discussion of the ethics of the built environment (or the ethics of building) to take off as a field of enquiry in its own right. With that guiding aim, this volume has brought together, on the one hand, a range of philosophers with an interest in architecture, planning and building and, on the other hand, a range of philosophically oriented architects, planners and other analysts of the built environment. This exploratory and invigorating aim is quite different from that of fulfilling the textbook function of attempting to provide a *systematic* introduction to an area of enquiry. But even though it has not been the task of this volume (and generally is not considered to be the task of edited collections) to present a systematic approach to the topic under consideration, it is nevertheless the case that the chapters presented here serve to define a very wide range of issues that any systematic exposition of the ethics of the built environment would need to cover. To that extent, they also serve to define an initial agenda for the future development of this field of enquiry.

Let me illustrate these last two points by briefly viewing some of the central topics covered herein through a more systematic lens. Ethics is standardly divided into *descriptive ethics*, *normative ethics*, *meta-ethics* and *applied ethics*. Descriptive ethics simply refers to the descriptive study of the ethical views that people *happen* to hold. Normative ethics, in contrast, refers to arguments for the sorts of norms, goals or standards that people *ought* to hold. As such, normative ethics lies at the heart of philosophical approaches to ethics and is what most people mean when they use the term 'ethics'. Meta-ethics refers to discussion *about* normative ethics, as opposed to arguments *for* a substantive normative position. Meta-ethics covers questions regarding such things as the meaning of ethical terms and how we come by knowledge of what is good or bad, right or wrong (i.e. meta-ethics picks up especially on the semantic and epistemological issues that arise *from* normative ethical discussion). Finally, applied ethics refers to enquiry into the application of normative ethical approaches in all manner of specific practical contexts. These range from A to Z (abortion, animal experimentation, ... business, computing, ... journalism, medicine, nursing, ... zoos), and from birth to death (prenatal testing, obstetrics ... euthanasia and physician-assisted suicide).

A systematic exposition of the basics of normative ethics, the heart of ethics, would typically begin by outlining the three main approaches to normative ethics:

1   ethics that focus on the cultivation of certain *qualities of character* (formally known as *virtue ethics*);
2   ethics that focus on the upholding of, or respect for, certain *principles* (formally known as *deontological ethics*, from *deon* duty, but a more user-friendly term is principle ethics). A principle ethics approach is concerned with the upholding of, or respect for, certain *principles* quite independently of the question of whether or not the *character* of moral agents is such that they personally *wish* to uphold these principles, and quite independently of the question of whether or not upholding these principles necessarily leads to the best *consequences* on each occasion;
3   ethics that focus on obtaining certain kinds of *outcomes* (formally known as *consequentialist ethics*, or just *consequentialism*).

This simple schema, based on whether the focus of an ethical approach is on the character of the *actor*, the principle that informs the *action per se* or the *outcome of the action*, respectively, opens out on to a wide range of questions for the ethics of building. For example:

• What kinds of personal qualities of character (or virtues) should planners, designers, architects and builders cultivate? More generally, what kinds of virtues should people in general cultivate in order to be more sensitive to the built environment (and *perhaps* by implication the natural environment)?
• What kinds of principles should we seek to uphold with respect to the built environment?

- What kinds of outcomes or consequences should we seek to promote with respect to the built environment?

Many of the chapters herein implicitly or explicitly address one or more of these systematically presented ethical questions. For example, Nigel Taylor argued that those charged with responsibility for the built environment should cultivate the personal quality of character (i.e. the virtue) of 'careful aesthetic attention' to the work they are undertaking, and that it is the degree of *care* shown in realising an aesthetic aim that brings design and construction into the realm of moral evaluation, since 'caring is a moral concept'. Thus, according to Taylor, we might not *like* a building on aesthetic grounds, but that does not by itself provide us with any purchase in criticising it on moral grounds. However, a building can legitimately be criticised on moral grounds when the argument can be put forward that the people responsible for its design and/or construction have shown a 'lack of *careful* aesthetic attention' to their work (my italics).

The virtue of careful aesthetic attention can be reframed so as to sound more like a principle that ought to be upheld, or perhaps even given an operational definition so that it can be evaluated in terms of outcomes or consequences. However, ethical discussions involving the notion of *care* (and, as it happens, there is much theorising in feminist ethical discussion in regard to the cultivation of this particular quality of character) are generally best viewed under the rubric of virtue ethics because the notion of care is *fundamentally* a personally realised quality of character rather than an impersonal principle to be respected or outcome to be realised.

Isis Brook similarly implies the endorsement of a virtue ethics approach when she suggests in the conclusion of her chapter that we need to become 'sensitive investigators' of place. Although she does not explore the question of how we might develop this personal quality within this chapter, she refers to another paper of her own that outlines a method that enables us to cultivate this particular virtue – a method that is generally discussed under the name of 'Goethean Science.' Christopher Day is in broad agreement with Brook's Goethean Science sympathies and the four-level approach he briefly outlines within his chapter as a way of cultivating the personal quality of greater sensitivity to the 'levels of being' of a place is representative of this Goethean Science approach. For Day, this method 'empowers and spurs inner growth in the individuals involved' and results in more sensitively designed places and buildings. Thus, Taylor, Brook and Day, to cite three examples herein, could all be said to endorse what might *formally* be described as a virtue ethics approach to the ethics of the built environment.

In contrast to the virtue ethics approach, but not necessarily in opposition to it, I emphasised a principle ethics approach in arguing that those charged with responsibility for the built environment ought to uphold the fundamental principle of *responsive cohesion*. As explained, upholding this principle entails endeavouring to ensure that examples of the built environment are responsive to, or answer to, their ecological, social and built contexts, and that they do so in that overall order of preference. To be sure, I think that respecting this principle will result in better outcomes with respect to the built environment than failing to respect it, but what makes this approach essentially a principle ethics approach rather than a consequentialist approach is that it is the principle that is fundamental. A consequentialist approach is (theoretically) free to pick and mix its principles – if it invokes 'principles' at all – in order to secure whatever set of outcomes are viewed as 'best' whereas a principle ethics approach sticks to its central principle(s) and determines judgements of better and worse in accord with that. Thus, in my view, if a particular outcome failed to exemplify (or was seen as deficient in exemplifying) the principle of responsive cohesion, then it *couldn't* be as good an outcome as one that did exemplify (or that better exemplified) this principle, since, according to my argument, it is ultimately on the basis of this principle that we ought to make our judgements of better and worse in the first place.

Other contributors such as Roger Talbot and Gian Carlo Magnoli, Bob Fowles and Paul Oliver perhaps implicitly straddle the approaches of principle ethics and conseqentialist ethics in regard to their respective emphases on the importance of including those for whom buildings are being built in the design process itself. On the one hand, these authors often justify the importance of such inclusion on the basis of the better *outcomes* that they see (or have seen) as resulting from it, as well as on the basis of the worse outcomes that they have seen to result when this is not done (e.g. see Chapter 9). But above and beyond this, there is also an overriding sense in these contributions that including people in the process of designing the buildings they will use is something that should be done in any case, as a matter of *principle*. This is surely right. If we consider human beings to posses an inherent worth or dignity, then it is generally held to follow that, as a matter of principle, we ought not to ride roughshod over their interests. We ought, at least, to take their interests into account in some way in actions we perform that are likely to affect them. Including people in the process of designing the buildings they will use is a straightforward way of trying to ensure that their interests are taken into account with respect to matters concerning the built environment. Conversely, given the pervasive effects that built environments have upon the people who live in them (to say nothing of their effects upon the rest of the planet and its other inhabitants), it might reasonably be considered that *not* including people in the process of designing the buildings they will use is tantamount to a violation of the right of human beings to a significant degree of self-determination. 'Unilaterally Imposed Building Practices as a Violation of Basic Human Rights' – now there's a provocative title for a paper whose time has surely come!

Yet other contributors, especially those most explicitly concerned with the mega-issue, the Ur-issue, of ecological sustainability (like Herbert Girardet, John Whitelegg, Tom Woolley, Terry Williamson and Antony Radford), were primarily concerned with the promotion of certain kinds of outcomes or consequences – sustainable ones! These authors were implicitly or explicitly endorsing a consequentialist approach to the ethics of the built environment. A number of these contributors invoked the ideal of respecting certain kinds of *principles* as the best way of ensuring practices that delivered sustainable *outcomes* (such as the now well-known 'precautionary principle'), but it is the fact that such principles are ultimately justified in terms of their consequences that leads them to be categorised under the heading of consequentialist ethics.

Viewed through a systematic lens, we can also see that the contributions to this volume cover, implicitly or explicitly, much more than just *normative ethical* considerations. For example, Simon Guy and Graham Farmer offer what could be viewed from an ethical vantage point as both a *descriptive ethical* and *meta-ethical* approach to the ideal of 'green building'. This is because they both describe and analyse in some (categorically organised) detail the various meanings that people concerned with the normative ideal of 'green building' attach to it. Isis Brook similarly offers both a *descriptive ethical* and *meta-ethical* approach to the 'proliferation of interpretations' of the long-standing idea of *genius loci*, 'spirit of place' or 'sense of place'. This is because she, too both describes and analyses the various meanings that people concerned with the normative ideal of respect for spirit of place attach to the concept of spirit of place – that is, to what it is exactly that they see themselves as respecting.

Broadly *meta-ethical* considerations are vigorously pursued by both Mustafa Pultar and Saul Fisher, who address essential framing questions: What is the full range of values that must enter into any comprehensive discussion of the ethics of the built environment? How do these values relate to each other? How can we map them? How are we to resolve conflicts between them? In which directions should we look in order to find the most fruitful way(s) of *approaching* normative ethical questions regarding the built environment?

Even broader philosophical questions, such as ontological and aesthetic questions, that *frame* the discussion of ethics in general are raised by other contributors. For example, Keekok Lee speaks to questions such as: What, if any, are the ontological differences – the essential differences in their modes of existence – between natural and built environments? And what are the implications of these differences for our actions in regard to them? Nigel Taylor's chapter speaks to questions along the border/fault line of ethics and aesthetics: Where do aesthetic concerns begin and end? Where do ethical concerns begin and end? Is it possible that some apparently aesthetic concerns are also, or even fundamentally, ethical concerns? And I ask (but answer in the negative) the reductionist question: Are allegedly ethical concerns about the built environment actually reducible to more familiar kinds of ethical concerns? Is the ethics of the built environment, in other words, 'surplus to moral requirements'?

Finally, when it comes to the domain of *applied ethics*, it is clear that *all* the contributions herein, by practitioners and theorists alike, are ultimately geared towards questions of application, including the honest exploration of the *difficulties* involved in applying the kinds of ethical principles to which we are personally and professionally committed.

The kinds of questions summarised in this conclusion, and which are implicitly or explicitly addressed in the contributions in this volume, clearly serve to define an initial agenda for the future development of this field of enquiry:

- What specific kinds of qualities of character, principles and outcomes should we strive to cultivate, respect or promote with respect to the built environment? (This question relates to the sphere of normative ethics.)
- How do these differ from the virtues, principles and preferred outcomes that presently pertain, if only by default, in regard to the built environment? (This question relates to the sphere of descriptive ethics.)
- What are the obstacles to moving from the present situation to a more ethically desirable situation and how can we best effect this shift? (This question obviously speaks to very broad political, economic, cultural and even psychological issues. But it also raises significant meta-ethical issues in that different people can mean different things by the same normative ideal, such as 'sustainability' and 'spirit of place', and so keep talking past each other.)
- How should we apply our normative ideals (virtues, principles, and outcomes) in specific, real-world situations regarding the

built environment? (This question relations to the sphere of applied ethics.)

- How and to what extent should the difficulties we encounter in applying these normative ideals to the built environment feed back to modify the normative ideals themselves? (The applied ethics to normative ethics direction of feedback.)
- What other questions do we need to ask that lie outside the frame of ethics as conventionally understood but which nevertheless impact upon the way in which we approach questions concerning the ethics of the built environment?

All of the chapters in this volume advance answers of various kinds to these kinds of questions. However, as with all worthwhile enquiry, none of the answers advanced here should be considered as final. Rather, these answers should be considered as both responses to the above kinds of questions *and* stimuli to the further pursuit of them. Given the importance of the built environment to all our lives and ultimately to the fate of the planet, including its non-human inhabitants, we urgently need to be able to explore, debate and put into effect the best answers we can find to these kinds of questions. These questions are obviously being pursued in various implicit and *ad hoc* ways at present, but formally recognising the field of the ethics of the built environment is a step forward in providing the intellectual space in which legitimately to pursue these questions. What is now to be hoped for is that this field of enquiry becomes a vigorous, inspirational and practically fruitful contributor to life in the twenty-first century.

INDEX

229